ATTENTION DEFICIT HYPERACTIVITY DISORDER IN ADULTHOOD

ATTENTION DEFICIT HYPERACTIVITY DISORDER IN ADULTHOOD:

A Practitioner's Handbook

Santo J. Triolo, PH.D.
Clinical Director, Adult and Child Psychological Services
Columbus, Georgia

USA	Publishing Office:	BRUNNER/MAZEL *A member of the Taylor & Francis Group* 325 Chestnut Street Philadelphia, PA 19106 Tel: (215) 625–8900 Fax: (215) 625–2940
	Distribution Center:	BRUNNER/MAZEL *A member of the Taylor & Francis Group* 47 Runway Road, Suite G Levittown, PA 19057–4700 Tel: (215) 269–0400 Fax: (215) 269–0363
UK		BRUNNER/MAZEL *A member of the Taylor & Francis Group* 1 Gunpowder Square London EC4A 3DE Tel: +44 171 583 0490 Fax: +44 171 583 0581

ATTENTION DEFICIT HYPERACTIVITY DISORDER IN ADULTHOOD:
A Practitioner's Handbook

1 2 3 4 5 6 7 8 9 0

Printed by Hamilton Printing Company, Castleton, NY, 1998.

A CIP catalog record for this book is available from the British Library.
♾The paper in this publication meets the requirements of the ANSI Standard Z39.48–1984 (Permanence of Paper).

Library of Congress Cataloging-in-Publication Data

Triolo, Santo J., 1954–
    Attention deficit hyperactivity disorder in adulthood : a
practitioner's handbook / Santo J. Triolo.
        p.   cm.
    Includes bibliographical references and index
    ISBN 0-87630-890-6 (case :   alk. paper)
    1. Attention-deficit disorder in adults.   I. Title.
RC394.A85T75   1998
616.85'89—dc21   98-24227
                                                                 CIP

ISBN 0-87630-890-6

Contents

Preface

Several years ago, in the midst of conducting research in the area of adult attention problems, my intern walked into my office to show me a cartoon published in *The New Yorker*. It was the first time I had seen anything on adult attention deficit disorder (ADD) directed at the general public. I remembered a feeling of uneasiness inside of me. Scientific knowledge on adult attention deficit hyperactivity disorder (ADHD) is far from comprehensive; however, I felt that Pandora's box was now open and a flood of publications, directed toward the general public, could be expected to hit the stands. This has happened, and it has exceeded my expectations.

There is nothing wrong with passing on information to the general public. However, this field is quite young, and many of the hypotheses presented today may not be validated by the data collected later. Unfortunately, even when the media inform the general public of the new scientific shifts and changes, old viewpoints are hard to kill. Perhaps the best example of this is the notion that diet and sugar are the reasons why children are hyperactive. Decades have passed since this hypothesis has been proven wrong, yet I still meet parents at workshops and in my office who maintain this old belief.

To consider a more recent example, I am often presented by my patients and, unfortunately, a few colleagues, with this notion that ADHD is due to a "chemical imbalance" in the brain. Although there is little doubt that ADHD is due to cognitive functions of the central nervous system, the term *chemical imbalance* is very misleading, and I am concerned about the impression it gives to the general population. A more comprehensive discussion is presented in this book, but for now it may be worthwhile for the reader to simply think about the implications of such a term. Many practitioners already may have blindly accepted this term as fact. If so, it may be worthwhile to think about what a "chemical imbalance" assumes. To have an imbalance of any kind, there must be some form of standard. In essence, one must know what is to be "balanced." To the best of my knowledge, science has not been able to come up with a valid description of a chemically "balanced" brain. I can only imagine the misperceptions and the potential psychological stressors the idea of a chemically imbalanced brain can produce. The damage may include both psychological and practical problems. Patients may see themselves as being "less human" or as missing parts of their brain. Practical implications can be seen with respect to potential employers or insurance companies inappropriately discriminating against this population. How many employers, for instance, would feel comfortable hiring someone who is described as having a "chemical imbalance" in the brain?

Another example of recent communication to the public is the notion that an ADHD diagnosis is made by interview only. Unfortunately, there are a number of practitioners who have also accepted this information as fact and, considering the recent popularity of ADHD, a diagnosis made by interview alone may be more unreliable today than it was just few years ago. Today, it is not unusual to meet very sophisticated patients who have read numerous articles and books on the subject. They run down the list of symptoms as if they had written the diagnostic manual themselves. The diagnostician is faced with a difficult task of deciding whether the reported symptoms are truly due to ADHD or whether the symptoms are being reported by someone who may be hypersensitive and tends to exaggerate, such as found in personalities with histrionic tendencies.

Thus, the motivation for writing this book is to help the practitioner through these problems and, in so doing, provide a more reliable method of diagnosing and treating people with ADHD. In fact, this book is not written for the general public. It is specifically geared toward the practitioner. It will offer the diagnostician practical guidance in properly diagnosing ADHD, with special consideration of comorbid and differential diagnoses. In doing so, it will challenge the practitioner to move beyond the current diagnostic criteria. It will also present arguments for standardized testing in addition to the usual interview. Finally, throughout this book, the reader will be challenged to look critically at the current literature. Although it may have been years since many clinical practitioners have conducted their own research, I ask the readers to at least take the position of being a good consumer of research studies and to not uncritically accept conclusions. A comprehensive analysis of all of the literature is certainly beyond the scope of this text. However, it will provide some important critical analyses that may motivate the reader to think through some of the current conclusions in the field.

The book is intended to be used as a reference source. Topics are presented to provide a natural flow from chapter to chapter; however, the reader is not locked into the book's sequence and is free to choose the chapters that are most pertinent to his or her present needs. Thus, practitioners can turn to the diagnostic chapters to refer to specific interview and testing procedures. Other practitioners may wish to refer to the treatment chapters regarding psychotherapy and medication treatments. Depending on the subtopic of interest, the chapters stand relatively independent from each other. If a subject matter presented in one chapter is presented more comprehensively in another, the reader is referred there.

The first chapter is a brief introduction of the study of ADHD. Special emphasis is given to the historical perspective and the limited study of the adult ADHD population. The second chapter reviews some of the theories of ADHD and presents some challenges to the reader in rethinking some of the old concepts. Also, the latter part of the chapter is dedicated toward a more systematic theory-building process. I strongly believe that we are not ready for a comprehensive theory of ADHD, especially in consideration of the lack of data on adults with ADHD. Alternatively, a structural model is offered for the systematic collection of observed data.

Chapter 3 is a critique of the *DSM–IV* criteria. Special consideration of the adult population is given. This is a short chapter that originally was included in the diagnostic process chapter (Chapter 4); however, I decided to extract it and make it a chapter of its own to provide an easier reference for diagnosticians. Chapter 4 incorporates some of the suggested changes from Chapter 3 in a six-step diagnostic process. I consider this process the most helpful in providing the most reliable method of diagnosing adults with ADHD. The process allows for some flexibility in individual preference styles but also recommends the inclusion of a number of necessary assessments.

Chapter 5 is dedicated to case studies. I purposely chose some of the more difficult cases to report because I thought it might be more helpful than presenting cases that are straightforward and reflective of ''textbook'' findings. I have often read nice, clean, and neat case studies of patients and wondered why I hardly ever get to see them in my practice. Real life private practice is plagued with complexities. Now, as an author, I realize how tempting it is to just share the ''few'' cases that are clean and neat. I decided to share the cases that presented the most uncertainties because they represent a more realistic perspective of a typical private practice.

Chapter 6 is dedicated to the psychotherapeutic interventions for ADHD adults. The most common comorbid conditions are discussed at length. Special sensitivity is given to the multiple needs of adult ADHD patients. Consequently, decisions with respect to different forms of psychotherapeutic interventions—individual, family, or both—also are discussed.

Chapter 7 is dedicated to the research findings on psychopharmacology for adult ADHD patients. Unfortunately, this field of study is still quite young, and there seems to be more emphasis on case study reviews rather than more appropriate control studies. Nevertheless, some general treatment trends and procedures are presented. Also, suggestions are given with respect to clinical judgments.

Chapter 8 is a discussion of some issues that may be addressed in future research. As in other young fields of study, I believe we are just beginning to formulate the right questions, and we may be a long way from all the answers. However, I also believe the newness of this field of study brings with it the excitement of exploring virgin territory. The hope is that future research will be sensitive to the practical needs of diagnosticians and therapists who work with ADHD adults every day.

Acknowledgments

Much of the content of this book comes from insights given to me by my ADHD patients. I have learned much from listening to their viewpoints and descriptions. They have not been passive recipients of testing and intervention; rather, they have taken an active role in the management of their lives and, in so doing, they have provided me with a richness in knowledge that simply could not be matched by only reading research studies and statistical reports. I thank them for this very valuable education.

The mechanical task of writing this book was made much easier by my transcribers, Anne Beyer, Lillian Sanchez, Gail Wingo, and Dawn K. Thompson. Anne was with me at the launching of the first outlines and early chapters. Lillian later took on the bulk of this work and patiently worked with me through a number of rewrites. Gail was responsible for the final adjustments, and Dawn helped with the compilation of the index. They are all still my friends.

From conception to final product, there have been a number of colleagues who have provided valuable professional assistance. In particular, Suzanne Martin, Stanley Levine, Genevieve Laforte, and Kevin Murphy have been most helpful in providing valuable research information and, from time to time, they have made themselves available for discussions of various professional topics. I thank them for their guidance and direction.

In addition, I wish to thank three anonymous reviewers for their review of this book. Their objective critiques and suggestions were most helpful and constructive.

I am particularly grateful to Lewis Lieberman for his critical review and valuable advice. I am very fortunate to have had him available over the years as supervisor, colleague, consultant, and friend.

I am most grateful to my immediate family: Joshua, Joseph, and my wife Janice. This book took three times longer to complete than originally expected. Their love, support, and patience gave me the strength and energy necessary to bring this project to a close. In particular, my wife has had to endure the burdens of family responsibility during many of my absences. Throughout this project, her love, understanding, and kindness has been constant and unwavering. I have been blessed.

Santo J. Triolo, Ph.D.

Chapter 1

Introduction

Attention deficit hyperactivity disorder (ADHD), the latest in a long string of names to describe this disorder, is at present the diagnosis given to individuals who present significant symptoms of hyperactivity–impulsivity and inattention. These problems are defined by a set of behavioral and cognitive symptoms that impair normal functioning. It is estimated that 3%–7% of the childhood population can be described as having ADHD (Barkley, 1990). It has now been well documented that ADHD persists into adulthood (Nadeau, 1995; Weiss & Hechtman, 1993; Wender, 1995); however, there is controversy with respect to the percentage of children who grow up to continue to have significant problems in adulthood. Schaffer (1994) presented the most conservative data, with the estimation that only 10% of ADHD children experience significant symptomatology in adult life. By contrast, Weinstein (1994) suggested that 79% of children diagnosed as having ADHD will continue to have significant problems in adulthood. The latest reviews (Barkley, 1997; Jackson & Farrugia, 1997) suggest that the best estimates, based on more objective prospective analyses, are somewhere between 30% and 50%. The variance in percentage may be explained partially by error due to different inclusion criteria over the years and by different operational definitions of significant symptomotology.

On the basis of more recent objective analyses, there is reason to believe that ADHD is underdiagnosed in adults because the *Diagnostic and Statistical Manual of Mental Disorders* (*DSM–IV*; American Psychiatric Association, 1994) uses symptom cutoffs that are based on childhood sample groups, as opposed to adults (Murphy & Barkley, 1995). Also, there is ample evidence to suggest that there are numerous ADHD adults who were never diagnosed ADHD as children and are now missed by clinicians normally trained to address "adult" problems such as alcoholism, personality disorders, marital conflicts, antisocial behaviors, mood disturbances, and anxiety disorders. Eyestone and Howell (1994) interviewed and tested 202 inmates from an all-male prison population and discovered that over 25% met the criteria for ADHD as adults and had presented significant ADHD symptoms during their childhood years. They identified 22 additional inmates who showed "varying patterns of ADHD symptoms throughout childhood and adulthood, but did not have sufficient symptoms to be diagnosed ADHD" (p. 187) based on the researchers' testing at the time of the study. Of the 202 inmates, only 40 reported no significant ADHD symptoms. The authors concluded that prisoners represent an untapped population of ADHD adults: people who have not been diagnosed and, consequently, moved away from mainstream functioning.

Similar arguments can be made for the population of drug abusers. There have been several researchers who have noted a high correlation between substance abuse and ADHD (Shekim, Asarnow, Hess, Zaucha, & Wheeler, 1990; Tzelepis, Schubiner, & Warbasse, 1995; Wood, Wender, & Reimherr, 1983). It has been hypothesized that many undiagnosed ADHD adults have turned to drugs as a way to medicate themselves. Again, this population of adults may be representative of a significant number of ADHD adults who have yet to receive appropriate professional help. Clinicians who are trained to work with adults are more likely to focus on typical adult problems, such as antisocial functioning, alcoholism, and mood disturbances, and may not consider ADHD.

BRIEF HISTORICAL PERSPECTIVE

Historical documentation of ADHD and, in particular, adult ADHD, has been presented elsewhere (Barkley, 1990; Jaffe, 1995). Barkley's (1990) review of this field's beginnings and historical achievements is quite comprehensive, except perhaps for the omission of his own contribution. He may be too modest to say it, but his work over the years has helped shape the landscape of ADHD research. In addition, Jaffe's (1995) chapter provides a special historical perspective on adult ADHD research. He documents the acceptance of adult ADHD by the professional community and its growing recognition by the general public.

The emphasis here will be on the presentation of two themes that have not been discussed extensively in earlier writings. First, the study of ADHD has received much popular attention, and this may present special challenges to the practitioner. Although media attention advances interest, it may very well be a source of bias that could get in the way of good clinical practice. Second, the history of ADHD is far from linear; it is important to keep in mind that researchers are influenced by the professional trends and perspectives of their time. Periods of progress have been followed by alternate periods of regression. These themes are important to understand, and they have great significance for clinicians who must address the practical matters of taking good care of their patients.

As mentioned earlier, ADHD is the latest of a long list of names that has included *minimal brain damage; hyperkineses* or *hyperkinetic syndrome; hyperactivity; attention deficit disorder* (ADD) *with or without hyperactivity;* and now *attention deficit hyperactivity disorder* (ADHD). It is important to understand that these names are reflective of limitations in seeing the "elephant" rather than any real changes in the "elephant" itself. The core observations of behaviors and cognitive tendencies have remained relatively stable throughout the years. Back at the last turn of the century, Still's (1902) description of problem children was remarkably similar to what is observed today. He recognized that these children had problems with moral conduct; they seemed to understand the behaviors that were expected of them, although they did not follow through with their actions. He also observed what was described as *volitional inhibitions*—an inability to control behaviors. Still recognized that these children were physically different and, in particular, noted their small bone structure and size with respect to age. He correctly recognized that there were more boys than girls with these types of problems and correctly speculated that the problems follow familiar lines. Still was remarkably accurate in noting that these children were unable to attend and focus as well as their peers, an emphasis that was seemingly missed by observers for several decades subsequent to his publication. Also, Still speculated that these problems were due to constitutional factors, a major emphasis in today's literature. The ADHD patient of today is obviously no different from the patient of almost 100 years ago. Thus, what has changed over time are the interpretations and emphasis of the particular behaviors.

Barkley (1990) suggested that interest in ADHD was sparked by the effects of the 1917–1918 encephalitis epidemic on the survivors. Many of the children who survived presented significant behavioral and cognitive problems similar to the symptoms of ADHD. Consequently, a logical connection was made between ADHD behaviors and brain damage. At first, children with a documented history of brain infection or injury were followed, and their ADHD-like behaviors were documented. As time passed, children who presented with ADHD behaviors were assumed to have experienced some kind of brain trauma, even if none was documented. Perhaps the term *minimal brain damage* (Strauss & Lehtinen, 1947), a very misleading label, was coined because clear historical documentation of brain trauma was not presented. The association between ADHD and brain trauma remained through the rationalization that the injury was minimal and, therefore, undetectable. However, concurrent and subsequent reviewers continued to argue that this label was misleading (Birch, 1964; Childers, 1935; Herbert, 1964) and, slowly, a new direction toward a more descriptive label was adopted.

By the 1960s much emphasis was given to environmental influences, and there seemed to be a trend toward behavioral observations. The ADHD child's most obvious problem, to observers, was the "hyperactive" component; consequently, a new label, *hyperkinetic reaction of childhood disorder* (American Psychiatric Association, 1968) won favor over the *minimal brain damage* label. To some extent the switch may have been influenced by the growing sensitivity toward the negative consequences of labels. Social consciousness and special emphasis on environmental influences seem to have been more prevalent during the 1960s and 1970s and, just as old genetic and organic origins of intelligence were challenged (Brody & Brody, 1976), similar challenges were introduced in the study of ADHD (Block, 1977). As Barkley (1990) correctly accounted, these challenges included the notions—which we know now to be false—that sugar and other nutritional factors were the cause of ADHD. This challenge also included the use of medication, and this time period marks the beginning of major debates about the merits of various treatments. Arguments that "proper" parenting and teaching are what is missing in ADHD children found their roots during this era. Possibly, the theme that medication treatment is used as a substitute for a lack of motivation on the part of parents and teachers can be traced to the political trends of the time.

Virginia Douglas has been credited for the movement away from hyperactivity and the rediscovery of attention factors involved with ADHD (Barkley, 1990). Through a series of objective observations, Douglas (1972) discovered that the level of activity alone could not differentiate ADHD children from non-ADHD children as well as behaviors associated with attentional components. Because of these efforts, subsequent research on components such as the ability to use time efficiently, screen away distracting stimuli, concentrate on tasks, and sustain focus with minimal external reinforcers became the prominent subject matter of research studies (Douglas, 1983). This shift away from simply looking at activity levels and toward the assessment of cognitive deficits, at least indirectly, may be responsible for the consideration of ADHD as a lifelong condition. Although ADHD children can eventually learn to compensate and reduce their level of overt activity as they get older, the core underlying cognitive deficits remain. Sensitivity to these deficits may have helped clinicians recognize that adults can continue to have problems (Kane, Mikalac, Benjamin, & Barkley, 1990; Morrison, 1979, 1980; Wood, 1986).

The shift away from hyperactivity toward attention deficit disorder was accepted into mainstream diagnostics in 1980 with the publication of the *DSM–III* (American Psychiatric Association, 1980). The new diagnostic name was *attention deficit disorder*. This new diagnostic label had two subcategories: with or without hyperactivity. Also, it was the first indication in mainstream diagnostics that children do not outgrow this disorder. A third category was introduced: *attention deficit disorder, residual type*. Full commitment to the diagnosis of adults as having this disorder apparently was withheld, but at least recognition was given to lingering symptoms beyond the childhood and adolescent years.

Adult treatment for ADHD began much as the treatment for children, with the use of stimulant medication by the presentation of case studies. Arnold and his associates (Arnold, Strobl, & Weisenberg, 1972) presented the results of dextroamphetamines treatment on a 22-year-old male patient. This patient had never previously been diagnosed as a child, but retrospective reports indicated that behavioral difficulties observed in adulthood originated in early childhood. The dependent variables included concentration, anxiety, depression, and self-esteem. In a single-subject double-blind procedure, the patient was observed on two different days on either dextroamphetamines or a placebo in each. Data were collected before administration of the drug and three other times: 2, 5, and 8 hr after the administration of the drug. In a repeated-measures design, significant increases in concentration and decreases in anxiety were reported, compared to placebo conditions. Also, the authors noted an increase in depression and no significant changes in self-esteem.

Later in 1975, David Wood and Paul Wender treated two women who presented ongoing symptoms and history of ADHD with methylphenidate, the now-preferred stimulant medication in the treatment of ADHD; the positive results motivated them to conduct an expanded double-blind study (Wood, Reimherr, Wender, & Johnson, 1976). They found that their patients responded positively to the stimulant medication, and these preliminary results encouraged them to further study the use of stimulant medication treatment on adults with ADHD (Wender, 1995; Wood, 1986).

From the mid-1970s to the early 1980s, much advancement in the field of ADHD took place. Barkley's (1981) publication of *Hyperactive Children: A Handbook for Diagnosis and Treatment* perhaps solidified him as a leading researcher in the field. He certainly helped set the pace for the move away from subjective analyses to quantitative objective study. One could argue that this period marked the most advancements and, since that time, there may have been some regressive trends.

In 1987, the next *DSM* edition (*DSM–III–R*) was published (American Psychiatric Association, 1987). The new diagnostic label was *attention deficit hyperactivity disorder* (ADHD). It was argued that

> in a field trial of several hundred children of the *DSM–III–R* criteria of attention deficit hyperactivity disorder, oppositional defiant disorder and conduct disorder, a clinical diagnosis of *DSM–III* category of attention deficit disorder without hyperactivity was hardly ever made. This suggests that with the revised and more inclusive criteria for attention deficit hyperactivity disorder there may be little need for this category. (APA, 1987, p. 411)

The key notation here is that the field trial included only children. Although by this time it had been recognized that ADHD is a lifelong condition for a significant number of patients, adults were excluded. Ironically, the "residual type" was dropped from this publication and replaced by the "undifferentiated type." This change in terminology, although perhaps a matter of semantics only, indirectly recognized and validated the diagnosis of ADHD in adults. *Residual* refers to a remnant of ADHD; *undifferentiated* is reflective of the fact that an ADHD diagnosis applies, although not all of the symptoms for the other ADHD categories are presented.

The latest edition of the *DSM,* the *DSM–IV* seems to be a compromise between the 1980 and 1987 editions (see Chapter 3 for a more comprehensive discussion); instead of exclusive categories—with or without hyperactivity—this latest edition uses the term *predominately* in descriptions of the subcategories.

In essence, the *DSM–IV* seems to have positioned itself somewhere between the 1980 and 1987 editions.

One of the major studies to usher in the 1990s was the work by Zametkin et al. (1990). Zametkin et al.'s analyses measured cerebral glucose metabolic functioning; they compared ADHD males to a comparison group of non-ADHD males and noted some statistically significant between-group differences. Through no fault of the researchers, who statistically were very conservative and responsible in the presentation of their data, this study has been publicized as a landmark finding in the answer to the missing link that associates ADHD with brain dysfunction. In many respects, the field today has come full circle, and the pendulum has swung back toward the minimal brain damage perspective of decades past. For at least a decade or so, a reductionist perspective has dominated, with special focus given to neuropathological functioning. There seems to be an emphasis again on examining that side of the "elephant."

Nevertheless, several positive advances took place during this most recent history, especially with respect to the study of ADHD adults. In 1989 and 1991, the first two clinics exclusively devoted to the study of ADHD adults opened at Wayne State University, in Detroit, Michigan, and the University of Massachusetts Medical Center, in Worcester. Slowly, adolescent outcome reviews (Klein, 1987; Lambert, 1988) began to document the risk of multiple negative consequences of ADHD. These include social disabilities, family conflicts, aggressive and violent behaviors that may lead to legal problems, substance abuse, psychiatric disorders in later adulthood (Morrison, 1980), and significant social economic limitations due to academic underachievement (Hinshaw, 1992). These negative outcomes have received support from long-term prospective findings (Barkley, Fischer, Edelbrock, & Smallish, 1990; Hechtman & Weiss, 1986; Weiss & Hechtman, 1993). At present, Weiss and her colleagues have provided the longest prospective analysis of the developmental course of ADHD. Her data include a series of follow-ups that cover more than 20 years, from childhood to adulthood. These efforts have provided insights into lifelong management strategies (Fargason & Ford, 1994).

More recent longitudal investigations are beginning to look at the multifactor conditions of ADHD. For instance, Greene, Biedorman, Faraone, Sienna, and Garcia-Jetton (1997) identified social disability as an important comorbid condition to the prediction of maladaptive functioning later in life. It is hoped that future follow-up studies will use the sophisticated designs necessary to accommodate the interconnecting pathways of multiple comorbid variables. Other studies may lead to a better understanding of the direct and indirect effects of ADHD over time.

CONTEMPORARY STATUS

Today, discussions regarding ADHD enjoy much media interest. Although it is inherently good to inform the general public, the practicing clinician has the added burden of clarifying numerous misconceptions caused by premature conclusions, simplification of findings, and the usual distortions inherited in a sound-bite delivery format. As is presented later in this book, this burden has added implications with respect to diagnosis.

A sampling of some of the popular issues include the use of stimulant medication for treatment, testimonials that advocate the use of untested or unproven treatments, and even general questioning of the existence of ADHD. For instance, Vatz and Weinberg (1995), in an article that appeared in *USA Today,* did all but literally state that the diagnosis of ADHD is manufactured for ulterior motives such as gaining entrance into medical schools, excusing antisocial behaviors, and lining the pockets of charlatans.

An article presented in the *Well Being Journal* (Santamarina, 1996) advocated the use of a dietary plan referred to as "God's Recipe" in place of Ritalin. In fact, the aim is to "rid the world of Ritalin" altogether. Such articles, as unbalanced as they may seem to the objective reader, are often influential to the uninformed public. Other reviews are more balanced and responsible in their reporting, such as the series of articles published in the July 18, 1984, issue of *Time* (Wallis, 1984); although some old issues that have long since been put to rest were readdressed in controversial fashion, much information was responsibly presented. A similar comment could be made of Hancock's (1996) *Newsweek* article, entitled "Mother's Little Helper" (referring to the Ritalin pill). The focus of this article was on the use of Ritalin, and some legitimate concerns were raised regarding the increasing number of people who are now prescribed this drug. Of course, with the advent of seeing ADHD as a lifelong condition and the greater awareness within the public domain, much of this increase can be explained. Just the same, the philosophical arguments against a society with these rising rates of prescription medication are healthy.

The most recent trend is the use of diagnostic procedures on adults suspected of ADHD that are more structured and objective. The first semistructured diagnostic procedure was introduced by the University of Utah research group (Wender, Reimherr, & Wood, 1981; Wood, 1986). This is a two-phase process designed to be more conservative than the *DSM–III*. Since then, standardized self-rating measures for ADHD adults have been introduced (Brown, 1996; McCarney & Anderson, 1996; Triolo & Murphy, 1996), and some validity has been reported with the use of continuous-performance tasks (Gordon, 1983; Greenberg, 1995). The diagnostic procedure introduced in this book combines structured interviews with standardized instruments to increase diagnostic reliability. Preliminary findings have been positive.

REFERENCES

American Psychiatric Association. (1968). *Diagnostic and statistical manual of mental disorders* (2nd ed.). Washington, DC: Author.

American Psychiatric Association. (1980). *Diagnostic and statistical manual of mental disorders* (3rd ed.). Washington, DC: Author.

American Psychiatric Association. (1987). *Diagnostic and statistical manual of mental disorders* (3rd ed., rev.). Washington, DC: Author.

American Psychiatric Association. (1994). *Diagnostic and statistical manual of mental disorders* (4th ed.). Washington, DC: Author.

Arnold, L. E., Strobl, D., & Weisenberg, A. (1972). Hyperkinetic adult: Study of the "paradoxical" amphetamine response. *Journal of the American Medical Association, 222,* 693–694.

Barkley, R. A. (1981). *Hyperactive children: A handbook for diagnosis and treatment.* New York: Guilford Press.

Barkley, R. A. (1990). *Attention deficit hyperactivity disorder (ADHD): A handbook for diagnosis and treatment.* New York: Guilford Press.

Barkley, R. A. (1997). Behavioral inhibitions, sustained attention in executive functions: Constructing a unifying theory of ADHD. *Psychological Bulletin, 121,* 65–94.

Barkley, R. A., Fischer, M., Edelbrock, C. S., & Smallish, L. (1990). The adolescent outcome of hyperactive children diagnosed by research criteria: II. An 8-year prospective follow-up study. *Journal of the American Academy of Child and Adolescent Psychiatry, 29,* 546–557.

Birch, H. G. (1964). *Brain damage in children: The biological and social aspects.* Baltimore: Williams and Wilkins.

Block, G. H. (1977). Hyperactivity: A cultural perspective. *Journal of Learning Disabilities, 110,* 236–240.

Brody, E. B., & Brody, N. (1976). *Intelligence: Nature, determinants, and consequences.* New York: Academic Press.

Brown, T. E. (1996). *Brown Attention-Deficit Disorder Scales: Manual.* San Antonio, TX: The Psychological Corporation.

Childers, A. T. (1935). Hyper-activity in children having behavior disorders. *American Journal of Orthopsychiatry, 5,* 227–243.

Douglas, V. I. (1972). Stop, look, and listen: The problem of sustained attention and impulse control in hyperactive and normal children. *Canadian Journal of Behavioral Science, 4,* 259–282.

Douglas, V. I. (1983). Attention and cognitive problems. In M. Rutter (Ed.), *Developmental neuropsychiatry* (pp. 282–329). New York: Guilford Press.

Eyestone, L. L., & Howell, R. J. (1994). An epidemiological study of attention-deficit hyperactivity disorder in major depression in a male prison population. *Bulletin of the American Academy of Psychiatry and Law, 22,* 181–193.

Fargason, R. E., & Ford, C. V. (1994). Attention deficit hyperactivity disorder in adults: Diagnosis, treatment, and prognosis. *Southern Medical Journal, 87,* 302–309.

Gordon, M. (1983). *The Gordon Diagnostic System.* DeWitt, NY: Gordon Systems.

Greenberg, L. M. (1995). Improving the clinical utility of continuous performance tests: A preliminary comparison of computer-based errors. *The ADHD Report, 6*(6), 7–8.

Greene, R.W., Biedorman, J., Faraone, S. V., Sienna, M., & Garcia-Jetton, J. (1997). Adolescent outcome of boys with attention deficit/hyperactivity disorder and social disability: Results from a 4-year longitudinal follow-up study. *Journal of Consulting and Clinical Psychology, 65,* 758–767.

Hancock, L. (1996, March 18). Mother's little helper. *Newsweek,* pp. 51–54.

Hechtman, L., & Weiss, G. (1986). Controlled prospective fifteen year follow-up of hyperactives as adults: Non-medical drug and alcohol use and anti-social behavior. *Canadian Journal of Psychology, 31,* 557–567.

Herbert, N. (1964). The concept in testing of brain damage in children: A review. *Journal of Child Psychology and Psychiatry, 5,* 197–217.

Hinshaw, S. P. (1992). Academic underachievement, attention deficits, and aggression: Comorbidity and implications for intervention. *Journal of Consulting and Clinical Psychology, 60,* 893–903.

Jackson, B., & Farrugia, D. (1997). Diagnosis and treatment of adults with attention deficit hyperactivity disorder. *Journal of Counseling and Development, 75,* 312–319.

Jaffe, P. (1995). History and overview of adulthood ADD. In K. G. Nadeau (Ed.), *A comprehensive guide to attention deficit disorder in adults: Research, diagnosis, and treatment* (pp. 3–17). New York: Brunner/Mazel.

Kane, R., Mikalac, C., Benjamin, S., & Barkley, R. A. (1990). Assessment and treatment of adults with ADHD. In R. A. Barkley (Ed.), *Attention deficit hyperactivity disorder: A handbook for diagnosis and treatment* (pp. 613–654). New York: Guilford Press.

Klein, R. G. (1987). Prognosis of attention deficit disorder and its management in adolescence. *Pediatrics in Review, 8,* 216–222.

Lambert, N. M. (1988). Adolescent outcomes of hyperactive children: Perspectives on general and specific patterns of childhood risk for adolescent emotional, social, and mental health problems. *American Psychologist, 43,* 786–799.

McCarney, S. B., & Anderson, P. D. (1996). *Adult Attention Deficit Disorder Evaluation Scale (A-ADDES) technical manual.* Columbia, MO: Hawthorne Educational Services.

Morrison, J. R. (1979). Diagnosis of adult psychiatric patients with childhood hyperactivity. *American Journal of Psychiatry, 136,* 955–958.

Morrison, J. R. (1980). Childhood hyperactivity in an adult psychiatric population: Social factors. *Journal of Clinical Psychiatry, 41,* 40–43.

Murphy, K. R., & Barkley, R. A. (1995). Norms for the *DSM–IV* symptoms list for ADHD in adults. *The ADHD Report, 3*(3), 6–7.

Nadeau, K. G. (1995). *A comprehensive guide to attention deficit disorder in adults: Research, diagnosis, and treatment.* New York: Brunner/Mazel.

Santamarina, G. (1996, July/August). Attention deficit disorder reversed. *Well Being Journal, 5.*

Schaffer, D. (1994). Attention deficit hyperactivity disorder in adults. *American Journal of Psychiatry, 151,* 633–638.

Shekim, W. O., Asarnow, R. F., Hess, E., Zaucha, K., & Wheeler, N. (1990). A clinical and demographic profile of a sample of adults with attention deficit hyperactivity disorder, residual state. *Comprehensive Psychiatry, 31,* 416–425.

Still, G. F. (1902). Some abnormal psychical conditions in children. *The Lancet,* i, 1008–1012, 1077–1082, 1163–1168.

Strauss, A. A., & Lehtinen, L. E. (1947). *Psychopathology and education of the brain injured child.* New York: Grune & Stratton.

Triolo, S. J. & Murphy, K. R. (1996). *Attention-Deficit Scales for Adults (ADSA): manual for scoring and interpretation.* New York: Brunner/Mazel.

Tzelepis, A., Schubiner, H., & Warbasse, L. H., III (1995). Differential diagnosis and psychiatric comorbidity patterns in adult attention deficit disorder. In K. G. Nadeau (Ed.), *A comprehensive guide to attention deficit disorder in adults: Research, diagnosis, and treatment* (pp. 35–57). New York: Brunner/Mazel.

Vatz, R. E., & Weinberg, L. S. (1995, January). Overreacting to attention deficit disorder. *USA Today,* pp. 84–85.

Wallis, C. (1984, July 18). [Series of untitled articles on attention deficit disorder.] *Time,* pp. 43–50.

Weinstein, C. (1994). Cognitive remediation strategies. *Journal of Psychotherapy Practice and Research, 3*(1), 44–57.

Weiss, G., & Hechtman, L. T. (1993). *Hyperactive children grow up* (2nd ed.). New York: Guilford Press.

Wender, P. H. (1995). *Attention-deficit hyperactivity disorder in adults.* New York: Oxford University Press.

Wender, P. H., Reimherr, F. W., & Wood, D. R. (1981). Attention deficit disorder ("minimal brain damage") in adults: A replication study of diagnosis and drug treatment. *Archives of General Psychiatry, 38,* 449–456.

Wood, D. (1986). The diagnosis and treatment of attention deficit disorder, residual type. *Psychiatric Annals, 16,* 23–24, 26–28.

Wood, D. R., Reimherr, F. W., Wender, P. H., & Johnson, G. E. (1976). Diagnosis and treatment of minimal brain dysfunction in adults. *Archives of General Psychiatry, 33,* 1453–1460.

Wood, D., Wender, P., & Reimherr, F. W. (1983). The prevalence of attention deficit disorder residual type or minimal brain dysfunction, in a population of male alcoholic patients. *American Journal of Psychiatry, 140,* 95–98.

Zametkin, A. J., Nordahl, T. E., Gross, N., King, A. C., Semple, W. E., Rumsey, J., Hamburger, S., & Cohen, R. M. (1990). Cerebral glucose metabolism in adults with hyperactivity of childhood onset. *New England Journal of Medicine, 323,* 1361–1366.

Chapter 2

Theory

Several years before the Hubble telescope was launched, and before the *Challenger* disaster, a local public television station aired a program on the Hubble project. Several noted scientists involved with the project were interviewed, and one in particular was asked to comment on the data-collecting potential of this new instrument, along with the potential challenges to his theories. He was introduced as a leading theorist in his field, who was enjoying international recognition for his proposed view of the universe. The question addressed was rather personal in nature: He was asked how he would feel if, after the Hubble telescope was finished collecting all its data, findings would refute many of his espoused theories. Without hesitation, he responded that he would be greatly disappointed if, after all this data collection, none of his theories would be significantly challenged.

His response produced a rather sobering self-reflecting moment, because it was such a contrast to the response style usually presented in the social sciences. How many "giants" in the field of psychology, sociology, psychiatry, and so on, have gone to their graves hanging on to their particular theories and belief systems, even when faced with an overwhelming accumulation of contradictory data? For many scientists involved in the study of human behavior, there seems to be an emotional connection to their respective theories, and any challenge presented to their theory is somehow translated into a personal assault. How ironic—or how appropriate—that scientists who are in the best position to understand the pitfalls of human subjectivity are so easily led by it.

Thomas Kuhn (1970), in his book, *The Structure of Scientific Revolutions*, put theory in its place as simply a conceptual tool used as a stepping stone to further knowledge. Kuhn wisely does not dispel the inherent subjective nature of humans conducting science. The accumulation and integration of knowledge, according to Kuhn, are not linear, nor are they stable. Theoretical concepts initially arise from a variety of observations to provide comprehensive understanding. If new data accumulate to fit the proposed paradigm, the concepts and their relations are strengthened. The continuation of data collecting may also provide challenges to theoretical concepts. Shifts are made to accommodate new data, or a blindness may be created to refute the validation of the new challenging observations. The former is usually associated with new theory and conceptual adjustments. The latter is usually noted if the theory is well established and considered part of mainstream scientific knowledge. Thus, any conflicting data must overcome the inertia created by established concepts. Only the power of science and objective inquiry can eventually break through the inherent complacency of established theory. Anomalies or observed violations of expectancy, based on the established theory, can find respect only through the rigors of objective inquiry. Still, Kuhn suggested that the move to reject old theoretical perspectives is not usually made until the new ones are ready to be accepted and only in light of a more comprehensive explanation of data observed. Kuhn seemed to suggest that a new theoretical perspective must be able to incorporate old as well as new observations. When this is so, a revolution is complete. It seems reasonable to conclude that no progress can be made without the chance of revolution and, in turn, the drive to use objective data for direction should ultimately be superior to the drive to maintain a harmonious status quo. Theory can provide the occasional needed refuge from the cacophony of observed data as long as it does not foster complacency and become a blinder to challenging horizons.

Decades ago, a professor of neuropsychology, Donald Meyer, proposed that theory is useful only as a stepping stone or perhaps as a place of rest along the path of scientific inquiry. He recognized its necessity to the human biology that hungers for unity and harmony. Ultimately, though, he also recognized its relative insignificance as he reminded his students that "theory is cheap."

This chapter discusses three main theoretical perspectives. The first is considered the oldest and perhaps the most accepted theoretical model of ADHD. It views ADHD as a disease and assumes a neuropathological etiology. The second theoretical perspective, by contrast, refutes the disease model and proposes a view of ADHD as a component of normative brain functions that can be seen as being adaptive within some environmental conditions. The third and the latest theoretical model is Barkley's (1994b, 1995, 1997) development of a new comprehensive theory of ADHD.

The final portion of this chapter presents the theme that ADHD is still too young a field of study for a comprehensive theoretical model. However, suggestions are offered with respect to theory construction.

RECENT THEORETICAL PERSPECTIVES

Neuropathological Theory

This theory adopts the medical "disease" model, in which ADHD is described as a dysfunction that is neurologically based and distinctively different from normal neurological functioning. This is perhaps the oldest model adopted to explain ADHD; it dates back to the earliest descriptions of ADHD children (Bradley, 1937; Kahn & Cohen, 1934; Levin, 1938; Still, 1902). Still (1902), almost 100 years ago, linked the behavioral disruptiveness now typical of ADHD behaviors to possible constitutional factors. The nonvolitional nature of the misbehaviors observed, as well as suspected family patterns, suggested organically based pathology and etiology.

The first major findings in support of this model came when positive results were reported from stimulant medication treatment (Bradley, 1937; Bradley & Bowen, 1940). With these reported successes, the neurogenic model gained widespread support and seemed relatively free from critical challenges. However, during the years that followed, shifts in perspective took place guided by more systematic observations. For instance, the popular minimal brain damage description eventually lost favor because of a lack of concrete evidence of any brain-related damage (Chess, 1960; Werry & Sprague, 1970). Until just recently, constitutional–organic factors were seen as contributors to ADHD, but the notion of brain damage seemed to be dismissed, or at least it remained dormant, perhaps because of a lack of neurological evidence.

During this period, the focus seemed to be on behavioral observations rather than brain functioning, and further shifts in perspectives were introduced. Douglas (1972) and her associates (Douglas & Peters, 1979) managed to demonstrate the importance of looking at the underlying cognitive functions and demonstrated that the ability to sustain attention and maintain vigilance were the major distinguishing factors in ADHD—more discriminating than activity levels. Her studies focused on children and their performances. Again, the assumption was made that ADHD was due to a neurological disposition, and Douglas's studies led her to believe that the cognitive functions underlying the observed hyperactive behaviors best defined the problems in ADHD.

The continued positive effects of medication treatment kept alive the search, or at least the hope, that specific neurogenic functions will eventually be found to be related to ADHD. One branch of this research involved the consideration of neurotransmitter imbalances. Wender (1971) was one of the first investigators to suggest that difficulties in attention may be related to the neurotransmitter system of the brain. Specifically, dopamine and norepinephrine were cited as specific neurotransmitters involved in attentional functioning. The hypothesis seemed to stem from the fact that stimulants such as methylphenidate and pemoline may be helpful in increasing the availability of dopamine and norepinephrine in the neuronetwork of the brain (Hunt, Cohen, Anderson, & Mineraa, 1987; Zametkin & Rapoport, 1987). A third neurotransmitter, serotonin, also was introduced as a possible contributing influence to ADHD (Wender, 1971), and some successes have been reported with respect to the use of antidepressants (Wender, 1995).

The use of antidepressants had been relegated to second-order medication treatment (Barkley, 1990), but they have recently gained popularity, especially with practitioners working with the adult ADHD population (Wender, 1995). This may be for two reasons. First, practitioners who are mainly trained to work with adults are likely more comfortable with the use of antidepressants instead of stimulant medication. Second, adults are more likely to present depression as a comorbid condition to ADHD, and the use of these medications may sometimes be seen as a way to efficiently manage adults with the dual diagnosis of ADHD and depression.

Within the last decade or so, newer neurological measuring tools have been introduced to this area of research. These include magnetic resonance imaging (MRI) and positron emission tomography (PET), which have allowed researchers to measure details of the brain previously undetected by other methods. The instruments themselves are not new, only their use and availability to the field of research in ADHD. This is an important point, because the technology may very well be far more advanced than the researchers' ability to interpret results. This point is discussed in greater detail later on in the **Critique of the Neuro-pathological Theory** section. For now, it is important to note that these instruments have helped researchers observe the functions of the ADHD brain. They have paved the way for Zametkin et al.'s (1990) critical PET scan study, which provided perhaps the first concrete evidence that brain functions are different in ADHD adults, when compared with a normative group. This latest shift within the neuropathological model has reintroduced the notion of pathological brain functioning, and in many respects the field has now come full circle. The concrete evidence missing during the early writings apparently has been provided through the new instruments.

Specifically, Zametkin et al. (1990) used PET scans to measure the rate of glucose metabolism in the brains of 25 ADHD adult patients. When compared with 50 healthy normal adults, the rate of glucose metabolism was lower for 30 of the 60 specific brain regions selectively targeted for comparisons. Lower rates were recorded in both cortical and subcortical regions. These findings have provided the evidence necessary to support the long-standing assumption that ADHD is due to a deficit of the brain. According to the neuropathological model, environmental conditions are secondary, and advancement in the study of ADHD may be best achieved by focusing research on the physiological functions of the brain.

Mirsky (1987, 1989) has provided a neuropsychological model of attention. Again, emphasis is given to specific functions of the brain, and the assumption is that problems related to ADHD are due to brain dysfunctions; therefore, the understanding of these brain-related dysfunctions can lead to a better understanding of the behavioral difficulties among ADHD individuals. Mirsky believes that the attentional system within the brain is varied and widespread. To some extent he follows Reitan and Wolfson's (1985) model that the concept of attention is reflective of a very global function of the brain. As Reitan and Wolfson explained, all specialized areas of the brain (e.g., linguistic skills, visuospatial skills) require some level of attention and concentration. Thus, some underlying features common to all specialized structures are responsible for attentional functioning.

Mirsky (1987, 1989) went further and identified four functions of attention that are distributed in various regions of the brain. His model is quite mechanistic in nature—more so than Reitan and Wolfson (1985) proposed—and follows the belief that varying functions of the brain can be traced to specific structural components. In fact, Mirsky offered a mapping of the four attentional components with respect to different structural areas of the brain.

The first of these attentional components was described as the capacity to focus on or select a particular aspect of the environment from the rest of the perceived environment. Out of an endless supply of environmental stimuli, the organism becomes aroused by one stimulus or a particular set of stimuli. In a sense, the organism sets a priority and makes a choice to attend to a particular stimulus. Brain regions involved in this function include the superior temporal cortex; the inferior parietal cortex; and structures of the corpus striatum, including the caudate, putamen, and the globus pallidus. Although research is certainly not conclusive, Mirsky (1987, 1989) hypothesized that this capacity to focus has specific implications with respect to the structures of the brain. For instance, the motor executive function of selecting and focus may be mediated by the corpus striatal region and the inferior parietal structures of the brain.

The second component was described as the capacity to sustain or maintain the focus. This component was perhaps best described by Douglas (1972) years earlier as the capacity to maintain vigilance and stay on track. Once a stimulus has been selected out of the environment and the organism is locked onto it, this next function allows the organism to maintain the focus or exercise some degree of concentration. In essence, after a particular stimulus is selected from the environment, the nonselected stimuli are perceived as a form of competition to the selected stimulus, and the brain is charged with the responsibility of sustaining the original focus. Mirsky's (1989) special contribution in describing this function is the identification of midbrain structures. In particular, it was proposed that the rostral midbrain structures, including the tectum, the mesopontine, the reticular formation, and the midline and reticular thalamic nuclei, are possibly charged with the responsibility of sustaining focus on a selected stimulus. This still-theoretical perspective is perhaps derived from more generalized midbrain functions dealing with basic autonomic maintenance functions.

The third component proposed by Mirsky is the ability to encode or manipulate information initially provided by the selected stimuli. Traditionally, this capacity is associated with cerebral functioning and, in particular, the prefrontal cortex (Fuster, 1989). However, Mirsky (1987, 1989) hypothesized that the hippocampus, which is considered essential for mnemonic functioning necessary for some aspects of attention, is involved in this encoding component.

The last of the four components is the ability to shift attention from one aspect of the environment to another. This last component allows for flexibility and adaptive response to the surrounding world. Mirsky (1987) clearly identified this component of the brain as part of its executive function. The area of the brain identified is the prefrontal cortex.

Mirsky's (1987, 1989) contribution to this neurogenic model links conceptualized functions of attention to structural areas of the brain. This has opened the door to research that specifically targets brain structures in ADHD individuals. Recently, a number of researchers have attempted to compare ADHD and non-ADHD subjects with respect to different brain structures. For instance, Castellanos et al. (1994) used MRI to measure the caudate nucleus in ADHD subjects and found it to be slightly smaller when compared with a non-ADHD group. The difference in size was statistically significant.

Computer programs, in conjunction with scanning instruments, have opened the door for other types of investigation. Again, structures of the brain are measured with respect to size—or, more accurately, volume—as well as functioning, usually the amount of glucose metabolism and general analysis of blood flow. With the aid of computer programs, numerous comparisons have been made between ADHD and non-ADHD groups (Akshoomoff & Courchesne, 1994; Ernst et al., 1994; Giedd et al., 1994; Matochik et al., 1994; Sieg, Gaffney, Preston, & Hellings, 1995).

This neurogenic model has also opened the door for neuropsychological testing. The assumption is that abnormalities in brain structures should yield deviant scores on tests designed to measure their respective functions. Denckla (1991) proposed specific tests to tap into the components described by Mirsky (1987, 1989). For instance, the Wisconsin Card Sorting Test (Heaton, 1981) was identified as an instrument that can tap into the capacity to select and focus. The Stroop Color and Word Test (Golden, 1978) also was identified as a good instrument that can measure the capacity to focus and select, but it is less a measure of executive functioning and more a measure of concrete management of stimuli. The Paper and Pencil Cancellation Tests (Shum, McFarland, & Bain, 1990) have been widely used as a part of a neuropsychological battery of tests as a means to assess selection capacity.

It is important to keep in mind, however, that other brain functions are involved in the performance on these tests. In essence, they are not a pure indication of the capacity to focus and select. The variant levels of difficulties and intrinsic behavioral aspects tap into other cognitive components. A good example is the required perceptual scanning capacity needed during the administration of one of the cancellation tests, in addition to the capacity to sustain attention.

Tasks requiring sustained attention, continuous-performance tests, have been well documented by Douglas (1972), and neuropsychological assessments of attention have included such tasks as part of their assessment batteries (Denckla, 1991; Gordon & Mettelman, 1988; Klee & Garfinkel, 1983). There are other tests to tap into vigilance and sustained attention. These may include Trail Making A and B (Reitan & Wolfson, 1985), the Stroop Color and Word Test (Golden, 1978), and the Attentional Capacity Test (Weber, 1988).

demonstrated later, have been quite open in putting into perspective their findings; it is interesting to note that many of the limitations they themselves communicated in their article have not been discussed by subsequent authors who have cited their work.

The 25 patient subjects of Zametkin et al.'s (1990) study fulfilled the ADD criteria necessary for the *DSM–III* (American Psychiatric Association, 1980) and met the Utah criteria, which require a definitive history of childhood problems. In addition, it is important to note that these patients were selected from a population of children with ADHD; the adults were actually the parents of ADHD children. The authors cited literature that suggests that approximately 28% of biological parents have hyperactive children, and they speculated that patients with familial hyperactivity might increase the likelihood of identifying a biological determinant of the disorder. Zametkin et al. were quite open in reporting that their sample of patients came from a particular subset of the adult ADHD population. The added criterion of having biological relations who also had been diagnosed as having ADHD was clearly reported, along with their hope of increasing the chances of finding neurophysiological determinants. However, this information is not readily cited in subsequent articles that discuss the findings of this study. Zametkin and his associates were quite responsible in reporting this special criterion in selecting their patient group, and it was a reasonable choice given that their intent was to explore the possibility of finding biogenic determinants. It must be kept in mind that the original goal was simply to find evidence of biogenic determinants and that it would be up to subsequent researchers to support and confirm exploratory findings.

These 25 patients in the ADHD group were also unique in that they had never been treated at any time with stimulant medication. The reasoning, of course, was to rule out the possibility of any influence due to stimulant medication that may have "normalized" brain functioning.

During this brief scanning time, patients and controls were administered an auditory continuance performance test because of reported previous testing that suggested that this task affects cortical metabolism. All subjects performed this task with their eyes covered, presumably to factor out possible cortical activity due to visual stimuli, and the task itself took a little more than half an hour to complete. This is an important notation considering the nature of ADHD. By definition, ADHD includes a difficulty in inhibiting extraneous stimuli and in sustaining concentration and focus over long periods of time. Many ADHD patients perform better if they are in situations in which extraneous stimuli are reduced and performance time is limited, as opposed to the less structural and ongoing day-to-day flow of stimuli. It is interesting to note that there was no significant difference between the ADHD and non-ADHD groups with respect to the Auditory Continuance Performance test. In fact, the control group had a greater number of errors than the ADHD group. This is consistent with the findings that such tasks are not very sensitive to special ADHD conditions (see Chapter 4 for a more comprehensive discussion).

The capacity to encode information seems to require multiple cognitive skills and may not easily be addressed by a single test. However, the variability of performances on several tests can provide some insight. For instance, the combined performance on the backwards portion of the digit span from the Wechsler scales (Wechsler, 1981) and the Matching Familiar Figure Test (Carins & Cammock, 1978), along with several verbal fluency measures (Denckla, 1991), can be helpful.

Many of the above tests can also provide information regarding the capacity to shift attention. For instance, flexibility and fluency are necessary to do well on tests such as the Stroop Color and Word Test (Golden, 1978) and the Wisconsin Card Sort (Heaton, 1981).

In sum, the neurogenic model, as explanation of ADHD, is perhaps one of the oldest and has experienced several shifts throughout the century. The early clinical reports of patients followed the classical "disease" or medical model. Constitutional factors were cited as explanations of behavioral anomalies. The concept of minimal brain damage was adopted, although no concrete evidence of any actual damage to the brain existed. The lack of concrete evidence eventually moved investigators away from the perception of a damaged brain. This theory was not completely dispelled, however, perhaps because of the continued successes reported with respect to medication treatment.

With the advent of PET and MRI scans, along with the more sophisticated computerized systems, the concrete evidence of possible brain anomalies was introduced. These initial findings spawned an acceleration of research and much support of the neuropathological model. In more recent years, a greater interest has been paid to the use of neuropsychological testing. A structural functional model seems to be used, linking the different structures of the brain to various facets of neurofunctioning. Neuropsychological testing, which has been traditionally used to measure such functioning, has been considered recently to measure cognitive functions related to ADHD.

Critique of the Neuropathological Theory

As mentioned above, this theory is the oldest and most established. It dates back almost a century, and it has received minimal challenges. Perhaps the last major challenges took place almost 20 years ago, before the present-day cognitive revolution and during a time when humanistic psychology and the study of environmental and social conditions were more prominent (Barker, 1968). A limited number of investigators (Block, 1977; Willis & Lovaas, 1977) proposed a learning theory to ADHD as an alternative. There were specific concerns that children who displayed impulsivity and hyperactivity were products of a disorganized home life, parents with emotional difficulties, or both. Subsequent investigations challenged this cause-and-effect relationship and, in fact, demonstrated that negative parental behaviors may be a consequence of the ADHD child's disposition (Barkley & Cunningham, 1979; Cunningham & Barkley,

1978). Specifically, parental functioning improved after ADHD children were treated with stimulant medication. These initial findings were later supported by subsequent studies that measured the effects of methylphenidate on mother–child interactions (Barkley, Karlsson, Pollard, & Murphy, 1985; Barkley, Karlsson, Strzelecki, & Murphy, 1984). These research findings not only challenged the social learning theory of ADHD, but they also provided additional support that ADHD is due to neurogenic dispositions, by demonstrating positive effects due to stimulant medications. In essence, this theoretical model survived the ecological psychology trends of the 1960s and 1970s (Barker, 1968), and it now enjoys much acceptance and widespread support. Its support is reinforced by present trends toward research on cognitive functions and a heightened interest in brain research.

As presented earlier, it is important to consider the possibility that the neuro-pathological theory of ADHD may predispose investigators toward the error of blind acceptance. For this reason, special time and energy will be spent looking closely at the research in this area of study. In particular, it is important to understand the kinds of measures and methods used in generating research findings. Research methodology is often not given as much attention by clinical practitioners as by the researchers themselves. However, clinical practitioners need to be, at least, good consumers of research, and it makes sense that they spend some time looking at the inner mechanics of research design.

PET scans involve a technique in which radioactive material is circulated in the brain through the bloodstream so that it can be traced and measured. It has a very short half-life, which means that the amount of time available for measurement is quite limited. During this short time period, however, numerous measurements can be made within different structures of the brain, and calibrations can be made to identify the more active from the less active structures of the brain. Measurements can also be used for comparative purposes between groups of patients. As indicated in the studies cited above, groups of ADHD patients have undergone this procedure, and their brain activity levels were averaged together and compared with those of a similar group of non-ADHD patients. It is important to note that a number of different measures and comparisons can be generated, depending on the researcher's wishes. Researchers may simply be interested in comparing activity levels within different parts of the brain. Alternatively, researchers may be interested in calculating the difference between selected structures of a single brain, then averaging these differences with respect to a particular group, and finally comparing group averages of these differences. Basically, this is how researchers concluded that ADHD patients tended to have brains with asymmetrical functioning levels. The differences found within various structures of the brain (i.e., right vs. left hemispheres) were greater within the ADHD population than in the non-ADHD population.

During this short span of time when scanning takes place, there are numerous measures that can be made, and many more comparisons are available because of the multiple calibrations that can be generated from measures. This is an important point, because the large number of comparisons available to researchers can almost guarantee that some difference can be found between any two groups. For this reason, it is important that researchers govern themselves by limiting comparisons to an a priori set of hypotheses. For instance, researchers can assume beforehand that ADHD patients may have problems with left hemisphere functioning and, before any data are collected, the researchers justify the calculations of comparing differences between hemispheric functioning. In essence, calculations are not generated endlessly solely to find significant differences.

Similarly, large numbers of measures can be obtained from MRI and, therefore, the same precautions must be implemented. The MRI scan, as suggested earlier, is not a new technology. For a number of decades, physical chemists and other researchers have been using this technique to measure chemical structures. The instrument has been known in the research field as nuclear magnetic residence (NMR); the name may have been changed to MRI when the technology was first used in the medical field on patients. It was imagined that the term *nuclear* was dropped because of its potentially negative image of being dangerous; some patients may be reluctant to allow themselves to be placed in a machine whose name includes the word *nuclear*. It is ironic that the technology is rather unintrusive. The scan involves a strong machine-generated magnetic field that can be sensitive to the magnetic fields of very small structures, such as chemicals, by calibrating the distortion in the magetic field when the structures are introduced into the field. Each chemical structure has its own unique magnetic field, somewhat like its own signature.

For medical purposes, MRI scans are calibrated to the magnetic field of water. This is because water is so abundant in the body. Rather than tracking the flow of blood, as PET scans do, MRIs are useful in providing information on even the smallest structures of the brain (or any other part of the body). In research on ADHD, the sizes of different parts of the brain are calibrated, and these measures can subsequently be used for comparison purposes. Thus, the volumes of different structures are measured, rather than activity levels, and it is assumed that the greater the volume, the greater the capacity or function. It is important to keep in mind that this relationship between structure and function is still quite theoretical.

Zametkin and his associates (Zametkin et al., 1990) conducted what is considered a landmark study by providing the first physical evidence in an effort to associate ADHD with neuropathological functioning. For this reason, this study is singled out for critical review. This research article has since been cited repeatedly in subsequent articles on ADHD, and it has enjoyed familiarity among researchers and practitioners interested in this area of study. The aim of this discussion is to use this landmark study as an example of proper assessment of research methodology and subsequent findings. Again, the theme that is communicated here is that practitioners, although not directly involved in research, should at least be good consumers of research studies. Zametkin et al., as is

Zametkin et al. (1990) were very responsible in reporting that they did not conduct a test–retest comparison to measure within-subject variability of glucose metabolism. Their reasoning was certainly understandable, because there was some concern of the ethics of exposing subjects to additional radiation. It seemed that the authors were at least aware of the possible problem of large within-subject variance and the questionable reliability factor associated with their measurement methods. This variability is certainly reduced by the special conditions each subject was given, such as the lack of visual stimulation and special focus on the continuous-performance task. However, additional validity questions can be raised in consideration of this special and quite artificial condition because ADHD is a condition that is best identified by the quality of interactions over time, with respect to day-to-day activities and responsibilities.

Nevertheless, Zametkin et al. attempted to at least make a mathematical correction for this limitation. For each subject and corresponding set of scores, they calculated a reference ratio. They did this by dividing each subject's absolute glucose metabolism rate for each region of the brain measured by his or her global glucose metabolism rate. The aim was to attempt to minimize the effect of individual variations by using the global glucose metabolism rate as a normalization factor and by tempering the variation found when the absolute regional glucose metabolism rates are compared.

Of the 60 specific brain regions studied, comparison of absolute regional glucose metabolism rates between the ADHD and non-ADHD groups revealed a statistically different rate in 30 regions of the brain. Thus, the absolute difference in comparing rates yielded exactly half of the regions as being significant. However, when the 60 regions were normalized by dividing their rate by the global glucose metabolism rate, only 4 regions of the 60 reached statistical significance.

Unpaired student's t tests were used to make comparisons between the ADHD and non-ADHD groups. The t tests were not corrected for the number of comparisons. This presents a major problem in interpreting findings. Using an alpha level of .05 to determine statistical significance, and making comparisons at 60 regions of the brain, almost guarantees a statistically significant finding. In fact, the probability of 4 comparisons reaching statistical significance because of random chance is still relatively high.

Zametkin et al. (1990) used their statistically significant findings between the ADHD and non-ADHD groups, especially considering the four regions identified after the reference-ratio calibration, to identify areas of the brain involved in the attending andfocusing functions. The premotor and superior prefrontal regions were identified, and the authors cited other research findings to further speculate that the premotor cortex may have a special influence on voluntary movements depending on external cues (Rizzolitti, Mataelli, & Pavesi, 1983). The authors added that differences in absolute metabolic rates were found in areas beyond the frontal regions. They may have implied that ADHD is complex and most difficult to incorporate into a single comprehensive theory. However, they assumed, without fully appreciating the limitations in methodology, that ADHD is due to pathophysiological functioning.

The assumption that ADHD is due to neuropathological functioning is still not supported by research findings. In fact, there is absolutely no research that can provide a clear understanding of normative brain functioning, glucose metabolism, or any other activity of the brain. Science has not advanced enough to provide the normal parameters of brain functioning. Without fully appreciating the range of neuroactivity of the human brain, it is impossible to identify anomalies. In other medical conditions, physical anomalies are identified by comparing physiological dispositions to a standard. For instance, hypertension is diagnosed by comparing blood pressure with a given standard. These standards may vary with respect to age, gender, and a combination of several other factors, but they must be available for comparative purposes. Such standards for brain activity do not exist. Thus, it would simply be misleading to suggest that differences in brain activities are proof of neuropathologies. First, measured activity levels within a control group certainly cannot be representative of the entire range of brain activity for a normal population. Second, it is imagined that measured activity levels within different control groups, across several studies, are quite variant. Third, it is important to keep in mind the special conditions under which measures are made. At present, the technology does not exist to measure brain activities of individuals as they live their lives. The reader is invited to conduct a simple subjective retrospective study. Consider the cognitive state of your mind while reading this book; then go back no more than 48 hours and roughly review the different cognitive states you experienced within this very short time period. Even if life has been relatively routine, it is imagined that much variety has taken place related to different experiences, such as social interactions, moments of quiet solitude, and intimate encounters. Even without the consideration of special experiences such as surprise birthday parties, special vacations, or the occasional disappointment—all still within the parameter of normal living—it is easy to understand how varied and complex the standard of normative brain activities can be.

One could argue that neuropsychological tests are normed and that the finding of a statistically significant difference between an ADHD group and a control group is evidence in support of a neuropathological disposition. However, many ADHD adults score within normative parameters, even though there may be a statistically significant difference measured (Arcia & Gualtieri, 1994). Again, statistical significance is not proof of neuropathology.

Neuropsychological tests, although found to be reliable in the detection of brain anomalies due to injury, have not been very useful in detecting ADHD (Barkley, 1994a). Neuropsychological testing emerged as a specialized field of assessment to detect and describe effects of brain injury long before there was an interest in ADHD. As suggested earlier, numerous neuropsychological tests are available that can identify anomalies such as a limited capacity to scan visually, asymmetrical physical dexterity, and significant limitations in recall and memory. Unlike the patients suffering from stroke, dementia, and so on, ADHD patients do not have a signature pattern from which a diagnosis can be made. In fact, head injury patients who suffer with similar symptoms (lack of concentration, lack of behavioral inhibitions, etc.) are qualitatively different from ADHD patients

Another consideration is that standardization for these instruments, although it has screened away subjects with a history of brain damage, has not done so for ADHD subjects. It is conceivable, in fact, that many undetected ADHD subjects have been included in the standardization of these tests.

It is striking that there is so much diversity in outcome in the research literature generated in this field. Minor shifts in focus or methodology can often produce widely different results. For instance, Ernst et al. (1994) tried to replicate Zametkin et al.'s (1990) study of glucose metabolism by means of a PET scan analysis, this time looking at an adolescent population. There were no statistically significant differences between ADHD subjects and the normal adolescent group with respect to glucose metabolism. Ernst et al. did find a difference between the two groups when the subjects were separated with respect to gender; a significant difference was found only between the ADHD and non-ADHD girls, with no difference between the boys. The variation in findings may be indicative of the statistical power of the methodological designs. Also, it may be important to speculate on the practical significance of finding metabolic differences among girls and not among boys.

Subsequent research by the Zametkin research group attempted to detect cerebral glucose metabolic changes with respect to stimulant medication (Matochik et al., 1993, 1994), but they were unable to find any significant difference. They concluded that the measurement of glucose metabolism in adults with ADHD may not be an appropriately sensitive measure of medication effects. This is an important conclusion, considering that there are ample studies in which significant behavioral effects due to stimulant medication were measured (Barkley, 1977; DuPaul & Barkley, 1990; Wender, Reimherr, Wood, & Ward, 1985). If brain activity levels are associated with ADHD behaviors, then it is reasonable to assume that behavioral changes due to medication treatment correspond to changes in brain activity levels.

It is important to understand that discrepancies in findings are not due to significant investigator neglect; rather, they may be a reflection of the complexity of this area of study. For instance, the variety of brain locations, identified in relation to attentional functions, seems to go beyond even the scope proposed by Mirsky (1989). This field of study seems to lack organizational cohesiveness and, consequently, different measures, along with different methodologies, often result in different findings. Sieg et al. (1995) found that their SPECT (single photon emission computerized topography) brain imagery suggested anomalies in the frontal and parietal regions of the brain of ADHD subjects. Anomalies were identified by measuring asymmetrical activity levels; specifically, the left hemisphere was considered abnormal in functioning compared to the right hemisphere and also compared to the overall symmetrical activity levels found in control subjects.

By contrast, Heilman and Van Den Abell (1980) proposed a pathophysiological model of ADHD that is primarily due to right hemispheric anomalies. ADHD is again considered a dysfunction that may be due to asymmetry or lateralized anomalies, but in the opposite direction. Heilman and his associates based their model on measured behavioral difficulties due to lesions of the right hemisphere. In addition, they suggested that left hemisphere lesions do not seem to present any behavioral difficulties with respect to attentional functioning. They studied patients with both right and left medial frontal lesions and noted that only the patients with right hemispheric lesions failed to demonstrate adequate attentional responses. It is noteworthy that the behavioral measures included go–no-go tasks and performance observations made during a clinically based neurological exam. These clinical observations are typically not quantified. One could argue that the methods of measurement used are the antithesis of the SPECT analyses and other rather detailed measures. Also, there were some questions with respect to the use of clear neurogenic dysfunctions to propose a theory of ADHD. Many of the tasks used by neurologists, which are most difficult to perform by patients with clear brain injury, are easily performed by patients without brain injuries, including patients who have been diagnosed as having ADHD (Arcia & Gualtieri, 1994). Another way of looking at this issue is to consider the discriminate power these tasks have in distinguishing patients with ADHD from patients without ADHD. As is explained in Chapter 4, even the more standardized neuropsychological tests have minimal, if any, discriminative power.

Also, it is important to appreciate the variety of brain structures cited as being associated with attentional functioning. For instance, other studies have identified the corpus callosum (Giedd et al., 1994) and the cerebellum (Akshoomoff & Courchesne, 1994) as structures involved in attentional difficulties. In fact, some anomalies have been suggested in brain stem functioning (Lahat et al., 1995). Measurements of brain stem waves, their latency, and transmission time were recorded for both ADHD and non-ADHD children. Although not universal, the general latency times were longer for the ADHD group when compared with the control group.

Depending on the research emphasis, cortical and subcortical structures have been implicated with variant descriptions of anomalies. Some structures seem to be implicated more than others, but findings are inconsistent. Much of this confusion may be due to the microperspective inherent in this field of study. The proper study of ADHD may require a more holistic perspective that encompasses the complex fluidity of interactions between organism and environment. To accomplish this, traditional procedures of looking for the pathological structures may need to be reconsidered.

Normative Theory

Over the last decade, the literature on ADHD has been saturated with the emphasis on "deficit" (Quinn, 1995; Wender, 1995; Zametkin & Rapoport, 1987; Zametkin et al., 1990). With the emergence of studies using CAT scans and other biology-probing instruments (Zametkin et al., 1990), the most popular lines of investigation have been in the neurobiology fields. G. Weiss (1990), in her critique of some of the neurobiological assessments, stated that it would be a mistake to reduce ADHD simply to the study of metabolic dysfunctions in the brain. Pellegrini and Horvat (1995) presented a convincing critique that the psychosocial portion of the equation has been de-emphasized in recent years, yielding to the more exotic and popular investigations of brain functions. They argued that the environmental context of ADHD individuals, although not entirely discounted, has not been given proper attention, especially during the last two decades of what has sometimes been called the cognitive revolution. Barkley (1990), in his review of outcome studies, emphasized the importance of environmental variables, such as the socioeconomic status of ADHD individuals. More to the point, his rather eloquent description of "goodness of fit" (p. 227) brought home the notion that the interaction between organism and environment is an important consideration. In his later writings (Barkley, 1994b, 1997), however, he gives very little attention to his model of ADHD with respect to environmental components.

Taking this theory one step further, Hartmann (1993) argued against the notion of "deficit" and rather boldly suggested that ADHD individuals have a functional advantage over others. Although Hartmann's arguments are not based on rigorous research findings, and he dispels a wealth of evidence that identifies disadvantages to having ADHD, his challenge to the established pathological theory of ADHD is worthy of consideration.

Two compelling issues must be reviewed here that may provide some sobering thought to researchers who have adopted the pathological–disease model of ADHD. First, all of the symptoms related to ADHD are readily observed in the normal population. The average adult, when asked, can identify with experiences of boredom, wandering attention, lack of concentration, and so on. The problem with the ADHD population is that of *degree* rather than presence of these symptoms themselves. The defect or disease model usually pertains to dispositions that are unique and qualitatively different from those of the average population. The disease element is actually an invasion into or an assault on the normal brain. This would include pathologies such as brain tumors, toxic chemical exposures, and so on. Second, all measures used to identify ADHD universally use components such as frequency of correct responses, Likert scales that emphasize the severity of difficulties, and accumulation of data from different sources (interview, psychological testing, etc.). The cutoff marker to designate significant problems is statistically set by convention rather than by some real indication of deficit or disease. Usually, 1.5–2.0 *SD* beyond the mean is used as the demarcation point (Murphy & Barkley, 1995).

The normative theory of ADHD suggests that ADHD behaviors are simply an extension of expected human functioning. Hartmann (1993) took this principle further by suggesting that ADHD behaviors are not symptoms of a dysfunction but behaviors that were necessary and quite functional in an ancient society of hunters. As human civilizations shifted from a predominantly hunting system to that of farming, a new set of adaptive behaviors was necessary, and the old set of behaviors eventually became secondary to survival needs. Hartmann invited his readers to consider a new perspective of ADHD. He asked that ADHD individuals are seen as "hunters" living in a world of "farmers." For Hartmann, this is not simply an analogy. He went to great lengths to point out that many of the skills necessary to become a successful hunter are behaviors now considered typical of individuals with ADHD. For instance, he noted that hunters, as opposed to farmers, are more likely to migrate from territory to territory rather than staying in one place and cultivate the land. The hunter tends to always be ready to be on the move in pursuit of prey, whereas the farmer is motivated to stay close to the land. Also, unlike the farmer, who adapts to the natural rhythm of the climate, the hunter is more likely to react on impulse to the acute changes in the environment.

Because the farmer is not likely to move, much investment and energy are spent cultivating and attending to the details of the immediate world. Long-term planning is a priority, and behaviors are adapted to a long-term reward system. By contrast, the hunter, always being on the move, tends to be more of a scanner of the environment and reacts to quick changes. The world of the hunter is less involved in long-term planning and more in tune to quick and immediate rewards. The hunter is more likely to take risks.

Hartmann recognized that the shift from a predominantly hunting way of life to that of cultivation took place thousands of years ago, but the shift has been gradual, and an argument has been made with respect to a complementary system between hunters and farmers. In essence, for centuries civilizations have benefited from both hunters and farmers working in concert. Individuals with ADHD are not simply considered descendants of an ancient hunting way of life. Hartmann invited his readers to consider a continuation of this shift through recent and contemporary history. He stated:

> An interesting footnote to this hypothesis is the observation that Europeans view Americans and Australians as "brash and risk-taking." Americans and Australians often view Europeans as "stodgy and conservative." Accepting the notion that ADD is an inherited trait, considering the types of peoples who would risk life and limb for a journey across the Atlantic in the seventeenth century—they'd have to be either desperate farmers or normal hunters. Similarly, Australia's white population is almost entirely descendent from prisoners sent there from England; the misfits and malcontents of British society. (I suspect a very large percentage were ADD hunters who couldn't succeed as the industrial revolution "farmerized" the British labor market and culture.) (pp. 22–23)

The theme presented is that ADHD behavior is embedded in the culture itself, and evidence of this is indirectly presented by the frequency of ADHD with respect to culture and society. American society, which has a much higher frequency of ADHD than Europe, can be described as being far more mobile and innovative than European society.

It would be interesting to run a sociological comparison between the two societies with respect to ADHD behavioral tendencies. Variables such as the frequency of impulsive marriages, homicides, and other negative social components that may be related to ADHD should be measured, along with some of the more "functional" components, such as the number of patents registered, the number of novel and innovative research studies conducted, the frequency of successful business ventures, and so on.

Hartmann (1993) not only placed ADHD within the realm of normal functioning but also suggested that there are a number of jobs within society for which ADHD lifestyles can be an asset rather than a liability. He listed jobs such as traveling salespeople, consultants, entrepreneurs, freelance writers, field reporters, and military combat personnel as requiring a lifestyle compatible with ADHD behaviors.

Critique of the Normative Theory

Hartmann's (1993) normative model of ADHD provides a healthy challenge to the more popular "deficit" perspective. The neuropathological theme has become so popular that there may be a danger of people accepting its assumptions blindly, without considering—or even perceiving—alternatives. A former patient at a local CHADD (Children and Adults with Attention Deficit Disorder) meeting also pointed out that Hartmann offered a positive inoculation against the more popular negative label of ADHD. From a patient's perspective, it may be good to know some of the things that can be advantageous because of ADHD, rather than continually hearing about the pitfalls. Hartmann may have offered more than hope by identifying ADHD individuals as having particular advantages, a concept that mainstream research has not adopted readily.

Typical of a minority voice, this theoretical perspective does not have much empirical support at the present time. Studies that test the hypotheses generated from this perspective must be able to encompass psychosocial and cultural variables, along with the usual biological components. If ADHD is considered, at least in part, a component of the norm of a culture, then research studies must include comparisons across different psychosocial and cultural boundaries.

The adoption of this perspective brings forth some interesting questions. For instance, is it more important to look at the interaction of biological dispositions and environmental demands than it would be to look at each of these components separately? How would a group of ADHD adults, transplanted from a society that measures time by the minute to a society that measures time by the seasons, respond with respect to their "symptoms"?

It would be most interesting to consider ADHD behaviors with respect to societal rather than individual functioning. For instance, can ADHD symptomatology be found in a culture, just as it is found in individuals? According to this perspective the American culture could be compared with the standards of the rest of the world with respect to attention span, tolerance for repetitiveness, tendency toward boredom, tendency to act impulsively, and so on. Would the norm for the American culture be significantly different in these areas, compared to other cultures (Asian, European, etc.)? If so, what implications can be made regarding today's theoretical models of ADHD?

It may be easy to label individuals as having a "chemical imbalance" and pathological; it may not be so easy to accept that an entire society or culture is prone to be chemically imbalanced or pathological. It would be interesting, for instance, if Zametkin et al. (1990) conducted another study using PET scan analyses to compare American brains with Japanese or Chinese brains. Samples from the different societies could be matched demographically, and analyses could be made with respect to glucose metabolism, as in the original study. The subjects selected would all be normally functioning individuals within their respective societies. That is, subjects would need to be free from any pathologies identified by their respective societies, and each would be a mainstream representative sample of his or her society. For example, the American sample may represent a cross-section of the country, with various occupations and lifestyles (i.e., business owners, bus drivers, custodial workers, evangelists, rodeo riders, sale representatives, disc jockeys, computer technicians, artists, etc.), all free from symptoms that would be deemed by American standards as pathological (e.g., seizure disorders, alcohol dependency, dementia, etc., including ADHD). The same would be true for the Japanese or Chinese samples. According to the normative model, a significant difference between societies is a reasonable and testable hypothesis.

Research in this area of study obviously requires the gathering of data on numerous variables across social–cultural boundaries. This grand undertaking may be most difficult, and the complexities involved may significantly challenge the skills of researchers. Meanwhile, on a less grander scale, it may be worthwhile to look at some of the assumptions Hartmann (1993) offered. For instance, do ADHD dispositions really make for better hunters, military personnel, police, and so on? More specifically, would it be advantageous to allow someone with impulsive tendencies to take on job-related responsibilities that require carrying a lethal weapon, as the military and police do? Even if the more primitive perspective is considered, arguments can be made that even ancient hunting methods often involved much patience and attention to detail, perhaps more so than other activities because of the potential life-and-death circumstances. In plain terms, would it be advantageous for someone to go hunting with an ADHD partner in a terrain that includes lions, venomous reptiles, and other potentially dangerous animals?

The Unified Field Theory of ADHD

A few years ago Barkley (1994b) proposed a unified field theory of ADHD. He theorized that all problems in ADHD can be reduced to a single underlying feature. Specifically, he believes that all the problems related to ADHD are due to a basic difficulty to inhibit or delay reactions to environmental situations. His discussion included references to numerous studies, mainly of children who continually demonstrate difficulties in delaying responses to various stimuli. He noted that "impairment in delayed responding creates a hyperresponsivity to immediate signals or events" (p. 14) and further stated that "the evidence for impaired delayed responding or motor dysinhibition as the cornerstone of ADHD now seems irrefutable" (p. 15).

Barkley (1994b) cited correlational studies and, in particular, gave much discussion to very strong associations of a diagnosis of ADHD with respect to impulsive–hyperactive symptoms as opposed to symptoms of inattention. Consequently, Barkley de-emphasized inattentiveness as a core problem. Symptoms of inattention, along with impulsivity and hyperactivity—at present identified as the central categories for diagnosis (*DSM–IV*, American Psychiatric Association, 1994)—can be reduced to basic problems in delay or response inhibition.

More recently, Barkley (1997) published a revision of his earlier thesis. He maintained that ADHD is due to difficulties of the inhibitory system of the brain. This new edition of his unified theory has been described conceptually as a hybrid model that combines Bronowski's (1977) theory of human cognition with Fuster's (1989) theory of prefrontal functioning. In addition, Barkley (1997) discussed developmental properties of ADHD with particular overlapping properties identified by both Bronowski's (1977) and Fuster's (1989) theoretical perspectives. Barkley's theoretical model is significant in that it attempts to pull together diverse fields of study under a single conceptual model. One could argue that his model combines the two perspectives presented earlier in this chapter: neurological and normative. The neurological perspective is provided by Fuster's (1989) review of prefrontal functioning, and the normative perspective is provided by Bronowski's (1977) model of human evolution as well as the normative process of child development.

Again, Barkley should be credited for his attempt to develop a rather comprehensive conceptual framework of ADHD. It is assumed that this project is not finished, and special effort will be made to discuss the processes involved in the development of his unified theory. The following section will present the earliest model, and the section after that will discuss the more recent adjustments and changes. In addition, a critical review of his theory will be presented, and it is hoped that the process of theory refinement will continue.

Original Unified Field Theory Much of Barkley's originally proposed theory relied heavily on Bronowski's (1977) philosophy of human functioning. In particular, Barkley relied on four cognitive abilities described by Bronowski that enable humans to delay responding to situations in the environment. These include separation of affect, prolongation, internalization, and reconstitution. Barkley went on to explain how these cognitive abilities are defective in individuals with ADHD and, in turn, these defects are due to an underlying defective ability to delay responses to stimuli.

A problem in separation of affect was supported by observations that ADHD children have a greater tendency toward outbursts of temper and in lower frustration tolerance (Barkley, 1994b). Barkley also cited evidence that ADHD children are more excitable compared to normal children. Although no empirical data were presented, Barkley suggested that numerous clinical descriptions of adults with ADHD include difficulties in controlling temper and a tendency toward emotional outbursts.

The second cognitive ability, prolongation, was originally described by Bronowski as a functioning property within the realm of linguistics that allows humans to refer backward and forward in time to measure and analyze stimuli before rendering a response. Crucial to this capacity are the use of memory and the ability to use hindsight, foresight, or both. Barkley correctly reported that ADHD children and adults are not generally impaired with respect to memory storage and recall, but they may be inefficient in the prolongation ability of making correct analyses. For instance, past experiences are usually not referenced efficiently to make appropriate judgments.

The next of Bronowski's described abilities, internalization of language, refers to the inner dialogue that is theoretically unique in humans. Through this inner dialogue, contemplation and self-reflection are enacted. Bronowski (1977) described this as "a cardinal feature of human thought that it can refer to itself, and of human language that it contains its own metalanguage" (p. 119). Barkley associated this functioning with what he refers to as an impairment in rule-governed behavior, which was first presented almost two decades ago (Barkley, 1981). The original description of children who lacked appropriate self-governing skills was well conceptualized, with much reliance on developmental data. The more recent arguments also seemed to be supported by observations of children as they reportedly struggle when facing novel environmental conditions that require synthesis of novel solutions by means of internal dialogue.

The last of Bronowski's proposed functions is reconstitution. Bronowski explained that reconstitution involves two procedures. The first is a seemingly cognitive mechanism by which messages are broken down into smaller parts, and the second involves a "procedure of synthesis" (p. 119) in which the parts are rearranged to form other messages. According to Bronowski's very elaborate descriptions, it is obvious that this is a highly complex function that can translate into a number of different performance abilities. For instance, the description of reconstitutional functions is highly reminiscent of Piaget's (1972) discussion of the evolution of intellectual process from adolescence to adulthood; it encompasses the assimilation and accommodation functions of the brain as it interacts with environment. Barkley correctly determined that reconstitution, according to Bronowski's definition, can affect problem-solving skills, verbal fluency, and even creativity. He also reported that, when compared with a non-ADHD group, there is evidence that ADHD children score lower in these areas (Barkley, 1994b).

In a later article, Barkley (1995) introduced a fifth cognitive component he identified as "motor control-fluency" (p. 3). This added component reflects the ability to control complex motor actions to maximize long-term rewards. Barkley reported that it requires self-regulation to delay immediate gratification and, under circumstances of competing short-term rewards, persistence and perseverance are required. The underlying theme is that individuals with ADHD may have defective inhibitory controls; they may have problems because they tend to succumb to the need for immediate gratification. The consequences are inefficient performance or a general behavioral failure to achieve long-term goals that require much persistence.

In his 1995 article, Barkley argued that ADHD is a deficit in "output" or what he identified as "a response planning-programming execution," rather than "input" or what he described as "a sensory-perceptual information processing" (p. 1) component. The emphasis seems to be based on the ADHD individual's performance and behaviors rather than on any internal processing problem. In fact, Barkley titled this article "Is There an Attention Deficit in ADHD?" and went on to imply that the answer is most likely "no." True to its name, the unified field theory of ADHD seems to include an exercise in reductionism, and Barkley certainly presented a rather bold theme by questioning the existence of attention deficit in ADHD.

Continued Refinement of Barkley's Unified Theory In his revision of the theory, it may be important to note that Barkley (1997) used the term *constructing* in his title, perhaps to suggest an ongoing process of theory building. This version continued to refer to Bronowski's constructs but also incorporated the neurogenic model of prefrontal cortex functioning.

Also, this version proposed a major shift in the conceptualization of ADHD. Two qualitatively different disorders were suggested. In this model, the predominately inattentive type subcategory of the *DSM–IV* is described as being significantly different from all the other subcategories. Barkley (1997) went on to explain that his proposed theory is now mainly limited to the latter subcategories of the *DSM–IV*, and it excludes inattention problems without major problems with hyperactivity–impulsivity.

Barkley reasoned that symptoms related to the predominately inattentive type of ADHD, such as daydreaming, a sense of confusion, and hypoactivity, may be due to a separate deficit. Individuals with these symptoms seem to have problems only in speed of information processing and are qualitatively different from people classified in the other *DSM–IV* categories. Thus, an argument was made to look at the inattentive type as a separate disorder that should not be clustered together with ADHD.

This separate category, Barkley (1997) went on to explain, does not include children who are originally diagnosed as having ADHD, combined type, and may be diagnosed later as predominately inattentive type as they get older because the hyperactive behaviors have subsided. Barkley (1997) suggested that these children have not changed types of ADHD and that the behaviors associated with inattention in these children are "still qualitatively different from the inattention manifested by children classified as the inattentive type" (p. 67) without a history of problems in hyperactivity, impulsivity, or both.

With this conceptual shift, Barkley's model of an underlying deficit in response inhibition remains the essential impairment of ADHD. This central impairment explains problems in all of the ADHD subcategories, with the exclusion of the inattentive type.

Behavioral inhibition, according to the theory, refers to three processes. These are explained as follows:

> (a) inhibition of the initial prepotent response to an event; (b) stopping of an ongoing response, which thereby permits a delay in the decision to respond; and (c) the protection of this period of delay and the self-directed responses that occur within it from disruption by competing events and responses (interference control). (Barkley, 1997, p. 67)

In essence, the capacity to exercise behavioral inhibitions first allows individuals to prevent premature reactions to initial stimuli, and second, it permits a delay in response, which will allow the individual time to cognitively evaluate and make the proper decision to respond; finally, it prevents competing—or perhaps distracting—stimuli from interfering once a decided response is executed. Behavioral inhibition was further defined as not being a component of emotional distress such as that found in very shy and withdrawn individuals. The emphasis, of course, is in the identification of an inhibitory system that is cognitively dysfunctional rather than pathological because of emotional difficulties.

With this necessary underlying cognitive component, five areas of functioning are discussed, many of which were presented earlier in the original model (Barkley, 1994b,c, 1995). Just as argued in the original model, these functions are described as being problematic in ADHD individuals.

Perhaps the oldest function is Barkley's discussion (1981) of emotional self-regulation. Inner drives and motivations are controlled and managed by this cognitive capacity to check emotional reactions and maintain appropriate objective and social perspectives. Much emphasis has been given to the need for ADHD individuals to manage and maintain emotional control. It was hypothesized that through this mechanismlong-term negative outcomes can be avoided (Barkley, 1994b,c).

Another component that is considered a byproduct of a properly functioning inhibitory system is the use of a working memory. This cognitive function is closely related to Bronowski's (1977) description of prolongation in that it allows individuals to refer backward and forward in time to develop functional perspectives with respect to cause-and-effect experiences. Working memory includes an ability to understand sequences of events and, in turn, to make adjustments to properly plan and predict positive outcomes. This cognitive function allows individuals to move beyond the here and now and use temporal awareness as a tool to shape behavioral strategies. Barkley (1994b) pointed out that people with ADHD are deficient in this ability and are often trapped, or at least excessively influenced by the present circumstances. Cause-and-effect sequences are often limited and predispose ADHD individuals toward negative behavioral outcomes. For instance, ADHD children do not seem to learn from their past mistakes as well as their non-ADHD peers.

The other three components presented by Barkley—internalization of language, reconstitution, and motor control-fluency—are as they were presented in his earlier writings (1994b, 1995). Of these three, internalization of language is best associated with behavioral observations of ADHD. This is presented as a developmental component; as children mature, they are able to use internalized language as a means of self-governing. Whereas in an earlier stage of life they required external reinforcers—usually an adult authority figure such as a parent or a teacher—they are now able to internalize expected standards of behaviors and, therefore, regulate themselves with minimal external reinforcers. The ADHD child, limited in this capacity, cannot rely on internal language to remain on task or follow the appropriate rules. Consequently, ADHD children require more consistent external reinforcers to compensate.

Barkley (1997) proposed that all of the cognitive functions described above fit into his hybrid model of normative cognitive functioning as described by Bronowski (1977) and prefrontal neurogenic activity as presented by Fuster (1989). Barkley proposed that these cognitive constructs provide rich ground for further research, and he further suggested that the concept of inattentiveness be considered a secondary condition influenced by the cognitive functions he had proposed.

In Barkley's conceptual framework, attention or persistence on task is either contingency shaped or self-regulated. Contingency-shaped attention is based on immediate environmental rewards, novelty of the task, and close temporal continuity of events. Under such contingencies, individuals with ADHD should have no problems and are considered indistinguishable from non-ADHD individuals. By contrast, self-regulated attention does not require the same contingencies, because this form of attention is the product of all of the executive functions presented in the theoretical model. Barkley (1997) stated that "it is this self regulatory type of sustained attention that is probably developmentally delayed in children with ADHD, not the type that is contingency-shaped" (p. 84).

In sum, the construction of a new theory of ADHD includes a restructuring of several conceptualizations. Symptoms of inattention that are without a history of hyperactivity–impulsivity are considered a separate disorder from ADHD. All other subcategories of ADHD are now explained as problems due to a single underlying feature: poor behavioral inhibition. With the use of cognitive constructs from Bronowski (1977) and research on prefrontal functioning, five neuropsychological functions are considered essential. These include self-regulation of affect, working memory, internalization of language, reconstitution, and the fluidity of complex motor controls. The unifying feature of ADHD is that problems are basically due to a defect in behavioral inhibition. In this respect, the new model follows the reductionist tradition of the neurogenic theory of ADHD. However, the model allows for a developmental understanding of cognitive functioning and, at least, implies that problems in ADHD fit into a continuum of normative functioning. Nevertheless, this model clearly places ADHD within the context of neurogenic functioning, and factors with respect to cultural and social standards are not considered defining properties of ADHD.

Critical Review of the Unified Field Theory

Before presenting any discussion on the content of Barkley's theory, it may be worthwhile to review the concept of the unified field theory and, in consideration of the fact that much of Barkley's theory originates from Bronowski's (1977) description of cognitive functioning, it may be prudent to take a closer look at Bronowski's work.

Foundations of the Unified Field Theory   The unified field phenomenon introduced by Barkley apparently was borrowed from the field of physics where, for almost a century, much effort has been expended on finding the single underlying property of the universe (Hawking, 1988, 1993). In Hawking's historical accounts, the strong and weak forces of physics have been unified, and interchanging models now can be adopted to explain one or the other. Later, the forces involved with electromagnetic fields—better known as chemistry—were eventually integrated into the unified field perspective where, again, the same underlying set of rules incorporated electromagnetic structures. The force of gravity is the only one that has yet to be incorporated into this unified field theory. Of all the forces, gravity is described as being the weakest and, because it requires the study of large masses—planets and galaxies—it has been difficult to apply experimental designs to it. Hawking, a noted contemporary theoretical physicist, has apparently spent much of his career looking for black holes in the universe, theoretical structures in themselves, which would have the mass necessary to perhaps explain some of the mysteries related to gravitational force. It was suggested that Albert Einstein spent the last years of his life engaged in the understanding of the force of gravity, again in an effort to advance the unified field theory.

Apparently, the search for a unified theory is not new to science. There seems to be a special attraction to and interest in the discovery of the most basic rule or property that can encompass all observed data. This special attraction is perhaps the single most motivating force for reductionism. It is believed that, if complex observations can be broken down to their simplest form, this will lead to the discovery of the most basic underlying explanation. The goal is to replace previous equations with a single and more general equation whereby all previous equations can be interchangeable. If this is accomplished, cohesiveness, and perhaps greater simplicity, can be realized. A unifying theory, almost by definition, brings harmony and a more esthetic understanding because it is able to resolve and reconcile previously orthogonal principles.

There may be an inherent motivational flaw to the search for a unifying theoretical perspective, however. The drive to achieve harmony and esthetic symmetry may be an inherent human need that could contaminate objectivity. Thus, it can be said that scientists are projecting themselves in search of a unifed theory. In plain terms, harmony may be a figment of their imaginations.

This human condition was perhaps best explained by Max Wertheimer and his associates Wolfgang Kohler and Kurt Koffka, who pioneered the experimental studies in gestalt psychology (Hothersall, 1984; Watson, 1978). Among numerous findings, these rather creative researchers noted and measured the power of human perception and its tendencies. A comprehensive discussion is beyond the realm of this book, but it is worth reviewing, in brief, some of the findings presented by these almost-forgotten researchers.

Gestalt psychologists have been instrumental in providing evidence that it is human nature to look for symmetry, closure, and harmony when explaining the environment. There seems to be a propensity to lean in this direction and, if no cohesiveness is found objectively, it is quite possible that humans will project it onto the world around them (Koffka, 1922; Kohler, 1929). Before World War II, gestalt psychology seemed to enjoy some level of prominence in the United States (Helson, 1925; Hothersall, 1984; Watson, 1978). It was perhaps unfortunate that this field of study emerged just before World War II. The principal researchers were Jewish, and politically they faced a very difficult time during the emerging Nazi regime. Also, the German name given to this field of study may have biased American researchers. Whatever the reason, there has been relatively minimal research in this field, and gestalt psychology does not seem to be a prominent focus of contemporary American social science.

Regardless, the principles brought forth more than 70 years ago are worth considering because of their power in clouding objective views. Toward the end of his life, Albert Einstein tended to be a critic of the emerging study of quantum mechanics. He seemed to be against the notions of quantum probability fields and that the forces of physics behave at random and often in haphazard patterns; as he remarked, "God does not play dice with the universe." Decades after his death, quantum mechanics has emerged as a prominent and respected field of study. In fact, there are scientists who proposed a future theory of chaos (Gleick, 1987) that even challenges the predictive equations based on random fields and may be the antithesis of a unified field theory.

Bronowski's Essays: Application to the New ADHD Theory   In consideration of the fact that much of Barkley's theory is derived from Bronowski's description of cognitive functioning, it may be prudent to take a closer look at Bronowski's work. *A Sense of the Future: Essays on Natural Philosophy* (1977) is a collection of essays that quite eloquently discuss development of human endeavors in reference to art and science. In the early portion of the book, Bronowski gives much time to his view of the development of science. The writings are much more than just a chronicle; he makes a point to integrate scientific development with his view of human evolution. The beginnings of scientific investigation for Bronowski were paralleled by an age of reason and a hunger for the discovery of underlying mechanisms. He dates the 17th through the 19th centuries as the first stage of science, when it was believed that anything could be understood if it were broken down into its basic components. The underlying assumption during this era of scientific inquiry was that the fundamental principles governing observed data can lead to a unifying principle that encompasses all observations. Thus, Bronowski suggested that reductionism was the main philosophical thrust to scientific inquiry by the beginning of the 20th century. However, he went on to explain that the world of absolute mechanisms gave way to a world of uncertainties and metaphors, as suggested above regarding the emergence of quantum mechanics in physics. The limits of reductionism were discovered, and a revolutionary new science of models and probabilities emerged.

It is somewhat of a paradox to read about Barkley's unified theory of ADHD, drawn from Bronowski's work, when Bronowski himself presented a historical critique of this kind of thinking. On the basis of Bronowski's own assessments, Barkley's theory of fundamental neurogenic functions—or perhaps a single inhibitory function—is destined to the same fate as early 20th-century reductionism.

Barkley drew much of his theory of ADHD from one particular essay, entitled "Human and Animal Languages." Bronowski's historical critique was presented in an earlier essay in the book, entitled "The Logic of Nature." Bronowski argued for the recognition of limitations to mechanical logic and reason yet the continuation of scientific discovery. Human capacity for self-reflection and creativity is offered as an explanation to differentiate formal logic from the logic of the mind. Bronowski went on to discuss the unique human advantages of language and outlined the processes toward a society of science. In these discussions, Bronowksi did not shy away from difficult topics such as human values and moral conduct. His very eloquent writings lead the reader by tying together the conceptual strings of philosophy, cultural development, and contemporary politics.

In his earlier writings, Barkley (1994b) gave credit to Bronowski for Bronowski's complex insights into human functioning. Rather than limiting a theoretical model of ADHD to a single essay, it may have been wiser to consider Bronowski's entire collection of essays and, in turn, propose a less mechanical model of ADHD. For instance, at first assessments, the two previous theoretical positions outlined in this chapter reflect divergent and opposing points of view. The first is based on neurogenic functioning and embraces a reductionist model of ADHD. The second is sensitive to normative social and cultural factors and embraces a more holistic view. Bronowski provided the conceptual framework necessary for the integration of both seemingly opposing perspectives. It seems Barkley missed this opportunity.

Assessing the Reconstruction of Barkley's Theory   Before advancing his theory, Barkley (1997) proposed a major conceptual change. He considered individuals who are inattentive, without any history of hyperactivity–impulsivity, qualitatively different from both individuals who are predominately hyperactive–impulsive and individuals who may be predominately inattentive but have had a history of hyperactivity–impulsivity. According to this new realignment, the inattentive type, without a history of hyperactivity–impulsivity, is reflective of an entirely different disorder, separate from ADHD. It may be appropriate to see these individuals as being qualitatively different from individuals in other subcategories of ADHD, but it seems premature to identify them as having a completely separate disorder, no longer under the ADHD umbrella.

An alternative model regarding all of the subcategories of ADHD is discussed later in this chapter. For now, it is important to understand that Barkley, with this rather radical conceptual change, has assigned his theoretical model to a new conceptualization of ADHD. In essence, the inattentive type without a history of hyperactivity–impulsivity is the "gravitational force" of ADHD theory. Unlike the theoretical physicists who are still working diligently to incorporate gravitational force into a unified field theory, Barkley has jettisoned this category as a disorder outside of the field of ADHD.

As is presented later, when the individual cognitive abilities are discussed, this conceptual shift freed Barkley from incorporating this expelled subcategory. In a purely theoretical model, this is certainly permissible. However, the reason for expelling an entire subcategory must be substantially more than just a better fit into a conceptual framework.

The above issue is extremely important to consider for the adult population. As Barkley (1997) described, the predominately inattentive type seems to develop later in life. Overall, there is an age-related shift away from hyperactivity–impulsivity and more toward symptoms of inattention. Consequently, the new proposed theory, along with its conceptual shift, may not be as applicable to adults with ADHD as it is for ADHD children.

It is important to note that much of the evidence in support of this theory has been presented with respect to studies done on children, rather than adults; consequently, emphasis has been on behavioral measures of impulsivity and hyperactivity. In consideration of the fact that hyperactivity and impulsivity in ADHD individuals is predominately related to age (McBurnett, 1995), the theme of one underlying factor, behavioral inhibition, as the cornerstone of ADHD may be based on skewed observations with respect to age.

Even with the exclusion of the inattentive type without a history of hyperactivity–impulsivity, the cognitive constructs proposed in this theory seem to be too broad to be useful in explaining ADHD. The problems in the cognitive abilities presented are found in a variety of other disorders; specifics regarding this issue are provided when each of the cognitive abilities is discussed.

One can also argue that the proposed theoretical model does not account for all of the observed ADHD behaviors, even if the focus is on symptoms of hyperactivity–impulsivity. Impairments in delayed responding—or, as it was later (1997) retermed, *behavioral inhibition*—assumes, by definition, that a stimulus or stimuli exist. In essence, to prevent onseself from responding, one must first experience some stimuli. The theory assumes that stimuli exist and that the ADHD individual lacks the appropriate restraints necessary to inhibit or delay responding. However, an argument can be made that there is a subset of ADHD individuals who seem to be hungry for stimuli. The problem is not in a defective capacity to inhibit responding but a need to seek out stimuli. For those who have the intellectual capacity to match their hunger for stimuli, this disposition may be quite functional. Unfortunately, there are many others who have a high arousal threshold but lack the cognitive abilities to manage effectively. The problem in this subset of ADHD individuals may very well be due to a mismatch between energetic drives and intellectual talents. This alternative model is presented later in this chapter. For now, it may be important to focus on the overinclusive theme of Barkley's model by reviewing the different proposed cognitive functions.

Although there may be some overlap between ADHD symptoms and affect control, there is no evidence to suggest that all ADHD individuals have problems with self-regulation of affect. Individuals who are diagnosed as predominately inattentive type, without many or any signs of hyperactivity–impulsivity, may be more likely not to display affect control problems. These individuals are not likely to present problems of emotional reactivity and impulsive behaviors due to their immediate emotional state, but they may still struggle with a lack of adequate focus in attention to tasks. They are sometimes described as being lost in a fog (Murphy & LeVert, 1995), a symptom predominately reported by writers who mainly work with adults (Brown, 1996; Quinn, 1994; Solden, 1995; Weiss, 1992) rather than children (Achenbach & Edelbrock, 1983). According to the reconceptualization of ADHD, this critique does not apply to the predominately inattentive type, without a history of hyperactivity–impulsivity, because this subcategory has now been excluded from the model. However, people who have been diagnosed with the predominately inattentive type, who have had a history of hyperactivity–impulsivity, are included in the model, and the above critique would apply to this subset of individuals.

Also, there is a great number of individuals who have problems with affect control, but are not ADHD. The fact that there are numerous other problems related to affect control that do not include ADHD does not invalidate the theoretical perspective. However, it would be interesting to test frequency levels of these different categories to compare them with the frequency of ADHD and affect control problems combined. According to the theoretical perspective proposed, the combined ADHD and affect control category should have a high frequency of occurrence. The fewest observations should be found in the category of ADHD individuals without affect control problems, because these individuals would be considered the exceptions to the rule. According to Brown (1996), however, these individuals may actually be in the majority, if the focus is on the adult ADHD population. He believes that the behavioral difficulties, such as impulse control problems or emotional controls, are less prominent among adults with ADHD compared to children with ADHD. Again, ADHD individuals who have never had a history of hyperactivity–impulsivity would be excluded from the analysis because of the model's reconceptualization of ADHD. However, it is still hypothesized that there are numerous adults with a history of hyperactivity–impulsivity during the childhood years who do not present any major problem in affect control. The test to the theoretical model proposed is based on the comparative frequencies of observations within each category. If the observed frequency of ADHD and affect control problems is relatively high, compared to the categories of affect control problems without ADHD and ADHD without affect control problems, then the utility of this cognitive function, in explaining ADHD, is validated. Further refinement can be achieved if age is considered a factor. Based on the above descriptions of adults with ADHD, it is further hypothesized that the utility of this cognitive function, if at all validated for children, will be less so for adults.

Compared to the other five cognitive functions proposed by Barkley, difficulties in working memory seem to best fit ADHD individuals. Again, the original thesis, as described by Bronowski's concept of prolongation, is embedded in the field of linguistics, but ADHD-related symptoms, such as difficulties in sequencing, planning ahead, and prioritizing needs and responsibilities, all seem to fit into the concept of prolongation and the efficient use of recall skills. For those who are versed in statistics, an analogy can be made to the use of partial correlations. Partial correlations are used to hold constant some variable while one looks at relationships between other variables. The exercise of choosing which variable should be held constant to make sense and untangle multiple associations with numerous other variables may be an exercise of statistical prolongation. An efficient working memory is necessary to coordinate all the details of daily life, and Barkley (1997) noted that this is a major problem with ADHD individuals.

It is important to understand, however, that working memory is reflective of a broad category of cognitive functioning and complexities. It would be more accurate to describe working memory as a set of cognitive functions rather than a single cognitive ability. Problems in these areas of functioning may be reflective of specific learning disabilities, independent of ADHD. Again, the utility of this set of highly complex cognitive abilities must be weighed with respect to potential confounding factors.

The risk of confounding factors can be reduced if the focus is on temporal functioning rather than on working memory. Problems regarding the efficient use of time seem to be uniquely associated with ADHD, at least more so than other disorders (Chee, Logan, Schachar, Lindsay, & Wachsmuth, 1989; Van der Meere, Van Baal, & Sergeant, 1989; Van der Meere, Vreeling, & Sergeant, 1992; Zakay, 1992). Regarding the adult population, the Consistency/Long-Term subscale of the Attention Deficit Scales for Adults (ADSA) provided the greatest discriminative power differentiating ADHD from non-ADHD adults (Triolo & Murphy, 1996). In this respect, this subscale was superior to the Attention-Focus/Concentration and Behavior Disorganized Activity subscales, which address problems in attention and hyperactivity–impulsivity, respectively. Although both of these subscales significantly discriminated ADHD from non-ADHD adults, it was hypothesized that future studies may eventually identify temporal consistencies (planning, appropriate follow-through in sequencing, etc.) as the "centerpiece behavioral issue regarding adults with ADHD" (Triolo & Murphy, 1996, p. 10).

The concept of internalization of language, with respect to ADHD, may be extremely misleading. For instance, with special focus on the adult population, Shekim, Asarnow, Hess, Zaucha, and Wheeler (1990) suggested that a sizable percentage of ADHD individuals may present symptoms of obsessive disorder. The implication here is that there is actually too much internal dialogue taking place, to the point where it becomes somewhat paralyzing. At least for the adult population, there does not seem to be a problem in delay reaction as a consequence of the lack of internalization of language. In fact, the exact opposite may be true when there is an excess of internalized language that may impede performance proficiency. Again, for the adult population, symptoms of inattention may be more prominent than symptoms of hyperactivity–impulsivity. Consequently, the new reconceptualization of ADHD automatically excludes a sizable percentage of adults who would otherwise be diagnosed as ADHD, inattentive type; however, the critique presented above is applicable to individuals who are at present inattentive but who have a history of hyperactivity and impulsivity.

Hofstadter (1979) perhaps provided an excellent insight into this phenomenon through his discussion of computer programs designed to play chess. He reported that, in the early days, programmers were optimistic and estimated that a recursion capable program—a computer form of internalized language—that can learn from its mistakes and make adjustments would eventually develop into an unbeatable chess program. At the time, programmers estimated that within a decade this computer program would be able to use move and countermove permutations, follow a multilayer decision tree, and always make the best move possible. Knowing that no human could possibly match the machine in attending to all of the possible permutations during a given game, there was a level of confidence established that the machine, in 10 years' time, would become the world champion of chess. More than a decade passed and, though chess programs were quite impressive, they were still not good enough to beat the expert players. The solution was to add more memory and develop a program to look at more moves and permutations. It was then estimated that the machine would eventually be champion within the next decade. Again, this did not happen.

After much frustration, a programming moratorium took place so programmers could analyze how the good players found ways of beating the machine.

It was a surprise to discover that the very good chess players do not spend much time in contemplation and hardly ever see beyond two or three moves. In fact, unlike the average chess player, they seem to have limited vision; somehow, they are unable to see bad moves. To explain this, an analogy can be made between the novice and the average everyday chess player. The novice is still learning all the moves on the board and may actually consider illegal moves (i.e., moving a rook diagonally). However, with experience, the average player no longer considers illegal moves and is automatically blinded to them. Likewise, the chess masters do not even consider moves that could place the game in jeopardy. In essence, their keenness in play allows them to see only one or two "good" moves and, if the game progresses to the point where all possible "good" moves are eliminated, they are more likely to resign rather than waste time following through to the inevitable end. To some extent the success of "Big Blue," the latest chess program developed by IBM, was the incorporation of numerous highly strategic games in its memory. This latest program was flexible enough to use a permutation matrix with reliance on strategies of past games. Rather than consider all the moves ahead with equal weight, the machine is now better able to consider only the "good" moves.

The important notation here is that performance efficiency is dependent on an uninhibited fluidity and, in fact, internal dialogue—likely the result of prolongation, memory functions, and other cognitive systems—may sometimes get in the way. Hofstadter (1979), in his discussion of artificial intelligence, speculated that computers would need to have the ability to step away from themselves—a form of internalized meta-language—to begin to think like humans. He further speculated that, if that would happen, computers would likely begin to lose the ability to run numerous repetitive calculations with the speed they can today. In a way, the door would be open to having machines begin to contemplate, second guess, and significantly slow down productivity. In theory, it could then be possible to have machines with ADHD, or at least the new disorder of inattention.

Regarding cognitive functions of reconstitution, it is important to understand that this is far removed from the original thesis of delay responding, or what has been recently named *behavioral inhibition*. A delay in responding is certainly necessary, but it is far from sufficient to demonstrate adequate functioning in problem solving and creativity, as prescribed by properties of reconstitution. This issue is reminiscent of the controversy surrounding the Wechsler Intelligence Scale for Children–Revised (WISC-R, Wechsler, 1981) third factor, Freedom from Distractibility (Kaufman, 1975), presented by Sattler (1982) with respect to clinical assessments. This factor includes three subtests from the WISC-R: Arithmetic, Coding, and Digit Span. Stewart and Moely (1983) questioned the validity of identifying scores in these subtests as the child's capacity to be free from distracting stimuli. It was later concluded that concentration and a general capacity to not be distracted may be necessary components to do well but that this third factor is reflective of far more complex abilities, and the distractibility component is confounded in this matrix of abilities (Ownby & Matthews, 1985). In plain terms, it is important to be able to concentrate and not to be distracted to do well on the Arithmetic subtest but, of course, it also is important to know how to do the mathematical operations. The argument here is that Bronowski's (1977) reconstitution function encompasses a rather long list of cognitive abilities typically associated with executive functioning (Fuster, 1989), some of which can be related to ADHD, but certainly not exclusively.

Again, the problem is that this cognitive ability, or perhaps set of very complex cognitive abilities, covers a broad range of functioning, and it may not be very useful in distinguishing ADHD from non-ADHD populations. Barkley (1997) cited studies of verbal fluency in which ADHD children did not perform as well as non-ADHD children. However, he admitted that these studies were not conclusive and that discrimination between ADHD and non-ADHD child populations were best seen when the focus was on subtle cues. The latter findings may be due to simple perceptual inattentiveness, such as a problem in visual scanning, as opposed to the complex properties of reconstitution. More important, age is reported as a factor; older ADHD children seem to have fewer difficulties (Grodzinsky & Diamond, 1992). Also, it may be prudent to keep in mind that Barkley (1997) presented studies on children with ADHD and there do not seem to be any studies on adults with ADHD, regarding verbal fluency.

Regarding cited evidence that ADHD children are not as "creative" as non-ADHD children, it is interesting to note that Howell and Ratey (1994), in their assessment of ADHD patients, stressed that ADHD lends itself to greater creativity. The disorder is not seen as being "all bad," and they reported that individuals with ADHD "see new things or find new ways to see old things . . . (because) they are also tuned in, often to the fresh and the new" (p. 37). More definitive research, with proper controls, is necessary in this area of study to address this controversy appropriately.

The study of motor control–fluency–syntax lends itself to scientific inquiry because of its inherent behavioral component, and it is less broadly defined than the other components. Issues of self-regulation, behavioral delays and satisfying immediate gratification, persistence, and perseverance with respect to long-term goals are all related to very observable behavior controls. As is elaborated on later in this chapter, the development of a behavioral model, through systematic observation, may provide a foundation for an eventual theory of ADHD. Much of this beginning groundwork is already available. For instance, observations of children with respect to rule-governing behaviors were documented by Barkley (1981) several years ago; however, the movement from problems in rule-governing behavior to defects in internalization of speech may be a premature leap. Again, the observations of poor rule-governing behavior, at this stage, can best define ADHD, at least better than such a broad category as the internalization of speech.

Barkley (1995, 1997) provided excellent insights into very common difficulties among adults and children with ADHD; however, he proposed that behavioral problems are mainly due to "output" difficulties rather than "input."

There is certainly evidence to suggest problems in output, and this may be easier to measure than potential problems in input. *Output* refers to the individual's behavioral responses to stimuli, or the capacity to stay on task without immediate reinforcers. It is a behavioral measure amenable to observations. By contrast, input functions are more difficult to measure because they refer to the ability to receive, organize, and categorize information. Although this is more difficult to observe because of its nature of internal functioning, there are numerous reports of adult patients who present difficulties in this area (Murphy & LeVert, 1995; Nadeau, 1995; G. Weiss & Hechtman, 1993; L. Weiss, 1992; Wender, 1995). Misplacing a household item, finding it difficult to settle down and start a project, and not being able to follow multiple directions may all be indirect symptoms of input problems. Rather than making direct observations of behavior, it is more likely that patients will need to report what is going on internally.

Taking this issue one step further, difficulties reported could easily be explained as a problem in fluidity between output and input processes, where a cognitive component such as prolongation is one of many steps necessary. In essence, it may be best to describe the continuous flow of input and output interactions with the environment rather than the separation of the two. Fluidity eventually need not be restricted to just behavioral measures. With perhaps special sensitivity to the adult ADHD population, consideration should be made to begin to measure internal cognitive processes. Perhaps at this stage of theory building, the cognitive components that emerge will be less broadly defined. The hope is to arrive at cognitive functions that can be described as true signatures of ADHD, distinct from other disorders. At this stage it may be reasonable to include the internal cognitive processes associated with the subcategory inattentive type, without history of hyperactivity–impulsivity.

Conclusions This field of study is certainly ready for the active and conscious work of theory building. However, at this stage of research it may be premature to arrive at a conceptual closure by means of a unified theory of ADHD. Research is just beginning to systematically observe and record data on adults with ADHD, and most of Barkley's conceptual framework (1977, 1994a, 1994b) has apparently relied on child studies. Much is still unknown regarding the adult ADHD population. For instance, researchers have yet to properly investigate populations of adults who have been incarcerated, have a history of substance abuse, or both, a potentially rich untapped area of study. This is an important issue because the behavioral course of ADHD apparently changes with respect to age, and a unifying theory must accommodate this added complexity.

Horgan (1995), in his *Scientific American* article entitled "From Complexity to Perplexity," addressed these kinds of problems. In essence, he asked if science can achieve a unified theory of complex systems. Horgan presented example after example of fields of study in biology and other areas that elude comprehensive understanding and perhaps frustrate those who seek harmony and closure. G. Weiss and Hechtman (1993) provided some wisdom on this subject matter. For decades, data have been gathered on hyperactive children who have moved into adulthood. The researchers have had access to numerous ADHD subjects throughout the years, and they have been diligent enough to follow them up, marking their progress periodically throughout the growing and adult years. The reports on the data collected clearly reflect much variety and complexity as the direction of ADHD children are influenced by numerous internal and external variables. In fact, G. Weiss (1990) reported that "It is likely that ADHD has no single cause, but represents a final common pathway of various interacting biologic and psychosocial variables" (p. 1413). She concluded by identifying ADHD as a diagnosis given to a heterogeneous population.

The theme of multiple orthogonal disorders may eventually be proven, but it is quite premature to draw any boundaries at this stage of research. Barkley (1997) regarded the inattentive type without any history of hyperactivity–impulsivity as a non-ADHD disorder. This is a major conceptual shift and quite premature considering the lack of data available. He considered the subcategory inattentive type a legitimate ADHD disorder, if there had been a history of hyperactivity–impulsivity. Thus, in Barkley's conceptual framework, these individuals are theoretically linked to other ADHD subcategories such as predominately hyperactive–impulsive and combined type (inattentive and hyperactive–impulsive). At this stage of study, such conceptual landscaping may be misleading and counterproductive.

The new proposed theory seems to be underinclusive in some aspects and overinclusive in others. The adoption of a single underlying impairment in response inhibition, by definition, assumes that a stimulus—or stimuli—exists. In essence, to inhibit a response, one must first experience some stimulus. The theory assumes that there is a stimulus and that the ADHD individual lacks the appropriate restraints necessary to inhibit or delay responding. However, an argument can be made that there is a subset of ADHD individuals who seem to be hungry for stimuli. The problem is not in a defective capacity to inhibit responding but an uncontrollable urge to seek out stimuli. This subset of ADHD individuals seems to have problems because of a lack of stimuli rather than a defective capacity to delay or restrain from responding to them.

At the same time, the identification of impairment in a behavioral inhibitory system as the underlying problem of all ADHD symptoms is simply too broad and general to be useful. As indicated in the discussion of different cognitive abilities, difficulties are not due exclusively to ADHD. In fact, difficulties in many of the described cognitive functions may be more prominently due to other difficulties, such as specific learning disabilities and emotional instabilities.

One can also argue that the function of behavioral inhibition is too basic to provide adequate differentiation between ADHD and other problems. For years it has been known that delays in gratification and the ability to inhibit emerge in the very early stages of development (Hoffer, 1950; Kessler, 1966; Piaget, 1954, 1976). Even a young hungry and crying infant can often be observed, for instance, quieting down just by observing the caregiver pull a fresh bottle of formula out of the refrigerator. The hunger pangs are still there for the child, but the ritual of taking the formula out of the refrigerator and warming it has been observed enough times to somehow provide the comfort necessary that relief from hunger is on its way. The young child stops crying because feelings of hunger are inhibited or suppressed. The child, although still very young, can be observed as at least being in the beginning stages of delay. According to some psychoanalytic theorists, the first significant indicator of ego development is literally the capacity to delay gratification (Erikson, 1946; Menninger, 1964). Very early in life the ego emerges to mediate between inner drives and external realities. Delay in gratification, although quite minimal in the early stages, has been regarded as a basic and rather primitive function of defense (Menninger, 1964).

Consequently, this primitive function could most likely be an underlying feature of a variety of difficulties, in addition to ADHD. For instance, problems with delay inhibition seem to be found in a host of psychological problems. Histrionic, paranoid, and borderline personality disorders all seem to have basic problems in delay, the ability to inhibit or postpone gratification (Millon, 1981). Among the personality disorders, this feature seems to cause particular problems in interpersonal relationships. A trademark among many personality disorders is an inability to set aside personal needs to allow oneself the full richness of interpersonal intimacies. Narcissistic goals are the enslavement of many personality-disordered individuals because of a basic inability to inhibit or delay.

In a different capacity, this same basic problem can be identified in patients with anxiety disorders. When faced with problems, many anxiety-prone patients react quickly to apprehension of disaster rather than take the time to think through the problems logically (Ellis, 1962; Kranzler, 1974; Marks, 1982). In fact, remedies for many of these patients involve mechanisms that can help them stop, think—perhaps exercising some of the cognitive mechanisms described by Bronowski (1977)—and respond, as opposed to reacting to the perceived threatening circumstances.

Even the disorganization in psychotic patients, to some extent, can be attributed to flaws in delay. The runaway tangential processes during conversations with psychotics may be a good example of problems in inhibiting stimuli, both internally, through the organization of thoughts, and externally, with respect to environmental distractions.

Thus, although problems of delay may be found in individuals with ADHD, this feature does not have the differential power to distinguish ADHD from other difficulties. It is, therefore, at risk of going the way of the term *minimal brain damage,* as reported by Barkley (1990) himself. He reported that this was a very popular concept decades ago but that it "eventually died a slow death (because)—it became recognized as vague, overinclusive, (and) of little or no prescriptive value ... '' (p. 10).

THEORY BUILDING

Pre-Established Factors

The study of ADHD is still in its infancy, a long way from any comprehensive theory. Some basic facts have been established, however. It is now clear that neurobiological functions are involved in defining ADHD. Thus, factors such as poor parenting, reinforcement of antisocial behaviors, and childhood psychological trauma have been ruled out as major determinants of ADHD (Barkley, 1990). Nevertheless, the neuropathological model of a diseased or chemically imbalanced brain has not been proven. Only a minority of ADHD patients have clearly defined neurogenic dysfunctions; in addition, this minor subset of the ADHD population may present neurogenic dysfunctions because of comorbid conditions. ADHD symptoms coexist within a larger set of neurogenic symptoms, apart from ADHD symptomotology. The majority of data observed from the ADHD population can best be explained by a normative continuum model. In fact, researchers have used the 1.5 *SD* above the mean of the population *average* as the conventional threshold for clinical significance regarding ADHD symptoms (Murphy & Barkley, 1995). More direct evidence can be seen by looking at the distribution of reported symptoms with respect to population frequency. In a normal population, the distribution of symptoms is expected to be normal, following a standard bell curve for a population frequency. However, for the ADHD population the distribution should be skewed, with the greatest number of ADHD individuals scoring closest to the average with respect to symptomotology and the fewest scoring the farthest from the average (see Figure 2.1). In a clinical setting, adults diagnosed with ADHD are more likely to have mild or moderate symptoms, rather than severe symptoms. ADHD adults with severe symptomotology are relatively rare.

Also, although ADHD dispositions are neurologically based, they are behaviorally defined by the expectations and standards of functioning within society and culture. This factor is the least studied and perhaps the most complicated. Unlike the concrete mechanics of MRI and PET scans, measures of social expectancies and cultural standards are a challenge to the most skilled empiricists. Nevertheless, it is important not to disregard this component. Almost all patients who have expressed concerns regarding ADHD symptoms, regardless of whether they are ultimately diagnosed as having ADHD, clearly define their problems with respect to perceived social standards, with reports that they are, in some way, not up to speed.

Understanding Normative Functions: Foundation for Theory Building

Barkley (1997) cast the latest revision of his unifying theory of ADHD as a hybrid of self-regulation found in developmental psychology and executive

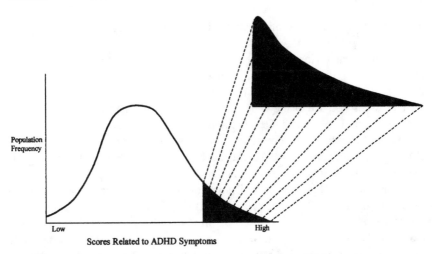

Population
Frequency

Low   High

Scores Related to ADHD Symptoms

Figure 2.1   Frequency distribution with respect to severity of ADHD symptoms.

functions of the brain as described in the study of neuropsychology. These two fields of study may be a good starting point to address normative functioning. According to developmental theory, symptoms related to ADHD are expected and normal among very young people, and these symptoms diminish or extinguish themselves altogether with maturation. The focal area of study is in cognitive development. The development of meta-cognition is of particular interest in regard to ADHD; Barkley (1981) referred to it as *self-regulation.* On the basis of a Piagetian view of cognitive development (Flavell, 1963, Elkind & Flavell, 1969; Piaget, 1976, 1978), several models have been constructed to further understand how humans begin to consciously recognize their own thinking and use this new development to self-regulate, monitor, organize, plan, and interact with the environment (Flavell, 1979, 1993; Piaget, 1976; Wohlwill, 1973). In more recent publications, researchers have tested the complex dynamics of meta-cognitive development, from its preverbal beginnings, through the stages of awareness of thought (Flavell, Green, & Flavell, 1995), and into the process of integration and self-regulation (Campos, Campos, & Barrett, 1989; Fox, 1994; Schwartz & Shapiro, 1978).

Studies in development are quite different from those found in the field of neurology. Emphasis is on normative functioning rather than on neuropathology. Unlike the comparative studies, which place emphasis on variable control through a reduction of variance, the study of development is usually correlational in nature. This form of research welcomes variability and does not consider it to be extraneous noise; usually, several variables are included in the research design, and correlational matrices are constructed to identify relationship strengths between variables. Variance, which is considered extraneous noise in experimental designs, typically is a useful observation in correlational studies. The reader is referred to Cronbach's (1957) article for further comparisons along with observation of its application to the theory-building process (Cronbach, 1975).

Correlational forms of research are certainly limited because they cannot provide direct evidence of cause-and-effect relationships between variables, but they can accommodate multivariable complexities. They may be applicable to ADHD issues because of the wide scope of behaviors related to ADHD, as well as the comorbid conditions. Developmental explorations often include complex regression formulas with comprehensive attention to numerous associated variables. Such a direction may be applicable to the study of ADHD, beginning with the study of normative cognitive functioning.

Demetriou and his associates (Demetriou, Efklides, & Platsidou, 1993) provided a beginning model in their research article, ''The Architecture and Dynamics of Developing Mind: Experiential Structuralism as a Frame for Unifying Cognitive Developmental Theories.'' They described a series of studies on self-regulation and capacity for self-monitoring behavioral management. They referred to these mechanisms as a form of ''hypercognition'' that is part of normal human development. Their normative developmental approach provides fertile ground to generate hypotheses that can help the understanding of different interrelating cognitive functions. True to a Piagetian approach, the biology is not the sole determining factor of behavior; environmental influences, however subtle, shape the developing biogenic functions. In this model of normative functioning, room is given to measure the possible influences that stem from social and cultural standards, as well as the neurogenic components.

In Barkley's (1997) revision of his unifying theory of ADHD, much emphasis is given to the prefrontal structures of the cerebral cortex, and references are made to Fuster's (1989) text on normative prefrontal functioning. Subcortical structures were not excluded, and particular attention was given to the interconnections between the executive properties of prefrontal structures and the more autonomic regulatory systems assigned to subcortical structures.

Fuster's (1989) text on the physiology and neuropsychology of the prefrontal cortex is also recommended reading for practitioners who are interested in the study of ADHD. Briefly, Fuster reported that

> the prefrontal cortex allows the organism to form the structures at the highest levels of that behavioral hierarchy and also facilitates the bridging of *temporal* discontinuities within them. The higher the level and the longer the discontinuity, the more essential is the role of prefrontal cortex. (pp. 159–160).

Fuster placed prefrontal functioning at the highest end of conscious processing—what is commonly referred to as *executive functioning*. He also took the time to explain which functions of the brain are not associated with prefrontal physiology. These include sensory reflexes, which are exclusive to spinal cord functioning, and classical conditioning, which has traditionally been delegated to subcortical structures. He cited animal studies in ruling out instinctual behaviors, or what he sometimes referred to as *stereotypical responses to external stimuli.*

Fuster (1989) spent much timediscussing prefrontal functions with respect to noninstinctual and complex behaviors. These prefontal functions are challenged by new situations, especially if they are fragmented by temporal lags. The longer the temporal lag, the greater is the need to engage in prefrontal functioning. The prefrontal cortex is described as the behavioral glue that can turn otherwise unrelated behaviors into a cohesive gestalt. Behaviorally, Barkley (1994b) explained this as the capacity to stay on target in spite of the fact that external reinforcers are unavailable. The prefrontal cortex can therefore be described as a structure of the brain that is most useful when external reinforcers and organized structures are unavailable. Fuster presented several animal studies to prove that the behaviors themselves are not extinguished because of prefrontal injury; on the other hand, the cohesiveness and organization of behaviors are clearly not present when prefrontal injury occurs. Also, there may be a deficiency in the utilization of memory (studies presented seem to focus on short-term memory only). The storage of memory is not associated with the executive functions of the prefrontal cortex as much as the necessary mechanisms to effectively recall stored memory when it is most needed.

Finally, the organizational properties associated with the prefrontal cortex are engaged in controlling both external and internal stimuli, especially those that may be interfering with conscious planning and unreinforced orientation to achieve a goal. Barkley (1997) referred to this as the *capacity to inhibit unwanted stimuli.* This inhibitory system may be associated with functioning within the orbital and perhaps the medial prefrontal cortex, and this identified executive function also includes the capacity to negotiate or even totally inhibit older behavioral patterns (habits) that have been delegated to autonomic functioning.

In sum, the prefrontal cortex can be described as the part of the brain that allows for meta-cognition. Its capacity to project forward into time enables a long and complex series of behaviors to be executed in an organized and hierarchical order. Unlike other, more autonomic functions of the brain, such as level of arousal, the prefrontal cortex is involved in the capacity to self-initiate and, as suggested by the interconnections to subcortical structures, it may also have the capacity to influence and regulate more autonomic functions (i.e., addressing emotional components related to the limbic system).

Lou, Henriksen, and Bruhn (1984) and Heilman, Voeller, & Nadeau (1991) have identified the striatum as a brain structure that is important in modulating and inhibiting unwanted kinetic reactions to stimuli. Heilman and Van Den Abell (1980) further suspected that the interconnections with the cerebral cortex—the right hemisphere in particular—are necessary to correctly transcode volition into appropriate actions. They hypothesized that defects lead to an inattention to details in the environment that require action as well as an inability to effectively inhibit behaviors due to distracting stimuli. Admittedly, the mediating functions proposed are not clearly defined, but it is reasonable to assume that the normative purpose for connections between higher cortical functioning and the lower brain are necessary to mediate impulsive tendencies, levels of arousal, and other components of brain functioning through the activation of structures usually associated with higher order cognitive functioning. Lou, Henriksen, Bruhn, Borner, and Nielesen (1989) placed special importance on striated dysfunctions in relation to problems in hyperactivity.

This model of integration and interconnecting regulatory systems between different parts of the brain goes beyond Mirsky's (1987) structural model. Mirsky (1987) did suggest that attentional components are different with respect to the structures studied; a variety of possible attentional functions was suggested, and ADHD may very well represent a set of varying problems. Nevertheless, it seems that normal brain functions must include the study of integration and interdependence between varying structures. In this respect, it may be best to focus research efforts on the investigation of the human capacity to integrate and mediate different cognitive functions. The study should not be limited to brain structures but should include other influences, such as hormonal involvement and the interactions between environmental standards and critical physiological development.

Behavioral Categories of ADHD

The previous sections emphasized the need to fully understand normative functioning. This task is most difficult because of the many unanswered questions. Also, special emphasis was given to challenging some basic assumptions that may be erroneous and misleading. One of these assumptions included the reasoning that no abnormality can be defined unless normative parameters are established. This is especially true in review of PET and MRI analyses.

In spite of handicaps, it would certainly be erroneous to conclude that ADHD does not exist unless proven by well-defined normative parameters and clearly measured functioning outside of these parameters. The analogy given earlier of hypertension can also apply to this line of reasoning. Even if the normative range of blood pressure readings were unknown, measures can certainly be made and associated with respect to medical consequences. For instance, even if normative parameters have not been established beforehand, a correlational analysis can easily be made with respect to the incidence of stroke and blood pressure readings. Likewise, behaviors related to ADHD can certainly be measured along with their associated risks. Therefore, although it is still premature and perhaps totally erroneous to talk in terms of brain pathology, behavioral observations of ADHD symptoms have certainly been made, and correlational analyses have associated these behaviors with real and often serious life conditions. In clinical terms, these include human suffering, such as an inability to fulfill career dreams, loneliness, conflictual relationships, and so on. Also, in consideration of some of the neurobiological models proposed, behaviors can now be associated with neuromechanisms suggested by these models. An attempt will be made here to integrate observed behaviors with respect to the various models and theories presented earlier in this chapter.

In 1980, the *DSM–III* changed the behavioral focus away from hyperactivity and more toward attention-related problems. The diagnostic name given was *attention deficit disorder* (ADD). Hyperactivity and impulsivity were certainly observed, but not in all cases that involved attention problems. Consequently, the ADD diagnosis was given along with the additional qualifier *with* or *without* hyperactivity. In the years that followed, the *DSM–III* was revised (American Psychiatric Association, 1987), and the division between the two qualifiers was removed. As presented in Chapter 1, this was because a diagnosis of ADD without hyperactivity was hardly ever made during the field trials. The major flaw in this argument is that the field trials were conducted on children, and there is now some evidence to indicate that many adults, even if they could easily be categorized as having been hyperactive during their early childhood years, may not present hyperactive behaviors during the years beyond childhood and adolescence (Brown, 1996). G. Weiss and Hechtman (1993) and Barkley, Fischer, Edelbrock, and Smallish (1990) have observed in their prospective follow-up studies that patients continue to struggle and suffer with attending symptoms, even though, for many individuals, hyperactive behaviors have disappeared over the adolescent and young adulthood years.

The *DSM–IV* (American Psychiatric Association, 1994), which also is discussed in Chapter 1, presents a reintroduction of the hyperactivity or without-hyperactivity categories that were presented 14 years earlier. Rather than definitive category boundaries, the term *predominantly* was introduced to cover overlapping behavioral symptoms. Also, hyperactivity and impulsivity were placed into a single category.

Additional discussions regarding the *DSM–IV*, especially dealing with practical diagnostic issues, are presented later in this book. For now it is important to recognize that behavioral observations of patients seem to cluster around two major categories. The more obvious is that of the classical hyperactive–impulsive behaviors. The less obvious catetgory, but perhaps the one that is more important to the older population, is the inattentive category. The present diagnostic descriptions suggest that there is certainly some gray area between the two categories, and some crossover in behavioral observations should be expected.

Subcategories: Divergent Features   Many of the behavioral features associated with hyperactivity–impulsivity, at first glance, appear to be the antithesis of behavioral features found in the inattentive category. Table 2.1 outlines some of these features. In reference to brain functioning and the understanding of developmental processes, an attempt will be made to explain possible associations between these seemingly divergent categories. However, it may be best to first describe some of the divergent features.

Table 2.1   ADHD Categories

Hyperactivity–impulsivity	Inattentive
Hungry for stimuli	Underaroused
Manic-like behaviors	Overwhelmed
Frustrated	Anxiety ridden
Master of shortcut tendencies	Obsessive–compulsive
Kinetically disorganized	Cognitively disorganized

Hyperactive–impulsive individuals are often described as having excessive energy and being hungry for stimuli. They may also be described as being "on the go," with a sense that they cannot possibly get enough stimuli to keep them from becoming bored. Throughout their lives, they are likely to sample many different experiences and adventures. By contrast, the predominately inattentive individuals tend to be underaroused. At times they may be described as having somewhat of a sleepy brain, and they are often caught daydreaming rather than paying attention to the world around them. There does not seem to be any drive toward additional stimuli as they are not able to manage even day-to-day responsibilities.

Emotionally, the hyperactive–impulsive types tend to present manic-like features. They seem to be racing about from one project to the next, trying to absorb anything and everything. Often, they are seen taking on much more than they can handle; however, rather than slow down they seem to be trapped in the mode of taking on even more. By contrast, the inattentive types tend to feel overwhelmed. It is likely that they cannot not absorb all of the stimuli presented to them. Their aim is to reduce their responsibilities to gain control and feel as if their lives are manageable. New adventures or responsibilities are usually not well received, and there may be an active behavioral tendency to avoid new stimuli.

Hyperactive individuals are often seen as being quite frustrated. Normal life is seen by them as being restrictive. By contrast, the inattentive individuals may very well feel much anxiety and inner tension in normal life. Rather than feeling restricted, they may present numerous reports of being stressed. For instance, hyperactive individuals may see their home life as being too boring, whereas the inattentive individual may complain that home life is too demanding. On the basis of clinical observations, hyperactive individuals tend to be masters of shortcuts. Often they report they cannot be bothered with many of the tedious details of their lives, and their work tends to be quite sloppy. They sometimes irritate supervisors and coworkers because they have a tendency to do just enough work to get by. They prefer to follow the path of least resistance and move on to something new rather than take the time to do a job well. The exact opposite may be true for the inattentive individuals. They may often develop obsessive–compulsive tendencies, perhaps as a way to compensate for their inattentiveness. Clinically, these individuals are often observed making lists and then checking and rechecking the lists to the point of exhaustion. They often become trapped in attending to insignificant details, which ultimately adds to their inefficiency. For instance, a student became so focused on a midterm essay question that she found herself with little time left to answer the other four essay questions. Although the hyperactive–impulsive type tends to act as if time is coming to an end, the inattentive type often loses track of time as if it is limitless.

Hyperactive–impulsive individuals tend to be kinetically disorganized. They may have problems with coordination and may be accident prone. Others may see them as being without any kinetic controls, and they could easily be described as being risk takers. By contrast, inattentive individuals tend to be cognitively disorganized. They are usually not seen as risk takers, but they may have problems processing stimuli such as verbal commands. Others may observe them as being somewhat scattered and they indeed may have problems organizing information internally in order to retrieve it and use it efficiently later. This is usually seen as a problem in recall.

Differences between the two categories can also be seen with respect to development. Younger children are more likely to be hyperactive and, as described earlier, they are more likely to receive the diagnosis of ADHD, predominately the hyperactive–impulsive type. Later on in development, there may be a gradual shift toward the inattentive type and, as Brown (1996) believes, hyperactivity and impulsivity during the adult years are not important problems. This belief is somewhat questionable, especially considering the fact that numerous ADHD adults with predominantly hyperactive–impulsive features are inaccessible to many practitioners who provide outpatient care. Because of incarcerations and a focus on more severe problems—brain injury due to risk-taking behaviors, drug overdose, resistance to treatment—it is difficult to tabulate the number of hyperactive–impulsive adults, and Brown's conclusion may very well be premature. Nevertheless, there is a trend toward this shift with age. This shift theoretically makes sense considering the processes involved in brain development. Hyperactivity and impulsivity seem to be features that pertain mostly to the subcortical autonomic domain of the brain. Attention-related features are usually related to cerebral functioning, and particular attention has been given to the prefrontal cortex. Brain development parallels the shift with respect to categories. Maturity of cerebral functioning takes place later in life (Demetriou et al., 1993; Elkind & Flavell, 1969; Welsh, Pennington, & Grossier, 1991).

Subcategories: Model Toward Integrated Features If subcortical and cerebral functioning are independent of each other, one might imagine that the above simplistic model explaining ADHD with respect to divergent features would be all that is needed. However, both structures of the brain are interconnected, and there is some evidence to suggest that the understanding of ADHD should include the understanding of these neuroconnections. In particular, as suggested earlier, the striatum has been considered an important structural component. These interconnections may explain the behavioral gray areas between these two categories. Although this adds complexity to the behavioral model, some hypotheses can be generated and tested with respect to behavioral frequencies. One hypothesis that has support from the observed data is the shift in frequency from hyperactivity–impulsivity to the inattentive category, with respect to brain development.

According to the projected model, functional difficulties at the subcortical level, including interconnecting structures, should correspond to behavioral problems in both categories. However, difficulties that stem from the prefrontal cortex should translate into problems with the inattentive category only. Thus, it is hypothesized that there is a nesting relationship between the two categories. Problems in hyperactivity–impulsivity, presumably set in subcortical structures, will also tax functioning related to the prefrontal cortex. However, the reverse may not be true. Difficulties exclusively associated within the higher cortical regions of the brain may not necessarily present behavioral problems associated with hyperactivity–impulsivity. These hypotheses could easily be tested through the use of standardized behavioral measures of both inattention and hyperactivity–impulsivity (i.e., Triolo & Murphy, 1996).

This new model of integrated features assumes a somewhat hierarchical structure of the brain, as implied in Fuster's (1989) text. However, the assumption of a strict hierarchical model of the brain may, in itself, be a mistake (Sperry, 1988). Again, it is important to consider the fluidity of interactions between different parts of the brain. More important, this fluidity of interrelated functions may challenge the present-day conceptualization of categories. For instance, Denckla (1989) revisited the concept of attention in terms of a continuous set of functions that were dependent on several components of the brain. In essence, Denckla proposed an "attentional matrix" (p. 158) to explain interconnecting neurofunctions. Thus, different aspects of attention involved different sets of brain structures. For instance, the motivational aspects of attention may be dependent on the limbic system. The basal ganglia, with particular attention again given to the striatum, have important integrative connections with the frontal lobes and can influence attentional components such as sustained focus, planning, and organization of behavior. In short, the meta-cognition described earlier is dependent on the integration of both cortical and subcortical processes.

Obviously, the work toward an integrated model is far from complete. This field of study is still in its infancy; however, hypothesis testing with respect to behavioral functions may be helpful in shaping our way toward a theory of ADHD. Instead of speculating on new categories and new conceptions of ADHD (i.e., splintering the concept of "attention" into subcategories), it may be first helpful to see how useful the concepts we now have are with respect to behavioral styles. The following is a simple model to test some behavioral hypotheses.

Proposed Hypothesis Testing   The testing of these hypotheses can be further advanced if behavioral measures are sensitive to activity and energy levels of individuals that do *not* present problems and, therefore, can be factored out.

Within the non-ADHD population, there is a great variety of behavioral styles that reflect varying degrees of energy levels. For instance, there are numerous individuals who can be described as being high drivers, highly motivated and achievement oriented. Like hyperactive individuals, they may seem to be hungry for stimuli and could easily become bored if not challenged. However, unlike hyperactive and impulsive individuals, they are very organized and very effective in their work. All tasks they take on seem to be accomplished with minimal difficulties. Although they may not be detail oriented, they are unlikely to be reckless and sloppy in their work. Others may see them as being full of energy, and they may even be admired for their many accomplishments and deeds.

At the other end of this spectrum are individuals who also do not have ADHD but are seen as having very low energy as they meet the day-to-day responsibilities of their lives. Tasks are achieved slowly and methodically, but they are achieved nevertheless. Others may see these individuals as not being very motivated to compete, as they may be quite content to keep a deliberate and slow pace. Long periods of rest may not be an unusual observation; they lead a life most others consider boring and unadventurous.

It is important to look at this energy factor without bias toward personality traits and emotional dispositions. The high-energy individual may at first appear to be the classical Type A personality, who is product oriented and fits into the usual capitalistic stereotypes (i.e., entrepreneurs, executives climbing the corporate ladder, etc.). This is not necessarily true. One of the most energetic individuals I know worked for the Catholic missions; she worked as a teacher during the day, spent her afternoon hours working at the local clinic, and somehow kept a very busy schedule contacting community leaders for financial support and assistance. It was noteworthy that she was unusually alert and attentive to the details of her many responsibilities and, in fact, she seemed to have a talent for remembering names of all the people with whom she interacted.

It is equally important to not mistake individuals who seem to maintain a low level of energy as unachievers, unmotivated, and lazy. For instance, one of the most low-key individuals I know—who somehow manages to take naps during the day—has also managed to run a very successful consulting business in computer programming.

The measurement of this factor, which does not contribute to ADHD-related symptoms, may help provide clearer associations and, in turn, greater reliability. Figure 2.2 depicts a three-dimensional model of the two ADHD-related categories along with the factor related to normative energy levels. This is nothing more than a visual model of a three-factor design. Each factor is continuous but, for descriptive purposes, the extremes of each factor in combination with the other factors is presented here. This generates eight possible behavioral combinations ($2 \times 2 \times 2 = 8$). According to the above hypotheses, two of these combinations should represent normative functioning. Four other combinations should represent different behavioral styles related to problems in ADHD. Finally, the last two combinations, according to the above hypotheses, should be rare or totally nonexistent, at least within the adult population.

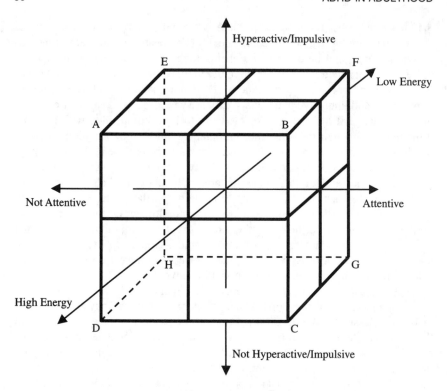

Figure 2.2   A three-dimensional model of ADHD and non-ADHD behavioral styles.

According to the model in Figure 2.2, the eight possible behavioral combinations are represented by the eight points of the cube and labeled with the letters A–H. Two of these (C and G) are the normative behavioral patterns described above. These are individuals who are observed as having high energy but are attentive and are not described as being hyperactive–impulsive (C) and individuals who may display a low level of energy but are also attentive to the environment and not hyperactive–impulsvie (G). The difficulty in making appropriate behavioral measurements may be in differentiating behaviors related to a high-energy disposition from behaviors related to hyperactivity–impulsivity. These two sets of behaviors may at first seem indistinguishable, but they can be operationalized with respect to two components. The first component is functionality. How functional are the behaviors observed with respect to goal attainment? Hyperactive–impulsive individuals are scattered and inefficient in achieving their goals, whereas others, who can be described as having a high energy level but are not hyperactive–impulsive, may be very focused and efficient in achieving their goals. The second component is whether the behaviors are considered ego syntonic (Millon, 1981). Individuals who are observed as having high energy, but are not hyperactive–impulsive, may tend to see their behaviors as being ego syntonic, as opposed to ego dystonic. The opposite is true for individuals who tend to be hyperactive–impulsive. A lengthier discussion is presented in Chapter 6 regarding ego-syntonic and ego-dystonic dispositions with respect to differential diagnosis between ADHD and personality disorders. For now it is important to understand that behavioral symptoms related to ADHD are considered to be ego dystonic; thus, individuals who tend to be hyperactive–impulsive do not like these behaviors in themselves, and there is a motivation to make appropriate corrections. Individuals who are described as being quite energetic but do not display hyperactive–impulsive behaviors are more likely to describe their behaviors as part of their personality (ego-syntonic) and tend to welcome these behaviors as a reflection of the self.

These two factors can also be used to differentiate between inattention and low-energy behaviors. Again, inattentiveness is considered dysfunctional, and the consequences include inefficiency in goal attainment. By contrast, non-ADHD individuals with low energy and a lethargic and methodical behavioral style may be quite functional in fulfilling individual goals. The non-ADHD individuals are quite organized; they may appear to others as being inefficient, but their slow pace may actually be functional because they are able to see solutions others miss. Salient details are not missed as would be the case for the inattentive individuals. The same ego-syntonic theme can be applied to this set of behaviors. Again, the lack of energy is seen as a desirable trait that does fit with the idealized self. An easygoing, low-energy lifestyle is more likely to be considered ego syntonic, an accepted trait that is very much part of the self.

The inattentive, hyperactive–impulsive, and high-energy individual (A in Figure 2.2) perhaps best describes the classical ADHD patient. This type is reflective of someone who is easily stimulated and highly distracted. Behaviors may include a tendency to try lots of different things in life; however, although lots of projects may be started, none seem to get finished. There may be an initial display of high energy, but these individuals seem to lose interest and look for other projects very quickly. In essence, problems may be seen in the ability to follow through with jobs and responsibilities. There may also be a tendency to not attend to the important details; it is quite likely that interests lie in looking at the big picture, and there is very little patience for attention to minor details. Individuals with this combination may sometimes become very excited with grandiose plans, but the lack of ability to follow through and attend to the practicalities of these plans is usually a setup for failure.

The inattentive, hyperactive–impulsive, and low-energy combination (E) is somewhat similar to the above descriptions. It is also likely that there is very little attention given to details, and there is certainly a lack of organization. Also, there may be a tendency to become distracted, suggesting the same tendency to move and wander from one stimulus to the next. However, this combination is suggestive of someone who is unlikely to initiate projects. Rather than displaying the same sense of grandiose excitement, it is more likely that there is a tendency to follow the most available lead, regardless of the fact that it may have negative long-term consequences. There may also be a tendency to take shortcuts when it comes to fulfilling responsibilities. Following the path of least resistance without attention to long-term consequences may be a central tendency, especially in areas where persistence is very much needed.

The inattentive, nonhyperactive–impulsive, and high-energy combination (D) is reflective of the attention deficit individual without hyperactivity. The behaviors involved may include all of the classical inattentive conditions, such as being forgetful, not paying attention to details, and so on. The high-energy component may also be reflective of a tendency to persist and follow through. It is also quite likely that energy is expended to compensate for the tendency to become inattentive. Thus, unlike individuals with hyperactive–impulsive traits, extra time is sometimes taken to check and recheck the work that is done. Much energy is often expended in compensatory strategies. For instance, it is not unusual to see individuals who are inattentive become somewhat obsessive–compulsive as a means to reduce errors. However, this combination may represent the greatest risk of developing classical neurotic traits. A more detailed discussion regarding this issue is presented later in this book regarding the comorbidity that exists between ADHD and anxiety disorders (Chapter 6).

The inattentive, nonhyperactive–impulsive and low-energy combination (H) also is reflective of the classical ADD without hyperactivity. This combination is usually associated with a tendency to daydream and fosters descriptions of being "spacy" or "lost in a fog." Rather than attending to responsibilities, it is likely that these individuals accomplish very little. Even if projects are initiated, it is unlikely that they are completed without outside direction, support, and reinforcement. In fact, without external structures, there may be problems in even normal self-maintenance—everything from doing laundry to putting gas in the car. Others may interpret this combination of behaviors as being lazy and irresponsible. Indeed, there may be a tendency to become dependent on others to the point of straining interpersonal relationships.

I hypothesize that the final two combinations, according to the proposed theoretical model, should not exist. The first of these two is the combination of attentiveness, with hyperactivity–impulsivity and a high level of energy (B). The second also includes attentiveness, with hyperactivity–impulsivity, however, with low behavioral energy (F). It will be interesting to see if future studies support this hypothesis.

CONCLUSIONS

At best, this chapter is reflective of some interesting conceptual adventures. The conceptual frameworks offered provide some explanation for ADHD. The oldest conceptualization of ADHD stems from a neurogenic model. This model has been challenged throughout the years, but is has withstood these tests and, in consideration of the present trend toward reductionism, it is at present enjoying much prominence. To ensure that alternative perspectives are not discounted, a normative theory was offered as a way to rethink some of the neurogenic assumptions. These include the concepts of deficits, disease, or both. Also, a conceptual shift was introduced away from the microanalysis (e.g., neurotransmitter functioning) of ADHD. It is important to enjoy the cohesive and esthetic comforts that are offered by the mainstream theoretical prospective, but it is more important to not be swept away to the point of blindness where alternative explanations are totally lost.

Barkley (1997) should be credited for perhaps the first attempt to provide an integrated model of ADHD. However, it was argued that the field of study, although quite popular, is still very young, and not enough data have been collected to provide the support necessary for a unified theory of ADHD. It has not been long since researchers have discovered that ADHD is a lifelong condition, for instance. The understanding of ADHD with respect to adult functioning is quite limited. For example, it was already noted in the first chapter that there may be untapped populations of adults that have yet to be studied.

Consequently, the field of study is in a very early theory-building stage. Especially in consideration of the adult population, it is important to realize that even the data that need to be observed have yet to be gathered. Rather than presenting a definitive theoretical model, a structural framework was offered to help organize and categorize observations. The structural model presented in Figure 2.2 is a simple three-factor suggestion to help untangle and make sense of the variety of behavioral styles. For instance, an additional factor implied but not included in the above model is age or, more accurately, developmental maturity.

From these simple models, data can be observed and correlated. At this next stage, integration can slowly begin. At this point, integration can include some of the established knowledge of brain functioning and, as suggested earlier, hypotheses can be established and tested accordingly.

The process proposed is laborious and long; it would certainly be tempting to draw premature closure and succumb to the need for a unifying explanation. However, delays in disclosure may ultimately provide greater rewards. The slow process, without premature closures, may provide the opportunity to gain insights that are now inconceivable.

REFERENCES

Achenbach, T. M., & Edelbrock, C. (1983). *Manual for the Child Behavior Checklist and Revised Child Behavior Profile*. Burlington VT: Author.

Akshoomoff, N. A., & Courchesne, E. (1994). ERP evidence for a shifting attention deficit in patients with damage to the cerebellum. *Journal of Cognitive Neuroscience, 6,* 388–399.

American Psychiatric Association. (1980). *Diagnostic and statistical manual of mental disorders* (3rd ed.). Washington, DC: Author.

American Psychiatric Association. (1987). Diagnostic and statistical manual of mental disorders (3rd ed., rev.). Washington, DC: Author.

American Psychiatric Association. (1994). *Diagnostic and statistical manual of mental disorders* (4th ed.). Washington, DC: Author.

Arcia, E., & Gualtieri, C. T. (1994). Neurobehavioral performance of adults with closed-head injury, adults with attention deficit, and controls. *Brain Injury, 8,* 395–404.

Barker, R. (1968). *Egological psychology.* Stanford, CA: Stanford University Press.

Barkley, R. A. (1977). A review of stimulant drug research with hyperactive children. *Journal of Child Psychology and Psychiatry, 18,* 137–165.

Barkley, R. A. (1981). *Hyperactive children: A handbook for diagnosis and treatment.* New York: Guilford Press.

Barkley, R. A. (1990). *Attention deficit hyperactivity disorder: Handbook for diagnosis and treatment.* New York: Guilford Press.

Barkley, R. A. (1994a). Can neuropsychological tests help diagnose ADD/ADHD? *The ADHD Report, 2*(1), 1–3.

Barkley, R. A. (1994b). Impaired delayed responding: The unified theory of attention-deficit hyperactivity disorder. In D. K. Routh (Ed.), *Disruptive behavior disorders in childhood* (pp. 11–59). New York: Plenum.

Barkley, R. A. (1994c). More on the new theory of ADHD. *The ADHD Report, 2*(2), 1–4.

Barkley, R. A. (1995). Is there an attention deficit in ADHD? *The ADHD Report, 3*(4), 1–4.

Barkley, R. A. (1997). Behavioral inhibition, sustained attention, and executive functions: Constructing a unified theory of ADHD. *Psychological Bulletin, 121,* 65–94.

Barkley, R. A., & Cunningham, C. E. (1979). The effects of methylphenidate on the mother–child interactions of hyperactive children. *Archives of General Psychiatry, 36,* 201–208.

Barkley, R. A., Fischer, M., Edelbrock, C. S., & Smallish, L. (1990). The adolescent outcome of hyperactive children diagnosed by research criteria: An 8-year prospective follow-up study. *Journal of American Academy of Child And Adolescent Psychiatry, 29,* 546–557.

Barkley, R. A., Karlsson, J., Pollard, S., & Murphy, J. (1985). Developmental changes in the mother–child interactions of hyperactive boys: Effects of two doses of Ritalin. *Journal of Child Psychology and Psychiatry, 26,* 705–715.

Barkley, R. A., Karlsson, J., Strzelecki, E., & Murphy, J. (1984). Effects of age and Ritalin dosage on the mother–child interactions of hyperactive children. *Journal of Consulting and Clinical Psychology, 52,* 1750–1758.

Block, G. H. (1977). Hyperactivity: A cultural perspective. *Journal of Learning Disabilities, 110,* 236–240.

Bradley, W. (1937). The behavior of children receiving benzadrine. *American Journal of Psychiatry, 94,* 577–585.

Bradley, W., & Bowen, C. (1940). School performance of children receiving amphetamines (benzedrine sulfate). *American Journal of Orthopsychiatry, 10,* 782–788.

Bronowski, J. (1977). *A sense of the future: Essays on natural philosophy.* Cambridge, MA: MIT Press.

Brown, T. E. (1996). *Brown Attention-Deficit Disorder Scales: Manual.* San Antonio, TX: The Psychological Corporation.

Campos, J. J., Campos, R. G., & Barrett, K. C. (1989). Emergent themes in the study of emotional development and emotion regulation. *Developmental Psychology, 25,* 394–402.

Carins, E., & Cammock, T. (1978). Development of a more reliable version of the "Matching Familiar Figures Test." *Developmental Psychology, 14,* 555–560.

Castellanos, F. X., Giedt, J. N., Eckburg, P., Marsh, W. L., Viatuzis, A. C., Kaysen, D., Hamburger, S. D., & Rapoport, J. L. (1994). Quantitative morphology of the caudate nucleus in attention deficit hyperactivity disorder. *American Journal of Psychiatry, 151,* 1791–1796.

Chee, P., Logan, G., Schachar, R., Lindsay, P., & Wachsmuth, R. (1989). Effects of event rate and display time on sustained attention in hyperactive, normal, and control children. *Journal of Abnormal Child Psychology, 17,* 371–391.

Chess, S. (1960). Diagnosis and treatment of the hyperactive child. *New York State Journal of Medicine, 16,* 2379–2385.

Cronbach, L. J. (1957). The two disciplines of scientific psychology. *American Psychologist, 12,* 671–684.

Cronbach, L. J. (1975). Beyond the two disciplines of scientific psychology. *American Psychologist, 30,* 116–127.

Cunningham, C. E., & Barkley, R. A. (1978). The effects of methylphenidate on the mother–child interactions of hyperactive twin boys. *Developmental Medicine and Child Neurology, 20,* 634–642.

Demetriou, A., Efklides, A., & Platsidou, M. (1993). The architecture and dynamics of developing mind: Experiential structuralism as a frame for unifying cognitive developmental theories. *Monographs of the Society for Research in Child Development, 58*(5, Serial No. 234).

Denckla, M. B. (1989). Executive function, the overlap zone between attention deficit hyperactivity disorder and learning disabilities. *International Pediatrics, 4,* 155–160.

Denckla, M. B. (1991). Attention deficit hyperactivity disorder: Residual type. *Journal of Child Neurology, 6*(Suppl.), S44–S50.

Douglas, V. I. (1972). Stop, look, and listen: The problem of sustained attention and impulse control in hyperactive and normal children. *Canadian Journal of Behavioral Science, 4,* 259–282.

Douglas, V. I., & Peters, K. G. (1979). Toward a clearer definition of the attentional deficit of hyperactive children. In G. A. Hale & M. Lewis (Eds.), *Attention in the development of cognitive skills* (pp. 173–248). New York: Plenum.

DuPaul, G. J., & Barkley, R. A. (1990). Medication therapy. In R. A. Barkley (Ed.), *Attention-deficit hyperactivity disorder: A handbook for diagnosis and treatment* (pp. 573–612). New York: Guilford Press.

Elkind, D., & Flavell, J. H. (Eds.). (1969). *Studies in cognitive developments: Essays in honor of Jean Piaget.* New York: Oxford University Press.

Ellis, A. (1962). *Reason and emotion in psychotherapy.* New York: Lyle Stuart.

Erikson, E. H. (1946). *Ego development and historical change: The psychoanalytic study of the child* (Vol. 2). New York: International Universities Press.

Ernst, M., Liebenauur, L. L., King, A. C., Fitzgerald, G. A., Cohen, R. M., & Zametkin, A. J. (1994). Reduced brain metabolism in hyperactive girls. *Journal of the American Academy of Child and Adolescent Psychiatry, 33,* 858–868.

Flavell, J. H. (1963). *The developmental psychology of Jean Piaget.* New York: Van Nostrand.

Flavell, J. H. (1979). Meta-cognition in cognitive monitoring: A new era of cognitive developmental inquiry. *American Psychologist, 34,* 906–911.

Flavell, J. H. (1993). Young children's understanding of thinking and consciousness. *Current Directions in Psychological Science, 2,* 40–a43.

Flavell, J. H., Green, F. L., & Flavell, E. R. (1995). Young children's knowledge about thinking. *Monographs of the Society for Research in Child Development, 60*(1, Serial No. 243).

Fox, N. A. (1994). The development of emotion regulation: Biological and behavioral considerations. *Monographs of the Society for Research in Child Development, 59*(2–3, No. 240).

Fuster, J. M. (1989). *The prefrontal cortex: Anatomy, physiology, and neuropsychology of the frontal lobe* (2nd ed.). New York: Raven Press

Giedd, J. N., Castellanos, F. X., Casey, B. J., Kozuch, P., King, A. C., Hamburg, S. D., & Rapoport, J. L. (1994). Quantitative morphology of the corpus callosum in attention deficit hyperactivity disorder. *American Journal of Psychiatry, 151,* 665–669.

Gleick, J. (1987). *Chaos: Making a new science.* New York: Penguin Books.

Golden, C. J. (1978). *Stroop Color and Word Test: A manual for clinical and experimental users.* Chicago: Stoelting.

Gordon, M., & Mettelman, B. B. (1988). The assessment of attention: Standardization and reliability of a behavior-based measure. *Journal of Clinical Psychology, 44,* 682–690.

Grodzinsky, G. M., & Diamond, R. (1992). Frontal lobe functioning and boys with attention-deficit hyperactivity disorder. *Developmental Neuropsychology, 8,* 427–445.

Hartmann, T. (1993). *Attention deficit disorder: A different perception.* Lancaster, PA: Underwood-Miller.

Hawking, S. W. (1988). *A brief history of time.* New York: Bantam Books.

Hawking, S. W. (1993). *Black holes and baby universes and other essays.* New York: Bantam Books.

Heaton, R. K. (1981). *A manual for the Wisconsin Card Sorting Test.* Odessa, FL: Psychological Assessment Resources.

Heilman, K. M., & Van Den Abell, T. (1980). Right hemisphere dominance for attention: The mechanism underlying hemispheric asymmetries of inattention (neglect). *Neurology, 30,* 327–330.

Heilman, K. M., Voeller, K. K. S., & Nadeau, S. E. (1991). A possible pathophysiological substrate of attention deficit hyperactivity disorder. *Journal of Child Neurology, 6,* 74–79.

Helson, H. (1925). The psychology of gestalt. *American Journal of Psychology, 36,* 342–370.

Hoffer, W. (1950). *Development of the body ego: The psychoanalytic study of the child (Vol. 5).* New York: International Universities Press.

Hofstadter, D. R. (1979). *Godel, Escher, Bach: An eternal Godel braid.* New York: Vintage Books.

Horgan, J. (1995). From complexity to perplexity. *Scientific American, 272*(6), 104–109.

Hothersall, D. (1984). *History of psychology.* New York: Random House.

Howell, E. N., & Ratey, J. J. (1994). *Driven to distraction.* New York: Pantheon Books.

Hunt, R. D., Cohen, D. J., Anderson, G., & Mineraa, R. B. (1987). Noradrenergic mechanisms. In L. Bloomingdale (Ed.), *Attention deficit disorder (Vol. 3): New research in attention, treatment, and psychopharmacology* (pp. 129–148). New York: Pergamon Press.

Kahn, R. L., & Cohen, L. H. (1934). Organic drivenness: A brain stem syndrome and an experience. *New England Journal of Medicine, 210,* 748–756.

Kaufman, S. (1975). Factor analysis of the WISC-R at eleven age levels between $6^1/2$ and $16^1/2$ years. *Journal of Consulting and Clinical Psychology, 43,* 135–147.

Kessler, J. W. (1966). *Psychopathology of childhood.* Englewood Cliffs, NJ: Prentice Hall.

Klee, S. H., & Garfinkel, B. D. (1983). The computerized continuous performance task: A new measure of inattention. *Journal of Abnormal Child Psychology, 11,* 487–496.

Koffka, K. (1922). Perception: An introduction to the gestalt-theorie. *Psychological Bulletin, 19,* 531–585.

Kohler, W. (1929). *Gestalt psychology.* New York: Boni and Liveright.

Kranzler, G., (1974). *You can change how you feel: A rational–emotional approach.* Eugene, OR: RETC Press.

Kuhn, T. S. (1970). *The structure of scientific revolutions* (2nd ed.). Chicago: University of Chicago Press.

Lahat, E., Avital, E., Barr, J., Berkovitch, M., Arlazoroff, A., & Aladjem, M. (1995). BAEP studies in children with attention deficit disorder. *Developmental Medicine and Child Neurology, 37,* 119–123.

Levin, P. M. (1938). Restlessness in children. *Archives of Neurology and Psychiatry, 39,* 764–770.

Lou, H. C., Henriksen, L., & Bruhn, P. (1984). Focal cerebral hypoperfusion in children with dysphasia and/or attention deficit disorder. *Archives of Neurology, 41,* 825–829.

Lou, H. C., Henriksen, L., Bruhn, P., Borner, H., & Nielesen, J. B. (1989). Striatal dysfunction of attention deficit hyperkentic disorder. *Archives of Neurology, 46,* 48–52.

Marks, I. (1982). Anxiety disorder. In J. H. Greist, J. W. Jefferson, & R. L. Spitzer (Eds.), *Treatment of mental disorders* (pp. 234–265). New York: Oxford University Press.

Matochik, J. A., Liebenauer, L. L., King, A. C., Szymanski, H. V., Cohen, R. M., & Zametkin, A. J. (1994). Cerebral glucose metabolism in adults with attention deficit hyperactivity disorder after chronic stimulant treatment. *American Journal of Psychiatry, 151,* 658–664.

Matochik, J. A., Nordahl, T. E., Gross, M., Semple, W. E., King, A. C., Cohen, R. M., & Zametkin, A. J. (1993). Effects of acute stimulant medication on cerebral metabolism in adults with hyperactivity. *Neuropsychopharmacology, 8,* 377–386.

McBurnett, K. (1995). New subtype of ADHD: Predominantly hyperactive–impulsive. *Attention!* 1 (3), 10–15.

Menninger, K. (1964). *The vital balance.* New York: Viking Press.

Millon, T. (1981). *Disorders of personality: DSM–III: Axis II.* New York: Wiley.

Mirsky, A. F. (1987). Behavioral and psychophysiological markers of attention disorder. *Environmental Health Perspectives, 74,* 191–199.

Mirsky, A. F. (1989). The neuropsychology of attention: Elements of a complex behavior. In E. Perecman (Ed.), *Integrating theory and practice in clinical neuropsychology* (pp. 75–91). Hillsdale, NJ: Erlbaum.

Murphy, K., & Barkley, R. A. (1995). Norms for the *DSM–IV* symptoms list for ADHD in adults. *The ADHD Report, 3(3),* 6–7.

Murphy, K. R., & Barkley, R. A. (1996). Prevalence of *DSM–IV* symptoms of ADHD in adult licensed drivers: Implications for clinical diagnosis. *Journal of Attention Disorders 1(3),* 147–161.

Murphy, K. R., & LaVert, S. (1995). *Out of the fog: Human options and coping strategies for adult attention deficit disorder.* New York: Skylight Press.

Nadeau, K. T. (1995). *A comprehensive guide to attention deficit disorder in adults: Research, diagnosis, and treatment.* New York: Brunner/Mazel.

Ownby, R. L., & Matthews, C. G. (1985). On the meaning of the WISC-R third factor: Relations to selected neurological measures. *Journal of Consulting and Clinical Psychology, 53,* 531–534.

Pellegrini, A. D., & Horvat, M. (1995). A developmental contextualist critique of attention deficit hyperactivity disorder. *Educational Researcher, 24,* 13–19.

Piaget, J. (1954). *The construction of reality in the child.* New York: Basic Books.

Piaget, J. (1972). Intellectual evolution from adolescence to adulthood. *Human Development, 15,* 1–12.

Piaget, J. (1976). *The grasp of consciousness: Action and concept in the young child.* Cambridge, MA: Harvard University Press.

Piaget, J. (1978). *Success and understanding.* Cambridge, MA: Harvard University Press.

Quinn, P. O. (1994). *ADD and the college student.* New York: Magination Press.

Quinn, P. O. (1995). Neurobiology of attention deficit disorder. In K. G. Nadeau (Ed.), *A comprehensive guide to attention deficit disorder in adults: Research, diagnosis, and treatment* (pp. 18–31). New York: Brunner/Mazel.

Reitan, R. M., & Wolfson, T. (1985). *The Halstead–Reitan Neuropsychological Test Battery: Theory in clinical interpretation.* Tucson, AZ: Neuropsychology Press.

Rizzolitti, G., Matelli, M., & Pavesi, G. (1983). Defects in attention and movement following the removal of postarcuate (area 6) and prearcuate (area 8) cortex in macaque monkeys. *Brain, 106,* 655–673.

Sattler, J. M. (1982). *The assessment of children's intelligence and special abilities* (2nd ed.). Boston: Allyn & Bacon.

Schwartz, G. E., & Shapiro, D. (1978). *Consciousness and self-regulation: Advances in research* (Vol. 2). New York: Holt.

Shekim, W. O., Asarnow, R. F., Hess, E., Zaucha, K., & Wheeler, N. (1990). A clinical and demographic profile of a sample of adults with attention deficit hyperactivity disorder, residual state. *Comprehensive Psychiatry, 31,* 416–425.

Shum, D. H. K., McFarland, K. A., & Bain, J. D. (1990). Construct validity of eight tests of attention: A comparison of normal and closed head injury samples. *The Clinical Neuropsychologist, 4,* 151–162.

Sieg, K. G., Gaffney, G. R., Preston, D. F., & Hellings, J. A. (1995). SPECT brain imaging abnormalities in attention deficit hyperactivity disorder. *Clinical Nuclear Medicine, 20,* 55–60.

Solden, S. (1995). *Woman with attention deficit disorder.* Grass Valley, CA: Underwood.

Sperry, R. W. (1988). Psychology's mental paradigm and the religion/science tension. *American Psychologist, 43,* 607–613.

Stewart, K. J., & Moely, B. E. (1983). The WISC-R third factor: What does it mean? *Journal of Consulting and Clinical Psychology, 51,* 940–941.

Still, G. M. (1902). Some abnormal psychical conditions in children. *The Lancet, 1,* 1008–1012, 1077–1082, 1163–1168.

Triolo, S. J., & Murphy, K. R. (1996). *Attention Deficit Scales for Adults (ADSA): Manual for scoring and interpretation.* New York: Brunner/Mazel.

Van der Meere, J., Van Baal, M., & Sergeant, J. (1989). The additive factor method: A differential diagnostic tool in hyperactivity and learning disability. *Journal of Abnormal Child Psychology, 17,* 409–422.

Van der Meere, J., Vreeling, H. J., & Sergeant, J. (1992). A motor presetting study in hyperactive, learning disabled and control children. *Journal of Child Psychology and Psychiatry, XX,* 1347–1354.

Watson, R. I. (1978). *The great psychologists* (4th ed.). New York: Lippincott.

Weber, A. M. (1988). A new clinical measure of attention: The Attentional Capacity Test. *Neuropsychology, 2,* 59–71.

Wechsler, D. (1981). *Wechsler Adult Intelligence Scales–Revised (WAIS-R) manual.* New York: The Psychological Corporation.

Weiss, G. (1990). Hyperactivity in childhood. *New England Journal of Medicine, 323,* 1413–1415.

Weiss, G., & Hechtman, L. T. (1993). *Hyperactive children grow up* (2nd ed.). New York: Guilford Press.

Weiss, L. (1992). *Attention deficit disorder in adults.* Dallas, TX: Taylor.

Welsh, M. C., Pennington, B. F., & Grossier, D. B. (1991). A normative–developmental study of executive function: A window on prefrontal function in children. *Developmental Neuropsychology, 7,* 131–149.

Wender, P. H. (1971). *Minimal brain dysfunction in children.* New York: Wiley.

Wender, P. H. (1995). *Attention-deficit hyperactivity disorder in adults.* New York: Oxford University Press.

Wender, P. H., Reimherr, F. W., Wood, D., & Ward, M. (1985). A controlled study of methylphenidate in the treatment of attention disorder, residual type, in adults. *American Journal of Psychiatry, 142,* 547–552.

Werry, J. S., & Sprague, R. L. (1970). Hyperactivity. In C. G. Costello (Ed.), *Symptoms of psychopathology* (pp. 397–417). New York: Wiley.

Willis, T. J., & Lovaas, I. (1977). A behavioral approach to treating hyperactive children: The parent's role. In J. B. Millichap (Ed.), *Learning disabilities and related disorders* (pp. 119–140). Chicago: Year Book Medical.

Wohlwill, J. (1973). *The study of behavioral development.* New York: Academic Press.

Zakay, D. (1992). The role of attention in children's time perceptions. *Journal of Experimental Child Psychology, 54,* 355–371.

Zametkin, A. J., Nordhal, T. E., Gross, M., King, A. C., Semple, W. E., Rumsey, J., Hamburger, S., & Cohen, R. M. (1990). Cerebral glucose metabolism in adults with hyperactivity of childhood onset. *New England Journal of Medicine, 323,* 1361–1366.

Zametkin, A. J., & Rapoport, J. L. (1987). Neurobiology of attention deficit disorder with hyperactivity: Where have we come in fifty years? *Journal of the American Academy of Child and Adolescent Psychiatry, 26,* 676–686.

Chapter 3

DSM–IV Criteria: Critique for the Diagnosis of Adults

CURRENT PROBLEMS WITH THE DIAGNOSIS OF ADULT ADHD

The identification of adults with ADHD is complex and needs the consideration of expanded criteria in addition to what is offered by the *DSM–IV* (American Psychiatric Association, 1994). As stated in earlier chapters, the *DSM–IV* does not offer a significant improvement over previous editions of the diagnostic manual. I argued that the *DSM–IV* categories provide some form of compromise between the viewpoints of the two previous editions.

The adult population with attention problems presents its own unique set of difficulties. It is important to realize that an adult who has not been diagnosed will most likely present comorbid issues that could very easily present a confusing picture. It is best to expect multiple layers of problems. Typically, attention problems predisposed ADHD adults, as children, to have significant behavioral problems in school (Fischer, Barkley, Fletcher, & Smallish, 1993; Weiss & Hechtman, 1993). It may be that ADHD children, without proper diagnosis, received much negative feedback from teachers, parents, and even peers. It is also quite likely that undiagnosed ADHD children may have accepted the negative feedback and self-reinforced it during the developing years. For instance, over time, they may actually have come to see themselves as negative people, and may have engaged in self-reinforcers, even at the absence of external reinforcers. Ironically, the more intelligent ADHD children are at higher risk than the less intelligent ADHD children in creating and maintaining these negative self-reinforcers. The intelligent ADHD children may be able to perceive, at some level, that something is wrong internally and may be more likely to accept themes such as being "stupid." Academically, it is well documented that children with attention problems are at risk of not reaching their academic potential (Hinshaw, 1992). Again, it is ironic that the brighter children are at risk of having a greater gap between intellectual potential and academic performance. Behaviorally, these children are sometimes seen as having conduct problems. To some extent, this label is usually perpetuated by the children themselves; after all, it is better to be seen as a "bad apple" than as someone who is too "stupid" to be academically successful.

Another subgroup, which may receive even less attention, would be children who tend to withdraw and perhaps even give up in making further efforts. They are not conduct-problem children who are at risk of developing the self-reinforcing "bad apple" persona; rather, they tend to shy away from the usual academic challenges, sensing that they are not up to speed with their peers. There is no definitive statistical proof, but it is reasonable to assume that these ADHD children did not receive the attention their conduct-problem peers did and were therefore overlooked. If anything, their quiet nature and poor academic performance are perhaps falsely attributed to intellectual "slowness." These are important points to consider, because it is obvious that only adults who have not been diagnosed as having ADHD as children are now coming in to be evaluated.

Barkley (1990b) introduced consistent data to indicate that attention-problem children are at great risk of academic failures and early withdrawal from school. Of course, the lack of education in a highly technical society opens the door to a cascade of problems. Before long, as these individuals move into adulthood, multiple problems can be expected in relationships, the job market, financial endeavors, and other adult arenas. In essence, the undiagnosed adult with attention problems has most likely traveled a path to other pathologies (Hinshaw, 1992).

These pathologies include marital conflicts; alcohol and other drug abuse; anxiety disorders; affective disorders; and the possibility of developing significant personality defects, such as borderline functioning and antisocial tendencies (Hallowell & Ratey, 1994; Wender, 1995). It is quite likely that adults with attention problems finally seek professional interventions because of these secondary issues. This may be less so as the general population becomes more aware of attention problems among adults. However, it is quite likely that they seek help from a professional who has been predominantly trained in treating adults. Thus, these professionals are more likely to focus on the secondary adult problems (i.e., marital conflicts, alcohol abuse, etc.) rather than to consider potential deficits in attention, an area in which they perhaps did not have much training. Of course, it is important not to discount any of the problems presented, but there is certainly a risk of missing the underlying factors that led to these traditionally "adult" problems.

Often, diagnostic interviews that are quite helpful for the child population are simply not available for the adult population. For instance, the usual proper procedure to make a diagnosis for a child with attention problems is to obtain information through collateral sources. Thus, histories taken from the child's parents and teachers are often available to provide additional information. Unlike children, adults with ADHD most often do not present with their parents. On a number of occasions, the spouse may be used as a collateral source of information; however, it is important to realize that many adults with ADHD may be separated or have never married. Also, they are likely to be quite mobile and be far from their home of origin.

Finally, the *DSM–IV* is still more sensitive to identification and diagnosis of children, rather than adults. In fact, the field studies for the *DSM–IV* did not include adult subjects (Lahey et al., 1994). This is quite irresponsible, considering that it had now been decades since first evidence of adult ADHD appeared.

THE NEED TO MOVE BEYOND THE *DSM–IV* CRITERIA

The most recent *DSM* provides four categories from which to choose a specific ADHD diagnosis. The first is Attention Deficit Hyperactivity Disorder, predominantly inattentive type. To meet the criteria for this diagnosis, at least six out of a list of nine symptoms of inattention, and fewer than six symptoms out of a list of nine symptoms of hyperactivity–impulsivity, must be met; the symptoms causing impairment must have been present before the age of 7, in at least two settings; and there must be evidence of clinically significant impairment in social, academic, or occupational functioning. The second category is Attention Deficit Hyperactivity Disorder, predominantly hyperactive–impulsive type. Criteria for this category include meeting at least six out of nine symptoms of hyperactivity or impulsivity, and fewer than six of nine symptoms of inattention. As in the previous category, onset of symptoms must be before the age of 7; impairments due to symptoms must be noted in at least two settings; and the symptoms must cause significant impairment in social, academic, or occupational functioning. The third category is Attention Deficit Hyperactivity Disorder, combined type. The diagnostic criteria include having at least six of nine inattentive symptoms and at least six of nine hyperactive–impulsivity symptoms. Again, the symptoms must have been present before the age of 7; the effects of the symptoms must be present in at least two settings; and the symptoms must cause impairment in social, academic, or occupational functioning. A fourth category, identified as Attention Deficit Hyperactivity Disorder, not otherwise specified, also is given as a diagnostic option for individuals with prominent ADHD symptoms that do not meet the criteria for any of the other three options.

McBurnett (1995) presented an interesting discussion on the new subtype of ADHD, predominantly hyperactive–impulsive type. According to his research data, this category best fits younger children (preschool age). He reported that, because of their age, these children may display several hyperactive–impulsive symptoms without presenting an opportunity to note symptoms of inattention. Children at this age are often not required to attend, or at least they are not placed in situations, like their older counterparts are, where they need to attend to schoolwork or home chores. Thus, he hypothesized that this is a developmentally based diagnostic subtype and, as these children grow older, they are more likely to present symptoms of inattention. Consequently, there may be a diagnostic shift with respect to age.

There has been a growing interest in the study of early signs of ADHD. Goldstein (1993) identified infant traits such as irritability, erratic sleep patterns, and feeding problems as possible signs of ADHD. The descriptions provided are reflective of classical studies of infant temperament (Thomas & Chess, 1977; Thomas, Chess, Birch, Hertzig, & Korn, 1963; Williams, 1956). Although some associations can be made between temperament and behavior disorders (Thomas, Chess, & Birch, 1968), predictive power is limited by numerous environmental interactions (Fagot & Kavanagh, 1993; Frankel & Bates, 1990; Thomas & Chess, 1977).

One can argue that this new diagnostic category has been added to the *DSM–IV* as a means of making it easier to diagnose younger children, and there may be some ethical concerns related to this issue that are beyond the scope of this text. However, the concept of diagnostic subtypes being developmentally associated may have some validity with respect to adolescent and adult populations. Barkley (1990a) suggested that the number of symptoms necessary for diagnosis should be dependent on age. It has already been demonstrated that ADHD symptoms—especially hyperactivity and impulsivity—are observed in greater numbers during the young childhood years and tend to decline in number during the growing years (Achenbach & Edelbrock, 1981). Barkley (1990a), therefore, suggested a higher cutoff score for the preschool age group (10 of 14 symptoms instead of the standard 8 of 14, as dictated by the then-diagnostic criteria in the *DSM–III–R* [American Psychiatric Association, 1987]). He went on to suggest that the middle childhood age group would use the standard 8-out-of-14-symptoms criteria of the *DSM–III–R*, but only 6 symptoms may be needed to make a diagnosis among the adolescent population.

In a more recent report, Murphy and Barkley (1995) suggested that the reduction of symptoms with respect to age does not stop at adolescence. On the surface, this evidence may appear to support the old notion that ADHD is a childhood disease, which somehow rectifies itself with maturity, and ADHD children eventually outgrow their problem once they reach adulthood. Unfortunately, this is not the case; in spite of a decline of overt symptoms, core impairments due to ADHD remain prominent and stable (Barkley, Fischer, Edelbrock, & Smallish, 1991). This point cannot be emphasized enough, because it presents a particular problem addressing the adult ADHD population. Many of the symptoms presented in childhood, such as behavioral disruptions, chronic interruptions, and impulsive acts, seem to be less overt in adulthood. However, the core problems related to ADHD do not disappear. The adult may make cognitive adjustments to reduce the frequency of impulsive, disorganized, or disruptive behaviors, but the inner struggles remain. In essence, what was once seen behaviorally may have been internalized during the adult years.

Murphy and Barkley (1995) provided evidence, based on their data analysis, for changing the cutoff criteria in the *DSM–IV* for adults. They took all 18 symptoms from the *DSM–IV* (9 inattention and 9 hyperactive–impulsive) and developed a rating scale to measure endorsement of items among the "normal" population. Using the criterion of 1.5 *SD* beyond the mean, cutoff criteria were established. Their preliminary results show that the *DSM–IV* standard of having 6 out of 9 symptoms for each of the inattentive and the hyperactive–impulsivity categories is too high for the adult population. In essence, the symptom cutoff level for adults may be producing too many false negatives: adults who have attention problems but fail to be diagnosed. Murphy and Barkley's data suggest new cutoff levels for the adult population. Again, using the 1.5 *SD* above the mean as a point of reference, they suggested that four or more symptoms from the inattentive category and five or more from the hyperactivity–impulsivity category best reduces the chance of false negative diagnoses. In fact, in the age group between 30 and 49, the cutoff criteria could be set at four for both the inattentive and the hyperactivity–impulsivity categories.

This statistical analysis brings forth another major flaw with the *DSM–IV* diagnostic criteria. There is now ample information on normative behavior among children and adolescents, if not for adults, predominantly taken in home and school settings, with respect to the average levels of attention, concentration, focus, and general activity (Conners, 1989; Reynolds & Kamphaus, 1992). It was originally hoped that the latest *DSM* would emphasize the use of standardized data. Unfortunately, the history of improving diagnostic procedures for attention problems may follow the same historical path as the diagnosis of intellectual deficits. There was a considerable lag of time between standardizations of cognitive functioning and the use of standardized instruments to make diagnoses of intellectual deficits. Today, making a diagnosis of mental retardation without the proper use of standardized tests would be considered malpractice; however, this was not always the case. In the not-too-distant past, clinicians were irresponsibly labeling patients as being mentally retarded without proper use of standardized instruments. Error in judgments resulted in serious consequences for patients. Eventually, proper corrections were made, and the use of standardized measures to assess intelligence were adopted as a necessary criterion. It is certainly hoped that a similar perspective will be adopted for the diagnosis of ADHD in the future.

At the present time there are a number of authors (e.g., Hallowell & Ratey, 1994) who have reported there are no instruments available that can help diagnose ADHD in adults. This is simply not true. If a clinician is looking for a definitive test, such as a blood test to diagnose pregnancy, then the authors' position applies. However, it would be a gross error to dismiss standardized measures (e.g., Brown, 1996; Triolo & Murphy, 1996) as not being useful for the diagnosis of ADHD, and the present diagnostic standard of the *DSM–IV* is seriously limiting reliability by the exclusion of such measures.

The *DSM–IV* criterion of having symptoms present in at least two settings, is a major improvement over previous *DSM* editions. The purpose of this criterion is to reflect the fact that symptoms are rather consistent across a number of different and varied settings. It is also reflective of the nature of ADHD in that it is mainly due to intracognitive functioning rather than environmental variability. Consequently, ADHD symptoms should cut across different settings.

This criterion may add to the validity of the diagnosis if it is more stringent. For years, one of the more useful ways to convince parents that the reason for their child's underachievement in school was not laziness or ''poor'' attitude was to identify similar behavioral problems in tasks the youngster normally enjoys. For example, the child who receives poor grades because he or she has a tendency to forget assignments and does not follow directions well, may also have problems forgetting sports equipment on the way to a play activity, something the child enjoys more than homework assignments. This same diagnostic criterion can be applied to adults. The same individual who forgets to stop by the grocery store on the way home, a task that usually is not very enjoyable, may also forget necessary camping equipment on a getaway weekend, a far more enjoyable activity than shopping. The aim is to see symptoms across more than one setting and situations, with at least one being described as a pleasurable task. This criterion will also help the diagnostician rule out alternative themes, such as passive–aggressive tendencies.

The last criterion of the *DSM–IV* can be very useful for the adult population. It simply requires the diagnostician to note impairments in social, academic, or occupational functioning, due to ADHD symptoms. In this area, the adult ADHD population can present a special history. One of the major themes presented by Weiss and Hechtman (1993) was that ADHD adults, over the years, have suffered from not reaching their full potential. Perhaps more so than any other age group, the adult population, especially if diagnosis has been made late in life, will present a distinctive feature of not achieving up to their full potential and talents. Special dreams, personal hopes, and achievement goals usually are not realized regardless of intellectual capacity. Test data may very well support this theme. For instance, it is not unusual for someone with above-average intellectual functioning to have had a history of dropping out of school early and to have had jobs that normally do not challenge individuals at this level of intellectual functioning. Thus, a special impairment with respect to underachievement may be a prominent condition for the adult ADHD population.

In summary, the *DSM–IV* is a long way from providing the diagnostician all of the necessary criteria for reliable and valid diagnosis of ADHD adults. Perhaps the most important fact to keep in mind is that the field studies for the *DSM–IV* did not include adults. The *DSM–IV* is a useful preliminary screening guide, but it should not be relied on exclusively to make diagnoses. To increase diagnostic reliability, several options should be seriously considered. On the one hand, the requirement to have six out of nine symptoms in either the inattentive or hyperactive–impulsive categories places the diagnostician at risk of making false-negative errors—failing to make the diagnosis of ADHD when it indeed applies. On the other hand, the lack of use of standardized measures places the diagnostician at risk of making false positives—failing to rule out ADHD. Additional suggestions designed to increase reliability include the presentation of symptoms during preferable and enjoyable activities, and an inability to fulfill potential with respect to intellect and talents.

REFERENCES

Achenbach, T. M., & Edelbrock, C. S. (1981). Behavioral problems and compentencies reported by parents of normal and disturbed children aged 4 through 16. *Monographs of the Society for Research and Child Development, 46(1)*, 1–82.

American Psychiatric Association. (1987). *Diagnostic and statistical manual of mental disorders* (3rd ed., rev.). Washington, DC: Author.

American Psychiatric Association. (1994). *Diagnostic and statistical manual of mental disorders* (4th ed.). Washington, DC: Author.

Barkley, R. A. (1990a). A critique of current diagnostic criteria for attention deficit hyperactivity disorder: Clinical and research implications. *Developmental and Behavioral Pediatrics, 11*, 343–352.

Barkley, R. A. (1990b). *Attention deficit hyperactivity disorder: A handbook for diagnosis and treatment.* New York: Guilford Press.

Barkely, R. A, Fischer, M., Edelbrock, C. S., & Smallish, L. (1991). The adolescent outcome of hyperactive children diagnosed by research criteria: I. An eight year prospective follow-up study. *Journal of the American Academy of Childhood and Adolescent Psychiatry, 29*, 546–557.

Brown, T. E. (1996). *Attention deficit disorder scales.* San Antonio, TX: The Psychological Corporation.

Conners, C. K. (1989). *Conners' Rating Scales manual.* New York: Multi-Health Systems.

Fagot, B. I., & Kavanagh, K. (1993). Parenting during the second year: Effects of children's age, sex and attachment classification. *Child Development, 64*, 258–271.

Fischer, M., Barkley, R. A., Fletcher, K. E., & Smallish, L. (1993). The adolescent outcome of hyperactive children: Predictors of psychiatric, academic, social and emotional adjustments. *Journal of the American Academy of Child and Adolescent Psychiatry, 32*, 324–332.

Frankel, K. A., & Bates, J. E. (1990). Mother–toddler problem solving: Antecedents in attachment, home behavior, and temperament. *Child Development, 61*, 810–819.

Goldstein, S. (1993). Young children at risk: Recognizing the early signs of ADHD. *The ADHD Report, 1(4)*, 7–8.

Hallowell, E. M., & Ratey, J. J. (1994). *Driven to destruction.* New York: Pantheon Books.

Hinshaw, S. P. (1992). Academic underachievement, attention deficits, and aggression: Comorbidity and implications for intervention. *Journal of Consulting and Clinical Psychology, 60*, 893–903.

Lahey, B. B., Applegate, B., McBurnett, K., Biederman, J., Greenhill, L., Hynd, G.W., Barkley, R. A., Newcorn, J., Jensen, P., Richters, J., Garfinkel, B., Kerdy, K. L., Frick, P. J., Ollendick, T., Perez, D., Hart, E. L., Waldman, I., & Shaffer, D. (1994). *DSM–IV* field trials for attention deficit hyperactivity disorder in children and adolescents. *American Journal of Psychiatry, 151*, 1673–1685.

McBurnett, K. (1995). New subtype of ADHD: Predominantly hyperactive–impulsive. *Attention!, 1(3)*, 10–15.

Murphy, K., & Barkley, R. A. (1995). Norms for the *DSM–IV* symptoms list for ADHD in adults. *The ADHD Report, 3*(3), 6–7.

Reynolds, C. R., & Kamphaus, R.W. (1992). *Behaviors assessment system for children.* Circle Pines, MN: American Guidance Service.

Thomas, A., & Chess, S. (1977). *Temperament and development.* New York: Brunner/Mazel.

Thomas, A., Chess, S., & Birch, H. G. (1968). *Temperament and behavior disorders in children.* New York: New York University Press.

Thomas, A., Chess, S., Birch, H. G., Hertzig, N. E., & Korn, S. (1963). *Behavioral individuality in early childhood.* New York: New York University Press.

Triolo, S. J., & Murphy, K. (1996). *Attention Deficit Scales for Adults (ADSA).* New York: Brunner/Mazel.

Weiss, G., & Hechtman, L. T. (1993). *Hyperactive children grow up.* New York: Guilford Press.

Wender, P. H. (1995). *Attention-deficit hyperactivity disorder in adults.* New York: Oxford University Press.

Williams, R. V. (1956). *Biochemical individuality.* New York: Wiley.

Chapter 4

Diagnosis

For practitioners who are in private practice, not linked to major university funding, and dependent on third-party payments, very realistic practical matters must be considered. In this day of managed-care companies that pressure clinicians to consider the most cost-effective avenues toward evaluating and treating patients, a balance must be struck between efficiency of services and adequate reliability. Unlike institutional settings, which are supported by endowments and research funds, the cost of evaluations burdens the patient. Most private practitioners are quite sensitive to the burdens their patients must endure. On the other hand, reliability of assessment is essential, and it should not be compromised.

Fortunately, reliability need not be compromised, because there are very practical methods to get around the cost-effectiveness problem. One of the most predominant themes throughout this chapter will be the notion of orthogonal testing. As much as possible, the evaluation process should include components that are independent of each other with minimal shared variance. For example, much has been written regarding neuropsychological testing (e.g., Barkley & Grodzinsky, 1994; Castellanos et al., 1994; O'Brien et al., 1992; Trommer, Hoeppner, Lorber, & Armstrong, 1988) and, as is presented later in this chapter, there are a number of new instruments now available to tap into attention-related cognitive functioning. In a university setting, funded by research grants, it may be appropriate to take an entire day to administer several of these instruments. However, a diagnostician in private practice may be wiser to choose carefully only one or two of these tests, especially if they cover the same territory (e.g., visual vigilance). This suggestion also applies to personality inventories. Again, there are a number of these tests available, but it would be somewhat of an overkill to bombard the patient with several of them, especially if the tests are highly correlated with each other. Thus, the theme is to choose tests wisely to cover different and independent aspects of the diagnostic process.

This procedure may actually be more reliable than the research models. Many of the patients who have gone through institutional settings are usually given an entire battery of tests with little variation from the other patients. The reasoning for this procedure is understandable, because the researchers are interested in collecting data in a uniform manner across a large subject pool. Of course, this uniform procedure sacrifices the needs of the individual. In a private practice setting, tests can be selected specifically to meet the needs of the individual patient.

On the other side of this argument, some practitioners may argue that there are no instruments available that can help diagnosis ADHD in adults. It seems there are a number of clinicians who have fooled themselves into believing that their "superior" interview skills are enough to make a reliable and valid diagnosis. This is unfortunate and a grave mistake. It opens the door to continued confusion and misinformation.

This issue is more important today than in previous years. A few years ago the public was not as informed, and patients presented ADHD symptoms ignorant of the literature in this field. Today, it is not unusual for patients to come to a doctor's office armed with numerous popular books and articles on the subject. Consequently, their responses to interview questions are almost tailor-made to the diagnostic criteria. It is good that the general population is no longer ignorant of ADHD; however, it is easy to see how such a popular topic can present a major challenge to the clinician interviewing a patient.

Later in this chapter the use of personality inventories to help circumvent this problem will be discussed. For now, it is important to understand that the use of more objective standardized instruments as part of the diagnostic process must be considered essential.

This subject matter is analogous to the use of instruments to fly an airplane. Today, the savvy pilot will certainly use all feedback that is available. Visual cues as well as instrument readings are integrated to ensure a safe flight. Also, it is important to have the knowledge and understanding that would be most reliable under different circumstances. Even in good weather, when visual cues are most reliable, the experienced pilot refers to instrument feedback as added insurance. Of course, it would be totally foolish to disregard the available instruments during inclement weather.

Diagnosticians should view the available assessment instruments in the same manner. One could argue that the experienced clinician has enough savvy to fly alone with just clinical impressions, and some level of success may be enough to reinforce the continuation of this practice. After all, unlike piloting a plane, the clinician does not crash with the patient. Consequently, there is greater room for error, especially among the most arrogant clinicians. In fact, because they do not crash with their patients, there is a greater chance of well-meaning and extremely experienced clinicians making the same errors repeatedly.

A legitimate argument can be made that this field of study is at a pre-Lindbergh stage, when there simply is not enough trust in the instruments provided. Certainly there are a number of articles and authors who have argued how useless available instruments are in doing proper diagnostics (e.g., Hallowell & Ratey, 1994). However, we have reached a time when we can prioritize instruments with respect to utility. Also, there is enough sophistication now to fully understand the power and limitations of the instruments available. For instance, there would be minimal usefulness in giving a patient a battery of neurological assessments, even if these instruments have been noted in the literature as being sensitive to attention problems. It would be like a cockpit being equipped with half a dozen horizon sensors. This would be not only redundant but also potentially tragic if they did not leave enough space for other instruments, such as a compass or an altimeter. Thus, the theme of having orthogonal purposes in instrumentation is more important than redundancy.

For the adult ADHD population, orthogonal purposes in instrumentation are extremely important. If ADHD is diagnosed in an individual for the first time during the adult years, it is almost certain that additional psychological problems will accompany the ADHD. The literature on ADHD in adulthood has been very attentive to this subject matter (Nadeau, 1995). Thus, a dual diagnosis is often indicated, and it seems reasonable to assume that testing would tap into a variety of psychological and cognitive spheres. In essence, the diagnostician working with adult ADHD patients almost always flies in inclement weather where nothing is purely as it seems and clinical visions are always clouded. Thus, to reject the power of instruments is analogous to landing a plane in dense fog with the naked eye.

At first, the diagnostician may be overwhelmed by the task at hand. However, there are some distinctive advantages to consider. As is demonstrated later, the diagnostic process itself need not be independent of diagnostic interviews for other dysfunctions. In essence, it is not necessary to have a patient come in for a specialized interview addressing ADHD symptoms, separate from other problems such as interpersonal difficulties, mood disorders, anxiety disorders, and so on. To some extent, the testing procedures should lend themselves to be sensitive to a number of disorders. The experienced practitioners, reading through the diagnostic process outlined in this book, will most likely recognize some very standardized clinical procedures.

DIAGNOSTIC PROCESS

The entire diagnostic process can be subdivided into six sequential components. They were first briefly presented by Triolo and Murphy (1996) as part of the interpretation chapter for the Attention-Deficit Scales for Adults (ADSA). They are as follows:

1 Rule out physical abnormalities.
2 Conduct clinical interview with patient to get a thorough history and also address *DSM–IV* (American Psychiatric Association, 1994) criteria.
3 Conduct an independent collateral interview.

4 Quantify subjective reports of ADHD symptoms with standardized measures.

5 Conduct brief analysis of personality traits and emotional dispositions.

6 If warranted, administer neuropsychological tests.

Medical Screening

It is important to rule out medical problems that may mimic ADHD symptoms. Overall, this is a relatively simple task that can often be accomplished by a routine physical examination. Among the school-age population, it may be important to rule out sensory deficit problems, especially auditory ones. For the older population, there may be less of a risk of overlooking this problem. Still, to ensure a comprehensive diagnostic analysis, this issue should be considered.

Studies with children have associated allergies with ADHD (Hartsough & Lambert, 1985; Szatmari, Offord, & Boyle, 1989; Trites, Tryphonoas, & Ferguson, 1980). These studies are not definitive, and data have shown that there are no significant differences between ADHD and non-ADHD populations with respect to frequency of allergies (Mitchell, Aman, Turbott, & Manku, 1987). Although the relationship between allergies and ADHD is still in question, it is best to be conservative and consider the possibility that some ADHD symptoms are due to allergies. That is, patients may be complaining that they cannot concentrate and have difficulty focusing on tasks such as reading, secondary to allergic reactions. A brief screening may be helpful in ruling out this possibility. For many allergy sufferers, predictable patterns can present themselves. For instance, frequency of symptoms may be seasonal. This is a good example of quickly ruling out ADHD, because attention problems are expected to be chronic.

Also, there has been an interest in linking ADHD symptoms with thyroid anomalies (Bhatara, Kumer, McMillin, & Bandettini, 1994). Hauser et al.'s (1993) study of both children and adults provided what is perhaps the best association of symptoms. In their studies, symptoms of ADHD were found among most of their sample of patients with thyroid disease. It must be noted that this study focused exclusively on generalized resistance to thyroid hormone, a subcategory of thyroid anomalies, but the evidence was convincing enough to suggest consideration. Even among other thyroid diseases, the frequency of ADHD symptoms is high enough to suggest a thyroid screening. This argument was presented, for at least the child population, by Ciaranello (1993). However, the overall consensus is that this screening is not necessary. Bhatara et al. (1994) pointed out that, although the incidence of ADHD symptoms among the population of thyroid patients is high, there is a very low frequency of ADHD patients who present thyroid anomalies. Perhaps it is best to simply be sensitive to the possibility of hormonal imbalances that cause behavioral problems that sometimes mimic ADHD symptoms. Among the adult population, special sensitivity may be warranted for individuals who have had a history of hormonal treatment, for instance. In such cases, the timing of symptoms with respect to life changes may be important to consider. Also, the chronicity of symptoms should be a major consideration, because it is likely that ADHD symptoms were not present in these patients during their developmental years.

Finally, disturbances in sleep due to neurogenic or medical conditions may produce daytime symptoms related to inattentiveness (Herman, Roffwarge, & Becker, 1989). Historically, ADHD has been associated with disturbances in sleep; disturbances in sleep was once used as a criterion for the diagnosis of attention problems (*DSM–III*; American Psychiatric Association, 1980). However, this criterion focused on behavioral patterns in children, especially those who were hyperactive and presented problems to their parents by becoming restless and oppositional at bedtime. Later editions of the *DSM* did not include sleep disturbances as a criterion. Nevertheless, Lavenstein (1995) identified sleep disturbances as perhaps a comorbid neurological condition of ADHD and reported that clinical reports suggest that a number of adults with ADHD symptoms also report erratic sleep patterns. Research in this area appears to be limited, and it is unknown if disturbances in sleep patterns are due to ADHD dispositions or whether ADHD symptoms are the result of specific neurogenic problems that interfere with sleep patterns.

A colleague who works with ADHD (personal correspondence, February 17, 1998) suggested there are two symptoms that can be used for differential diagnosis. The first is snoring on a regular basis, which can suggest problems with sleep apnea. The second is involuntary shaking limb movement while asleep, sometimes described as restless leg syndrome. If neither symptom is present, the patient's problems with attention may not be due to sleep disturbances. For assurance, however, it may be prudent to consult with a specialist in this area of study. Ideally, the patient may benefit from a collaboration of experts who collectively have expertise in ADHD and sleep disturbances.

In conclusion, medical dispositions may be contributing factors in mimicking ADHD symptoms, but they can easily be ruled out. It is certainly important to exercise good judgment. Common-sense considerations such as making note of prescription medications and possible side effects should be considered for all patients, regardless of their presenting problems. For instance, drowsiness is a common side effect of any number of medications, and it makes sense that patients taking these prescriptions report difficulties with concentration and attention.

The same consideration should be given to other physical conditions, such as sensory deficits. This is done routinely for children because it is correctly assumed that children are not sophisticated enough to recognize and communicate hearing loss and other difficulties. However, it may not be wise to assume that adults are quite capable of recognizing sensory deficits or that they will report them without specific questions. Thus, it may be prudent to at least query about this issue to assure a more comprehensive understanding of the presenting complaints.

The overall differential diagnosis issues with respect to physical problems should be straightforward. Some authors have presented a long list of physical problems along with discussions regarding differential diagnosis (e.g. Lavenstein, 1995) that may overwhelm many readers. Issues are considered with respect to epilepsy, stroke, tumors, Tourette's syndrome, and even multiple sclerosis. Most of these physical impairments can easily be ruled out by history, and they may not meet the chronicity criterion necessary for an ADHD diagnosis. Those impairments that may very well meet the chronicity criterion can be differentiated by the symptoms themselves. For instance, multiple sclerosis involves far more global impairments of cognitive functioning than would typically be found in ADHD. Also, the hyperactive component, which includes behavior problems such as impulsivity, excessive energy, and random responses to extraneous stimuli is obviously not expected in a patient with multiple sclerosis. Thus, there is no need to be overwhelmed by the extensive listings of possible confounding physical problems.

Perhaps the only category exception would be in the differentiation between ADHD and sleep dysfunctions. As suggested earlier, research in this area is not definitive. It is conceivable that many adults diagnosed as having ADHD, especially the inattentive type, may eventually be discovered to have an underlying sleep problem. Conversely, many patients who have been described as having sleep disturbances may very well have attention-related problems that are undetected. The primary concern should be to attend to sleep disturbances. Once they are corrected, ADHD symptoms, if they are still present, can be addressed next.

Clinical Interview to Address Symptoms and Their History

During an interview, it may be best to keep in mind two extremes in regard to the presentation of symptoms. The first is the patient who perhaps has read much about adult ADHD and, after reading one or two popular texts, is either convinced that this is "the" answer to all experienced problems or, at least, there is a suspicion that ADHD is a real issue that needs to be investigated. At the other end of the continuum is the patient who presents with traditional "adult" complaints (i.e., cannot get along with spouse, feelings of depression, alcohol abuse, etc.) but is not aware of ADHD. Thus, ADHD symptoms, if at all presented without specific questioning, may be mixed in with other symptoms. In a general clinical practice, both of these extremes must be considered along with every other condition in between.

In the case of the former extreme, where a patient is somewhat convinced that the problems are due to ADHD, it is quite likely that all of the *DSM–IV* symptoms are presented. It is also quite likely that the patient would make statements such as "I have read this book (sometimes bringing in a copy with highlighted sections), and it explains my whole life." At this stage it may be tempting to challenge the patient with alternative themes, but it is perhaps best to spend the initial time gathering information without giving any feedback other than acknowledgment of his or her described problems. This is simply good general practice; all patients would like to feel as though they have had an opportunity to express themselves and explain problems as they see them. Therefore, if the patient brings along the latest book on ADHD, it is a very good idea to allow the patient to point out all of the problems indicated in the text that fit with his or her life experience. There are a number of recent popular books on the market, and it may be a good idea to at least familiarize yourself with them. For instance, Weiss (1992) has an entire adult assessment section in her book and a checklist of symptoms for the reader to review and make a self-assessment. Hallowell and Ratey's (1994) book, which also is popular among the general public, has a table of "Suggested Diagnostic Criteria for Attention Deficit Disorder in Adults" (pp. 201–202), in which 20 symptoms are presented, and ADHD is suggested if 12 or more are identified by the reader. It is interesting to note that Wender (1995) recently published his "Utah criteria" in what will most likely be a very popular book. These books, and others, provide valuable resources to the general population; however, they may also be a source of hindrance. Two points should be kept in mind while listening to a patient describe symptoms. First, what percentage of the endorsed symptoms are secondary to ADHD? Second, are these proposed symptoms excessive, and do they significantly impair the patient's life?

In Weiss's (1992) book, the primary symptoms, such as "easily distracted," are mixed in with secondary symptoms, such as "tends to blame others" (pp. 167–168). It is extremely important to listen carefully and tabulate which of the symptoms are endorsed most. This same problem can be seen in Hallowell and Ratey's (1994) categories. Again, primary symptoms, such as "impatient," are presented with a rather long list of secondary symptoms, such as "a sense of under achievement ... often creative ... a sense of insecurity" (pp. 201–202). The second question is most concerning; Hallowell and Ratey seem to arbitrarily come up with 12 symptoms as the threshold of problems. Likewise, Weiss, without any standardized measure against which to compare symptoms, identified the endorsement of 40% of the symptoms as the threshold level of significance. This second question cannot be addressed properly unless standardized measures are implemented; it is important to keep in mind this lack of standardization while gathering interview information, especially when the patient is describing life interferences and general quality of day-to-day functioning.

At the other end of the extreme, the patient may not present any symptoms of ADHD and, just as recommended previously, it may be good to simply listen and allow him or her to communicate individual feelings and perspectives. Even if there are growing suspicions that many of the patient's problems are due to an underlying ADHD disposition, it may be best to simply allow the patient to communicate to you, rather than to introduce the ADHD theme. During this time of data gathering, it may be important to focus on historical patterns and behavioral tendencies. In some cases, patients can be very helpful in providing reports of difficulties stemming back to their childhood years. However, it would not be a surprise to learn that patients simply do not have this level of insight and cannot recall childhood difficulties. For instance, a man in his late 20s was referred for therapy by his new spouse because of ongoing interpersonal difficulties. Many of these difficulties came about when others became angry with him for not following through with promises and for being forgetful regarding day-to-day duties. It was quickly learned that interpersonal problems extended beyond the marriage to on-the-job difficulties, getting along with coworkers and supervisors. Time was spent learning about his childhood years, but he simply could not remember, stating that it was "one big blur." It was very fortunate in this case to have excellent collateral interviews and even some supporting documentation from old report cards, but the patient, by his very nature of impulsively plowing through life, was actually a poor historian. Therefore, as a general rule, it may be wise to focus on the present problem (i.e., marital conflict) and simply follow up on your suspicions of ADHD by patiently gathering additional data along the way. Additional data such as collateral interviews and standardized measures could be most helpful, as is presented later.

Regardless of which end of the continuum the patients represent, it is important to keep in mind that the *DSM–IV* diagnostic criteria should be used only as a guideline. As mentioned earlier, there should be less focus on reaching the critical number of symptoms; on the other hand, it is extremely important to be attentive to the strength of the symptoms. One measurement of their strength is chronicity. Statements such as "I've always had this problem" are important to note. Also important with respect to strength of symptoms is assessment of their pervasiveness and stability across different situations. As stated earlier, it is very important to note problems during activities the patient sees as being leisure time or a time of relaxation. Thus, a patient who reports being distracted at work should also provide some insight into how distractible he or she is during other enjoyable activities, such as hobbies and relaxing home projects. In fact, a lack of symptoms during enjoyable activities may be a way to rule out ADHD. For example, a young man who had had a difficult time throughout his school years and showed much impatience attending to job responsibilities reported that he could spend hours on end putting together model ships and planes. For this young man, it was eventually discovered that symptoms were due to temperamental issues rather than ADHD. This subject matter related to temperamental factors has received very little attention with respect to differential diagnosis and, unfortunately, much attention has been given to it as one of the symptoms of ADHD, which is very misleading. This issue is addressed more extensively later.

For now, it is important to keep in mind the robust nature of ADHD symptoms across time and different settings. It is therefore strongly recommended that the patient be asked questions about leisure time and enjoyable activities. Sometimes a simple question such as "what do you do for fun?" followed by "are there any problems related to the fun activity?" may be helpful in gaining insights. For patients who have already concluded that ADHD is their problem, and it is not, this might be an important issue to present—at the appropriate time—as a way to have them possibly rethink their ideas. Often patients present symptoms exclusively in relation to their work, academic activities, or both. Thus, it may be important to ask them "Okay, you told me all about your problems dealing with academics. Tell me about problems you are having outside of the academic sphere, in things that you enjoy." For instance, a young lady who reported numerous problems dealing with her college studies and seemed to be rather disorganized attending to job duties was amazingly organized at leading children in camping trips. She remembered individual schedules and even medication for the children under her care without any problems, and there was never an occasion when she forgot items (can opener, utensils, sleeping bags, etc.) in spite of the amount of attention to details this responsibility required.

At this point, it may be noteworthy to the reader that the usual queries dealing with academic life and job and career history have not been given as much emphasis here as found in other literature related to ADHD. The aim is not to discount these very important issues but to more efficiently use the interview time available. It is easy to see how numerous non-ADHD adults would report problems dealing with job duties and academic responsibilities. In fact, any activity that is considered a "chore" would understandably be described as being somewhat of a bore and problematic in terms of keeping vigilant attention and focus. On the other hand, if non-ADHD adults are asked about their leisure time, it would be rather unusual to hear extensive reports of having difficulty with attention and other ADHD-related symptoms. This is obviously not an absolute diagnostic criterion, but it certainly should be considered as a focal point of consideration during a clinical interview.

Assuming that symptoms are pervasive and the chronicity criteria are satisfied, it may be important to probe further regarding the quality of functioning. For instance, in addition to describing usual problems with completing job-related duties, it may be helpful to ask for examples of difficulty. It may make a difference if the job requires the patient to sit behind a desk for several hours of the day, as opposed to being on the road.

Another point to consider is the extent of responsibility asked of the patient. With a trend toward corporate downsizing, it is not unusual to find employees burdened with additional responsibilities, beyond what is normally expected. On the other hand, it would be significant if patients reported difficulties keeping up with daily details that have not changed throughout their work experience. If the patient works with several other employees as a team, it may be helpful to learn how the project duties are divided among the members of the team. For instance, one bright woman began to realize as she was explaining her work responsibilities how inefficient she was working alone, especially if long-term persistence were required. By contrast, she noted that projects were completed in less than half the time if she had a partner. She went on to explain that the partner did not take over her job; rather, she was able to use her coworker as someone to help her keep pace, concentrate, and stay on task.

Considering the extent of responsibilities also is a way to rule out ADHD. In another example, a man in his 40s, who reported numerous ADHD symptoms, gave reports of unrealistic expectations when he was asked to explain some of his troubles. It was later discovered that he had won several awards for his work and was considered by his employer as being one of the best and most efficient workers. Unfortunately, it was not good enough for this man, and he was looking for medication to enhance his abilities. Murphy (1994) wrote about such patients in his article, which discusses the dangers of the overdiagnosis of ADHD in adults. Sometimes patients' perceptions that they are not achieving are unrealistic and are related to personality or emotional problems rather than ADHD.

Similar in-depth analysis should be given with respect to home life. It may be important to look at all the stressors affecting the patient's life. This would include a family systems analysis, which should be part of any initial interview. Thus, information can be gathered regarding marital status, living arrangements in the family, traumatic experiences (i.e., recent death in the family), and physical and mental dispositions of family members. For concerns addressing possible ADHD, it may be helpful to learn who in the family is in charge of day-to-day tasks such as shopping, cleaning, and running errands. How the finances are managed is a major issue for most families, especially if funds are limited. Again, it is important to get examples of how budgets are kept and followed. It is not unusual for an ADHD patient to report that his or her spouse is responsible for balancing the checkbook and that tight reins have been placed on the patient with respect to spending. One 33-year-old man admitted that he had no idea how the family budget was maintained. He went on to explain that, in his first year of marriage, he was in charge of the finances, and it was disastrous. By the end of the second year, his wife took over and, after 7 years of marriage, he meekly reported, "We don't have any problems in this area, but don't ask me why."

In conclusion, the overall theme is to not be very concerned over the quantity of symptoms but to pay close attention to the breadth and depth of symptoms. Whenever possible, it is highly recommended that the patient is asked to provide examples of the problems, especially within different settings and circumstances. Patients who appear to be convinced that they have ADHD should not be discounted, but time should be taken to consider alternative explanations. Murphy (1994) presented five considerations to guard against the overdiagnosis of ADHD. First, it must be remembered that ADHD is a neurobiological disorder that cuts across different settings and circumstances in a patient's life. It is also chronic and pervasive, stemming back to childhood. Second, it is important to keep in mind the primary symptoms of inattention, impulsivity, and hyperactivity. Thus, patients who present mainly secondary symptoms such as moodiness and low self-esteem, although they are sometimes part of a published set of criteria, may not necessarily have ADHD. Third, it is important to be alert for patients who may be looking for what Murphy referred to as "performance enhancement"; these patients may have other psychological problems, perhaps dealing with self-esteem, but they may not have ADHD. Fourth, it may be wise to be aware of the patient's motivations. Some patients may wish to have an ADHD diagnosis for secondary gain. These patients may be unusually prepared during the interview to provide the right answers. Finally, it is important to pay attention to alternative diagnoses that may very well account for reported ADHD symptoms.

At the other end of the spectrum, where patients are unaware of ADHD, the core symptoms of ADHD should be kept in mind throughout all initial interviews, regardless of the psychological problems presented. ADHD could quickly be ruled out; this is especially so if the symptoms do not meet the chronicity criterion. However, long-term alcoholism, chronic depression, and a number of other problems could easily disguise an underlying problem with attention, and it is important to probe further.

Observations

There are some special observations to keep in mind when ADHD is considered, but they can easily be included in a typical mental status examination or diagnostic interview. On occasion, significant behaviors can be observed even before the formal interview. For instance, there have been patients who have called repeatedly to check and recheck their appointment times. There have been other patients who showed up late for their appointments with numerous apologies. They often state that they lost track of time. On several occasions, the secretary of the office has taken it upon herself to call and remind the patient of the appointment simply because the patient sounded "somewhat scattered" over the telephone when first contact was made. One patient arrived on time but was one day early.

Even the way patients present themselves as they search for their insurance card and fill out initial forms can provide valuable information. It is not unusual for patients to omit questions as they fill out forms and never remember to go back to complete what was omitted. It seems, more than any other problem, ADHD patients tend to forget to turn to the other side of the page when completing inventories. Obviously, none of these observations by themselves are enough to make a diagnosis, but they are certainly noteworthy.

During the interview itself, the organization of thought can be monitored through the patient's verbal communications. In their zeal to explain themselves, it is not unusual for some patients to jump from one topic to the next. By contrast, other patients may describe themselves as being totally disorganized, but their level of presentation and communication skills are quite superb. In fact, it is as if they have practiced their presentation. Therefore, it may be important to compare what is observed with the content of described problems. This is an important point and a theme that will thread through all of the diagnostic components. In essence, what is observed is somewhat of a validity check on what is being told during interview. An opportunity for additional validity checks will be offered when results from standardized tests are compared with interview notes; thus, conclusions should not be drawn prematurely. It may be prudent to simply make note of whether observations fit verbal reports .

For many patients, however, it must be kept in mind that attention difficulties subside during one-on-one interactions. A clinical interview may be able to provide enough structure to take care of tendencies to become disorganized and lose focus. This issue was presented quite eloquently by Sleator and Ullmann (1981) over a decade ago with respect to the child population. Although there are no data to substantiate the claim, it is probably more true for the adult population than for children and adolescents.

As suggested earlier, it is equally important to consider other observations related to intelligence, abstract thought processes, mood, memory, and general psychological functioning. The general procedure is to be open to the entire array of psychiatric disorders, and it may be best to first consider and rule out disorders of greatest impairment and global dysfunctions, such as psychosis and significant intellectual deficits, and then to move toward the less impaired disorders (i.e., adjustment disorder). For most patients, the more global and severe impairments can easily be ruled out. For instance, most patients present no signs of hallucinations or delusional thought processes, and it is obvious from the flow of conversation that mental retardation is not an issue. However, disorders of less impairment are usually more difficult to rule out, and it is best to allow additional data from other sources to provide more definitive insights. Moving from the most impaired categories to the least impaired categories can provide some assurance that important diagnostic issues are not overlooked. It is not unusual for patients who initially present minor adjustment difficulties to be later found to have a rather severe personality disorder; thus, it is prudent to guard against drawing diagnostic closure prematurely.

In conclusion, observations are helpful in providing the first validity check on the content presented, although they are not conclusive. They certainly are useful in ruling out severe impairments by following the typical outline of a mental status exam, and they can help formulate hypotheses to be addressed during the testing portion of the evaluation.

Collateral Interview

A collateral interview is recommended for two purposes. First, it can help fill in the information gaps left after an initial interview. Second, it can validate information already received.

If a collateral interview is conducted with someone who has known the patient through his or her growing years (i.e., a parent), questions should be asked regarding developmental processes. There appears to be no definitive study of association, but Goldstein (1993) suggested possible early childhood risk factors that could predict ADHD. From clinical experience, an interesting question to ask might be when the patient first started sleeping through the night as an infant. It has been somewhat remarkable to learn that some patients had much difficulty; one mother smiled and answered, "I don't ever remember him sleeping through the night, and he never took a nap." Perhaps a more subtle clinical finding, but equally as interesting, would be the reports of patients being extremely "good" babies. This description reflects the opposite extreme. These patients are often described as having been easy to handle, never crying, with reports like "you might even forget he was around." Again, there is no study to provide predictive power but, on the basis of clinical cases, a hypothesis worth pursuing is the association between behavioral extremes during infancy and later problems with hyperactivity and inattentiveness.

Developmental query can certainly provide some information regarding the presented symptoms. Given that chronicity is an important diagnostic criterion, interview findings may provide some information regarding onset of problems. It is important to keep in mind that the troubles presented in adulthood may be behaviorally different from those during childhood, but the essence of the problems should be consistent. Thus, the adult patient who impulsively runs up charges on a credit card may be represented by a childhood history of engaging in stimulating activities without first asking permission.

Making a decision regarding time of onset is not straightforward; not only are the behavioral changes to the underlying problems sensitive to age, but so are the circumstances. One mother reported, for instance, that her son did not have any problems until he entered fifth grade. No unusual circumstances in school were reported, but it was later learned that her child had received much special attention during the early grades, especially dealing with homework assignments and preparation for weekly tests. By the time he entered fifth grade, the mother was pregnant and having some medical problems. This is a case in which judgment must be sensitive to a number of possibilities. On the one hand, the child may have been sensitive to his mother's medical needs, and his poor performance in school, including the ADHD symptoms, may have been a reaction to her medical condition. Furthermore, the new baby significantly changed the atmosphere of the family, presenting a significant adjustment for the son after years of being the only child in the family.

On the other hand, the mother may have been extremely indulgent with her first and only child, and this might have helped compensate for real cognitive difficulties. The structured world of the child helped disguise problems in remembering assignments, following through with directions, and so on. One possible resolution to this dilemma is to look at the consistency of reported symptoms. For instance, from fifth grade on, was there a period of time in which no problems existed? Significant gaps of time in which there is a relief from symptoms may be an indication of alternative problems to ADHD. Again, this is not straightforward, because a good analysis of the "structure" of the patient's environment must be considered. In essence, the "behavioral" symptoms—as opposed to the underlying struggles in attention—may appear or disappear depending on environmental circumstances. Thus, it is important not to dismiss the possibility of ADHD simply because there was no evidence of behavioral symptoms during a particular period of time.

Perhaps the best example is that of a parent who came in with old report cards dating back to the kindergarten years. In kindergarten, and to some extent the first grade, the patient was described as being a pleasant child with some problems sustaining attention. Then, complaints of inattentiveness seemed to disappear, but they resurfaced again by the end of sixth grade; this time teachers were complaining of a "bad attitude" in addition to not following directions and not staying on task. A closer look at the years between first and sixth grade revealed numerous comments made regarding the child's efforts. After further questions, it was discovered that the patient had made a concerted effort to do well in school by spending extra time and being extra vigilant, only to experience somewhat of a burnout because of the stress and emotional drain. By the time the child completed the sixth grade, feelings of burnout were perceived by the teacher as a problem with attitude. The developmental history should include significant events in the patient's life, such as illnesses, previous interventions and evaluations, and important changes in the environment (e.g., death in the family, divorce, additions to the family, moves, changes in schools, etc.).

In a number of cases, the collateral interview cannot provide developmental history, but almost all collateral interviews can provide some insights into current functioning. If the collateral interview is conducted with someone who lives with the patient, it is extremely important to learn what it is like to live in the same household as the patient. There is at present no study that fully addresses how people who live with ADHD adults feel and manage their own lives. However, it has been well documented that ADHD children significantly affect the lives of those around them (Cunningham, Benness, & Siegel, 1988). Therefore, it is reasonable to assume that interactions may sometimes be strained and that adjustments need to be made among people who live with ADHD adults. Someday this issue may be studied fully, with an adult population, in a more controlled manner. For present purposes, it may be important to note that it can be quite enlightening to listen to the people who live with ADHD adult patients. Almost universally, they report major adjustments that need to be made in their own lives and frustrations that they have had to endure. The clinical conclusion is that it is extremely difficult to live with or interact in a consistent manner with an ADHD adult. In fact, it would be highly unusual and quite suspicious if no problems were reported.

Just as suggested in the discussion of patient interviews, it may be important to question how the daily chores and other routine responsibilities are divided among the members of the household. This portion of the interview can provide support for the patient's report and may add additional information regarding the quality of functioning. For example, a patient stated that he was in charge of managing the household funds, which included balancing the checkbook and paying the bills. Later, his wife reported that he indeed had this responsibility but that she reminded him when bills are due and actually attended to the mail when it came in, sorting bills and organizing them with respect to level of priority.

All collateral interviews are done independent of patient interviews. However, there may be some discrepancies with respect to reported symptoms, and it may be prudent to settle these discrepancies by later presenting them to both the patient and the collateral source together. This is usually done after the collateral interview is complete. The mechanics of doing this may be somewhat awkward and cumbersome, but it is often worth the effort. Sometimes this process is rather short, with only two or three points to address. If the patient is waiting just outside the office, a few minutes can be taken out at the end of the collateral interview time to have the patient join in the conversation. It is, of course, important not to be confrontive or challenging. The aim is to better understand the patient, and this motivation should be communicated. Simple statements such as "There's just a couple of areas I'm not quite sure about," or "Please help me clear some points up," may provide the appropriate atmosphere of open exchange.

It is sometimes the case that the patient has no idea how much of a problem exists among the members of the household. Thus, this revelation may be difficult to accept, especially in front of a stranger. It goes without saying that sensitivity and respect should be exercised throughout the entire diagnostic process, especially during potentially embarrassing moments. For instance, a patient was able to provide numerous symptoms of ADHD when discussing job-related duties and household projects that he considered "chores." He was unable to provide similar problems in other circumstances and settings that he considered leisure or relaxation time. Later, his wife made it a point to report that there is no such thing as relaxation time for her husband. She went on to explain that his restless and random behaviors put her and the children on edge even when there was nothing to do. This was an important issue, in consideration of the above criteria for making a diagnosis, and it was therefore discussed with both husband and wife present. It was embarrassing for the patient to learn of his wife's perception for the first time. In fact, she convinced him that her perception was more accurate by reminding him of the times when he had been asked to release some of his excess energy by running some errands outside and away from the household. This discussion was difficult for her as well as her husband, because she obviously loved her husband and did not want him to feel hurt. Extra time was taken to again assure them the purpose was to solve problems rather than exploit. In this case, both husband and wife came from a caring position that made it easy to deal with this sensitive topic.

As a final note, there are some practical issues to consider. As discussed earlier, a collateral interview may not be possible in all cases. Valid diagnoses can be made without such interviews, but it is highly recommended that some effort be made to explore resources. For instance, a young lady sharing an apartment with her schoolmate talked about the problems she was having keeping the place clean. An attempt was made to at least have a short interview with her roommate (with the patient's permission). For patients living miles away from their childhood home, it may help to have a telephone interview with a parent or significant other. These are not ideal conditions, but they can help in solving the diagnostic puzzle.

Use of Standardized ADHD Inventories

At this stage in the diagnostic process there should be some impressions made regarding the patient's possible diagnoses. If the patient does not meet some of the basic ADHD criteria, the clinician may opt to move in an entirely different direction, away from standardized inventories that address ADHD symptoms. If an ADHD diagnosis is still a possibility, it may be prudent to keep in mind the alternatives and possible comorbid conditions.

Choosing the correct instruments to attend to problems in attention can be somewhat difficult and confusing. As mentioned earlier, there are a number of popular publications that have introduced their own set of "checklist" items (e.g., Hallowell & Ratey, 1994; Murphy & LeVert, 1995; Weiss, 1992). These item checklists and questionnaires can be useful, but it is important to understand that they are not standardized, and they should never be used in place of standardized measures. Some of these nonstandardized checklists have their own particular cutoff points, but it is extremely important to understand that they are arbitrary and based on the personal judgment of the author(s) rather than any statistical analyses. Thus, they may serve a purpose in the clinical realm of the evaluation, but they should not be used as a standardized measure.

The above point cannot be emphasized enough, because some of the new checklists and questionnaires can sometimes appear to be statistically developed with normative parameters, although they are not. For instance, Owens and Owens (1993) introduced their Adult Attention Deficit Disorder Behavior Rating Scales and manual for scoring and evaluation. Their scoring sheet is complete with ranges of scores from "normal" to "at risk" to "very high risk," which suggests that some measures of the normal population were taken. However, this was not the case; in fact, it was reported in the manual that "the format for the adult scale is the same as the child scale and measures the same behavior. The same profile sheet is used for both scales" (p. 14). Looking back at the parameters chosen for the child scales, it was literally stated that the aim''was to find the most common behaviors of a child suffering ADD, so, it was not normed for the general population.'' Thus, it seems the main purpose for the development of these scales was originally to look at what particular problems within the ADHD population are most prominent. The same reasoning was used for the adult population, and the authors assumed that the same behaviors would be troublesome among adults. Thus, not only is this not a standardized instrument, but its design and purpose were not intended to help make diagnostic decisions.

Gilliam's (1995) Attention-Deficit/Hyperactivity Disorder Test was one of the first standardized instruments designed to address ADHD problems in adults. However, the same items that are used for children as young as 3 years old are given to adolescents and adults. More important, this test is standardized only up to the age of 23.

On the basis of the criterion of having a standardized instrument, designed to be sensitive to the entire age range of adults, and specifically developed to help make diagnostic decisions, only three instruments are available. These are the Adult Attention Deficit Evaluation Scale (A-ADDES; McCarney & Anderson, 1996), the Brown Attention-Deficit Disorder Scales (Brown, 1996), and the Attention Deficit Scales for Adults (ADSA; Triolo & Murphy, 1996). A computerized version of the ADSA is now available (Triolo & Murphy, 1997). It is not necessary to administer all three of these instruments; one standardized tool that can adequately measure ADHD-related symptoms may be sufficient.

The A-ADDES was constructed according to *DSM–IV* criteria. They were nationally normed on adults ages 18 and older, and diagnostic validation was achieved by a significant statistical ($p < .001$) comparison with 97 ADHD adults. The 97 ADHD adults were previously diagnosed by psychiatrists or psychologists on the basis of interview behavior rating and *DSM–IV* criteria.

Three versions of the scale are available. The first is a self-report version, which includes 58 items and is administered to the patient. The second is a home version, which includes 46 items and can be completed by the patient's spouse, roommate, or friend. The third is a work version, which includes 54 items and is designed to be completed by a coworker or a supervisor. Thus, standardized ratings are provided with respect to different settings and different perspectives. In addition to the self-report, independent information can be accumulated with respect to domestic behaviors (home version) and job-related responsibilities (work version). Also, the standardization sample is large (self-report: 2,211, home version: 2,008, work version: 1,868) and includes adults from 46 states.

The breadth of information across different settings and the large sample size seem to be the strengths of the A-ADDES. As indicated earlier, it is important to detect difficulties across various settings, and this is one of the positive changes of the *DSM–IV* criteria. Also, independent standardized measures can allow for objective validation checks. Ideally, all three versions of this scale should yield equal findings. Differences in perceptions between versions may help raise important diagnostic questions.

McCarney and Anderson (1996) identified their use of a frequency reference quantifier in their scale as an advantage. They stated that, compared to nonfrequency quantifiers in other scales (Gilliam, 1995; Triolo & Murphy, 1996), their scores yield greater reliability and circumvent the risk of the subjectivity of imprecise quantifiers used to measure frequency of impairments or degree of severity. However, they presented no statistical analyses to demonstrate greater accuracy and reliability. They reported that a field test found that their frequency-based quantifier system was adequate in assuring accuracy and objectivity. However, again, statistical analyses such as correlations between scale scores and field test findings were not presented to demonstrate accuracy objectively.

There are two major problems with the A-ADDES. First, the *DSM–IV* criteria were used to construct the scale. McCarney and Anderson (1996) considered the close association between scale items and the *DSM–IV* criteria a strength. However, as suggested earlier, there are some major flaws regarding the *DSM–IV* criteria. As a review, these include criteria based on field studies of children rather than adults. Consequently, items from the A-ADDES such as "I move about while seated (e.g., fidget, squirm, etc.)," "I move about unnecessarily (e.g., I have difficulty sitting still, I leave my seat, I walk around, etc.)," and "I make excessive noise (e.g., interrupt, hum, talk excessively)" may be more appropriate for children than adults. The development of items based on *DSM–IV* criteria, in the long term, may be a major error. Research regarding ADHD in the adult population is far from comprehensive. It is hoped that the significant flaws identified in the *DSM–IV* criteria will be addressed in later editions. Therefore, the A-ADDES may be at risk of being left behind with the *DSM–IV* as not being current and appropriately sensitive to ADHD adults.

Second, as provided in the *DSM–IV*, scores in two subcategories (Inattentive and Hyperactive–Impulsive) are generated by A-ADDES. Each item fits under one or the other subcategory, and there are no items that pertain to neither subcategory. Also, the respondent can clearly identify two sets of items on the questionnaire. Consequently, practical clinical situations such as malingering may be difficult to identify. The well-read patient who has a conviction that ADHD is the correct diagnosis, for instance, can very easily inflate the scores on the A-ADDES. However, this second problem is not as severe, because the clinician can provide validity checks by comparing scores on the self-report version with scores on the home and work versions.

Brown's (1996) Attention-Deficit Disorder Scales were designed to measure inattentiveness rather than hyperactivity. They were originally constructed for older children and adolescents. Brown and Gammon (1992) subsequently administered this instrument to 42 adults ranging in age from 18 to 72 years old. The subjects were referred to Brown's private outpatient practice because of suspicions of ADD. All of these subjects met *DSM–III* criteria for ADD without hyperactivity. Scores were then compared with those of a sample of 50 adults (nonclinical group) who also had been administered the Brown scales. A significant difference between the clinical and nonclinical comparison groups was found. This led to a subsequent publication of the scale with the use of 142 subjects in the clinical population, compared to 143 nonclinical subjects. A significant difference was also found between these two groups when the average scores were compared.

Brown's Attention Deficit Scales for Adults, although originally designed to tap into attention problems without hyperactivity, provide information on five subscales. The first, Activating and Organizing to Work, focuses on symptoms such as procrastination, difficulty getting started, difficulty setting priorities, and other day-to-day problems that limit the efficiency of getting responsibilities completed. The second subscale, Sustaining Attention and Concentration, focuses on problems related to excessive daydreaming, being distracted, and difficulties with listening. The third subscale, Sustained Energy and Effort, focuses on symptoms related to feeling sleepy during the day, inability to finish tasks, and a general sluggishness in processing information. The fourth subscale, Managing Affective Inferences, addresses possible depressed moods, sensitivity, and irritability. The last subscale, Working Memory and Accessing Recall, addresses memory skills and possible associated difficulties in memorizing information and misplacing items.

Brown's Attention Deficit Scales for Adults have an advantage in that they provide some insight into cognitive functioning. Specifically, a subgroup of 29 of the original clinical subjects were given the Wechsler Adult Intelligence Scale–Revised (WAIS-R; Wechsler, 1981) and the Bannatyne Conceptual Categories (Kaufman, 1990) were scored. The three factor scores were compared and, as expected, the score for the Sequential category was significantly lower than those for both the Conceptual and the Spatial categories. It is important to note, however, that the sequential scores were still within the average range. Also, IQ scores in Brown's sample were unusually high. For instance, of the 142 clinical subjects, 52 had an IQ within the average range, and 90 had an IQ of 110 or greater. This may present a problem regarding generalizability. Another problem with the generalizability of this instrument is that the scale focuses on problems in attention without hyperactivity. In his manual, Brown (1996) suggested that inattention, not hyperactivity and impulsivity, is theoretically considered the primary deficiency. Thus, the scales, by design, are not sensitive to behavioral difficulties of hyperactivity and impulsivity. By contrast, the scales are sensitive to a broad range of cognitive difficulties that are not explicitly included in the *DSM–IV* diagnostic criteria. Unlike the A-ADDES, this break away from the *DSM–IV* may afford greater sensitivity to the adult ADHD population.

The ADSA (Triolo & Murphy, 1996) was specifically designed to address ADHD problems within the adult population. Items were developed by first interviewing adults with attention-related complaints. The goal was to understand the kinds of struggles they face day by day in their adult world. Also, items were developed to reflect how some of the very common problems found in children with ADHD might manifest themselves in adulthood. For instance, a child who constantly forgets homework assignments from school may develop into an adult who tends to forget important paperwork from the office. Rather than first focusing on the clinical population, as represented by the Brown scales, Triolo and Murphy tried to first develop normative levels of cognitive functioning and behaviors among adults. The theoretical position taken was that it is important to first understand what are the average functioning levels related to

ADHD symptomotology. Consequently, the ADSA was first administered to a norm group of 306 adults. Criteria necessary to enter into a normative group were as follows: (a) 17 years old or older, (b) no childhood history of problems with attention or hyperactivity, (c) an IQ of 80 or above as estimated by the Shipley Institute of Living Scale (Shipley, 1940), (d) no reported history of drug or alcohol abuse, and (e) no reported history of a felony conviction. The IQ criterion was implemented to capture the cognitive and behavioral styles of the "average" population. It must be kept in mind that ADHD symptoms can also be found among individuals with borderline or impaired intellectual functioning, and this criterion was included to avoid confounding effects.

The fourth and fifth criteria listed were included to reduce the risk of including undiagnosed ADHD adults in the norm population. It has been over a decade now since it was hypothesized that many ADHD adults turn to alcohol or other drugs to self-medicate (Carroll & Rounsaville, 1993; DeMilio, 1989; Shemic, Asarnow, Hess, Zaucha, & Wheeler, 1990; Wood, Wendor, & Reimherr, 1983). It was decided not to include subjects in the norm group with backgrounds of substance abuse, to eliminate the risk of including individuals who have ADHD but have not been detected. The same reasoning was exercised for the last criterion, because a number of reasearchers have suspected undetected ADHD dispositions among convicted felons (Amando & Lustman, 1982; Eyestone & Howell, 1994).

By contrast, subjects were not eliminated from the normative group if they reported allergies (26.1%), a history of learning problems in school (10.5%), a history of anxiety or other emotional difficulties (6.2%), family members with drug or alcohol problems (34%), and major mental disorder in the immediate family (6.9%).

After normative statistics were gathered, 97 clinical subjects were administered the ADSA for validity purposes. These subjects came from two main sources: They were either referred to a private practionier or they were outpatients from the University of Massachusetts Medical Center ADHD Clinic. All of the clinical subjects were diagnosed as having ADHD prior to involvement with the validity study of the ADSA. All of the clinical subjects were 17 years or older, and the diagnostic criteria included the following: (a) fulfilling *DSM–III* or *DSM–III–R* criteria (depending on the date subjects presented for evaluation) according to a clinical interview that investigated presenting symptoms; (b) a review of each individual's history; (c) at least one collateral interview with a significant other; (d) consultation with a referring professional, usually a physician; and (e) support of clinical impressions by a battery of tests. These included a continuous-performance task, an intellectual assessment, and a personality inventory. The actual tests administered varied with respect to individual needs.

In addition to a total score, the ADSA provides an internal consistency check and scores on nine subscales. As is presented below, some of the subscales

Table 4.1 ADSA Subscales and Description

Subscale	Description
Attention-Focus/Concentration	Tendency to daydream, difficulty with persistence, lack of concentration, difficulty screening away distracting stimuli, etc.
Interpersonal	Short-lived intimate relationships, a lack of patience with people, lack of long-term friendship ties dating back to childhood, etc.
Behavior-Disorganized Activity	Restless activities, moving from one task to another without completion, needing constant encouragement from others to stay on task, agitation, risky management of daily responsibilities, engagement in dangerous and risky activities, etc.
Coordination	Accident prone, clumsy as a child, feeling clumsy and awkward, etc.
Academic Theme	Difficulty explaining ideas to others, underachievement.
Emotive	Feeling overwhelmed by responsibilities, a tendency to become agitated, easily excitable, feelings of boredom, feeling stressed by the demands and expectations of others, etc.
Consistency/Long-Term	Following directions in sequence, finishing home projects, persisting with long-term goals, follow through with ideas, etc.
Childhood	Described as being clumsy during childhood, underachievement in school.
Negative Social	Short-lived intimate relationships, lack of patience with people, not keeping in touch with friends and relations, etc.

Note: ADSA = Attention-Deficit Scales for Adults.

represent core symptoms of ADHD, whereas others represent secondary symptoms of ADHD. The items are not designated by subscale, and the respondent does not know which item goes with which subscale. Consequently, the profile from the entire set of subscales may be helpful in reducing errors in diagnosis. Chapter 5, on case studies, provides some discussion on profile interpretation. The subscales and their descriptions appear in Table 4.1. Differences between the norm and the clinical group were highly significant in all of the subtests and the total score (see Table 4.2).

Finding a significant difference between the two groups provides proper validation. In essence, the differences in scores with respect to the two groups are far greater than expected by random chance. However, the question remains from a more pragmatic diagnostic point of view of how useful this instrument

Table 4.2   Differences Between Groups With Respect to ADSA Total Score

Group	No. subjects	M	SD	SE
Norm	306	141.0359	19.495	1.114
Clinical	87	186.0230	24.952	2.675

Note: $t(117.45) = -15.52$, $p < .000$. ADSA = Attention = Deficit Scales for Adults.

can be in providing the clinician help in making proper diagnoses. Elwood (1993) stated that

> Statistical significance merely indicates the likelihood that observed difference is due to chance, given that the null hypothesis is true (i.e., that the means of the respective populations are essentially equivalent). However, significance alone does not reflect the magnitude of group differences nor does it imply that the tests can discriminate individual patients with sufficient accuracy for clinical use. (pp. 224–225)

In consideration of Elwood's (1993) argument, special effort was made to go beyond statistical significance and to investigate the utility of the ADSA instrument.

It was demonstrated earlier that finding a significant difference between a norm and clinical group with respect to brain activity does not necessarily mean that brain scans can now be used as diagnostic instruments. A measure of utility is required, in which the instrument itself is put to the test to see if it can blindly differentiate clinical from nonclinical subjects. In essence, now that a significant difference has been found between two known groups of subjects, can the process work backward by using the instrument to differentiate between clinical and nonclinical subjects? This is, of course, the dilemma that faces clinicians, especially in a general practice where a variety of problems can be expected to be presented.

This argument was made in terms of making clinical decisions with respect to neuropsychological tests; however, it can be generalized to all clinical testing (Baldessarini, Finklestein, & Arana, 1983; Rosnow & Rosenthal, 1989). One of the major concerns presented is the use of cutoff rates based on mean differences but without sensitivity to prevalence of the targeted disorder in the general population (Meehl & Rosen, 1955). This problem is further complicated if identifying symptoms of the disorder are common in the general population, as with ADHD, and the diagnosis is very much dependent on the strength of symptoms rather than their presence. Additional complications can easily be identified if the symptoms themselves, as found in ADHD, are variable within a population of patients—for that matter, within each individual ADHD patient—as well as between normal and clinical populations. Consequently, cutoff scores calculated

Table 4.3   Results of Discriminant Analysis

Actual Group	No. cases	Predicted norm	Predicted clinical
Norm	306	278 90.8%	28 9.2%
Clinical	89	16 18.0%	73 82.0%

Note: Percent of "grouped" cases correctly classified: 88.86%.

purely from measured statistical differences between groups may be inherently simplistic and, as Meehl (1960) suggested decades ago, more fluid cutoff parameters need to be considered, especially attending to clinical decisions.

With the above cautions in mind, a stepwise discriminant analysis was conducted on the ADSA subscales. The stepwise procedure included the Consistency/ Long-Term, Attention-Focus/Concentration, Behavior-Disorganized Activity, and Negative Social subscales (in that order) as the best subscales that can discriminate between ADHD patients and non-ADHD subjects.

Using these four subscales alone, the next step in the procedure was to see how well the total subject pool could be classified in either the ADHD or non-ADHD group. Thus, beyond the parameters of group differences, the procedure reflects the clinical dilemma of making diagnostic decisions, as would be expected in a general practice. In essence, it is working backward; instead of having two identified populations (ADHD or non-ADHD) and seeing if there are differences in scores, the scores themselves are used to see if they can help in making proper diagnostic decisions.

In this subject pool, 88.87% of the subjects were correctly classified. Table 4.3 presents the breakdown of percentages with respect to actual and predictive groups. Of the 306 subjects in the norm group, 278 (90.8%) were classified correctly, reflecting the specificity of the ADSA. The remaining 28 subjects (9.2%) from the norm group were erroneously classified as clinical cases; this is reflective of the ADSA's false-positive rate. Of the 89 clinical subjects, 73 (82%) were classified correctly, reflecting the sensitivity of the ADSA. The remaining 16 subjects (18%) from the clinical group were classified as being normal, and this would reflect the instrument's false-negative rate.

Again, even with statistical analyses supporting the utility of the ADSA, cautions must be considered with respect to the complexities involved in making an ADHD diagnosis. It is certainly recommended that clinicians not abandon all other data collected. Nevertheless, it is encouraging that a rather high classification rate was achieved with only four subtest scores, independent of added information from clinical interview, collateral sources, and other resources.

Beyond the statistical analysis, the ADSA may prove to be helpful in providing valuable information with respect to different behavioral styles within the

ADHD population. The Attention-Focus/Concentration and Behavior-Disorganized Activities subscales were specifically designed to help differentiate cognitive difficulties in attention from the more behavioral differences such as those found in hyperactivity and impulsivity. Using the *DSM–IV* nomenclature, a high score on Attention-Focus/Concentration may be reflective of ADHD, predominantly inattentive type (American Psychiatric Association, 1994, pp. 78–85). By contrast, a high score on the Behavior-Disorganized Activities subscale may reflect ADHD, predominantly hyperactive–impulsive type. Of course, a dual elevation of these two subtests may be suggestive of ADHD, combined type (American Psychiatric Association, 1994, pp. 78–85). Although these two subscales are reflective of the *DSM–IV* subcategories, it is important to remember that their original design preceded present-day nomenclature, and there are some important differences, independent of *DSM–IV* categories, that can help diagnosticians identify specific subtypes from a more operant perspective. For instance, one of the main dividing factors between the Attention-Focus/Concentration subscale and the Behavior-Disorganized Activities subscale is that the former contains items that address cognitive functioning, such as "I tend to daydream," and "While reading, my mind wanders." The latter subscale was constructed of items that are behaviorally oriented, such as "I get restless easily," and "I jump from one task to another." Another way of looking at the differences between these two subscales is to consider the former as a set of items that reflect internal factors that perhaps are not readily observed by others. For instance, a patient may be observed quietly reading but, in fact, is not concentrating on the reading material and may actually be struggling with internal distractions. On the other hand, the Behavior-Disorganized Activities subscale has items that are distinctly behavioral and can be observed by others. Thus, items such as "I jump from one task to another," and "I get restless easily" can be observed and behaviorally measured. This kind of differentiation does not exist between the inattentive and the hyperactivity–impulsivity subtypes of the *DSM–IV*.

It is equally important to remember that the ADSA items were constructed by asking ADHD adults about their problems, and many of the *DSM–IV* items—especially in the hyperactivity–impulsivity subcategory—are geared toward children. Consequently, items such as making excessive noises, which could be important for a grade school child, may not be relevant during the adult years.

Also, it is extremely interesting to note that the subscale that best discriminates between the norm and clinical groups, according to statistical analyses, is Consistency/Long-Term. This is a unique factor and component of the ADSA. Triolo and Murphy (1996) argued that

> Since adults have a much longer history to review than children, this subscale may possibly provide a special diagnostic perspective for the adult population . . . the statistical analyses suggest ADHD adults may have more subtle symptoms that may be missed by short clinical assessments or by their performance on relatively brief neurological tests. (p. 21)

Such sensitivity is not found within the *DSM–IV* criteria; however, it is hoped that future editions can be more sensitive to the adult population, and preliminary findings suggest that symptoms that address consistency issues and long-term functioning may eventually be central ADHD signatures for the adult population.

Analysis of Personality and Emotions

It is difficult to give specific recommendations in regard to tests for personality traits and emotional dispositions. Clinicians have their own level of comfort with different instruments, and there are certainly numerous tests from which to choose. Also, the choice of tests administered often depends on the circumstances of each individual case.

The single most important principle to keep in mind is that these tests are administered to provide an additional validity check on previously administered procedures. There are two aspects of this principle that should be considered. First, it may be important to address the general disposition of the patient with respect to reported symptoms. For instance, an extremely high F scale score on the Minnesota Multiphasic Personality Inventory, second edition (MMPI-2; Hathaway & McKinley, 1989), in contrast to an extremely low F score, would certainly make a difference in how reports of multiple symptoms and multiple elevations in other inventories would be interpreted. In essence, the validity configuration on a standardized measure such as the MMPI-2 can provide valuable information with respect to the interpretation of clinical scores. The second aspect reflects a more classical interpretation style of testing. Here reports of symptoms, especially those beyond core ADHD-related problems (depression, anxiety, etc.), can certainly be supported by projective findings.

There is no definitive rule with respect to the extent of projective testing necessary. However, interviews, especially the MSE (Mental Status Exam), should provide some insight into the kind and number of tests necessary. For patients who have presented a reasonably stable lifestyle with no major suspicions of severe underlying personality difficulties, one or two projective instruments may be sufficient. On the other hand, if personality problems are suspected, especially antisocial features, it may be worthwhile to administer a more extensive battery of tests. For example, a young lady presented numerous signs during an interview of very poor interpersonal adjustments, and there were suspicions that she had the capacity to dehumanize and manipulate others to her gain without any feelings of remorse. She was also seen as being relatively free from anxiety, although she professed otherwise. For this individual, it was decided that the Thematic Apperception Test (TAT; Murray, 1943) and the Rorschach inkblot test (Rorschach, 1921), using the Exner (1986) system, would be administered, in addition to the MMPI-2. Both the TAT and the Rorschach are usually not given as part of the battery for adults who claim that they have attention difficulties. However, in this case, the TAT was administered with particular attention given to the quality of interactions between characters of her story. The Rorschach was administered because this test is difficult to "fake," and it can provide some insights into the quality of human feelings, such as the capacity to attach to and have compassion for others. Findings from these tests were helpful in determining personality features. In this case, suspicions were well supported by test results, which suggested a personality free from anxiety, unlike the patient had claimed. Although she may have been capable of connecting with others socially, additional projective findings suggested that her relationships were rather superficial and self-serving. Most important, there were indications that she was a very controlled individual with minimal signs of impulsivity, although her history was reflective of someone who may have a tendency to act on impulse. It was eventually concluded that many of her ADHD symptoms were deliberate and that a diagnosis of ADHD would be erroneous.

In conclusion, projective testing is considered a necessary component of the diagnostic process, but the extent of testing, as well as the individual tests that are chosen, are dependent on each individual case. Further discussions of the use of projective testing are deferred to Chapter 5, in which case studies are presented and emphasis is placed on the integration of information and test findings.

Neuropsychological Testing

By this stage of the diagnostic process, there should be enough information already gathered to assure some level of certainty whether ADHD exists. If a clinician were left to make a diagnosis at this point of the evaluation, a fair amount of reliability in making a correct diagnosis can be expected. After all, the process, up to this point, is far more extensive than required by the *DSM–IV*, and it usurps criteria set by more recent publications (i.e., Nadeau, 1995; Wender, 1995). However, considering the trend toward cognition and special focus on brain functions with respect to ADHD (Benson, 1991; Fuster, 1989; Zametkin et.al., 1990), there seems to be an increased interest in neuropsychological tests and their potential contribution to the diagnosis of ADHD (Biggs, 1995; Palumbo et. al., 1995). This section first discusses some of the noted problems of using neuropsychological instruments; it then discusses some ways in which neuropsychological instruments can be used productively to further support diagnostic impressions.

Unfortunately, the preliminary reviews of using neuropsychological tests to help diagnose ADHD have not been very favorable. Barkley (1994) addressed the utility of using neuropsychological tests on children as a means of being able to discriminate between ADHD and non-ADHD individuals with a variety of neuropsychological instruments, and his discriminant statistics were described as being quite "sobering to any one believing that most neuropsychological tests are useful in helping in the clinical diagnosis of ADD/ADHD" (Barkley, 1994, p. 2). Of all the instruments evaluated, the continuous-performance task seemed to get the highest marks. Continuous-performance tests may be relatively new to the ADHD market, but the neuropsychological concept and the task itself date back more than 40 years (Rosvold, Mirsky, Sarason, Bransome, & Beck, 1956). The original purpose was to detect brain damage. Barkley (1994) used the Gordon Diagnostic System (GDS; Gordon, 1983) as a measure of continuous performance; although it was measured to be the best over other neuropsychological instruments, this test has been criticized with respect to its utility in making proper diagnoses (DuPaul, Anastopoulus, Shelton, Guevremont, & Metevia, 1992). The controversy involves the high number of false negatives (the number of ADHD individuals who score within the normal range).

In spite of the problems that plague neuropsychological tests, there seems to be a trend toward marketing at least the continuous-performance tasks for the diagnosis of ADHD. To some extent, this trend may be fueled by the computer industry, as there seem to be a number of continuous-performance tasks on the market today that use computer hardware. For instance, Sandford and Turner (1994) marketed a computerized visual and auditory continuous-performance task through a company called BrainTrain. The American Guidance Service, Inc., has recently publicized their computer program Test of Variables of Attention (TOVA; Greenberg & Dupuy, 1993; Greenberg & Waldman, 1993). This test is advertised as a comprehensive measurement for ADD/ADHD for ages 4–80.

Some other old instruments are now recycled with computer program additives. For instance, Duffy (1982) introduced his Brain Electric Activity Mapping (BEAM) technology and suggested that this is a clinical diagnostic tool that can eventually identify problems in ADHD and learning disabilities. An EEG output is entered into a computer program that transfers cerebral electroactivity into multicolor images; it was initially reported that ADHD subjects presented asymmetrical activity with respect to cerebral hemispheres. Again, to the best of my knowledge, there have been no studies to support the utility of such exotic instruments in making an ADHD diagnosis.

Neuropsychological tests are expensive, especially if the new computer programs are implemented, and they do not seem to provide much in terms of discriminant power (Barkley, 1994; Barkley & Grodzinsky, 1994). Nevertheless, it seems that the computer industry may have spawned the production of newer and perhaps more exotic tests of attention. If the clinician insists on using them, it is recommended that test results be interpreted with much caution.

Perhaps a better understanding of the problems that plague these tests can be found by re-examining the nature of ADHD. It is important to keep in mind that the problems that ADHD patients have are embedded in their interaction with the environment, whether at work or at home with the rest of the family. Although the problems stem from neurofunctioning, they manifest themselves with respect to the fluidity of everyday life. Consequently, it is difficult to capture this in a sterile laboratory-like task. One ADHD patient explained this issue quite simply after completing a continuous-performance task almost flawlessly.

She stated, "I actually like things like this (GDS-Distractibility Task) because I know what I am supposed to do and I am free not to concern myself with anything else; but with kids and stuff, life's not that easy."

Another problem with neuropsychological tests is that they were originally designed for the purpose of detecting brain dysfunctions. For instance, the Auditory Selective Attention Test, by Goldman, Fristoe, and Woodcock (1974), was originally designed for speech and language pathologists to detect auditory language discrimination problems. The patient is asked to point to pictures of items heard on a tape. Background noise is eventually introduced as a form of distraction, and this background noise increases in volume throughout the task. Three separate scores are derived from three different types of background noise experiences. They are fan noise, cafeteria noise, and a voice narrative. On the surface, this test seems appropriate, especially if the patient complains of auditory distractors. However, patients without any problems in auditory language discrimination usually do very well, often performing without any errors. In this test, there is little margin for error, and two or three mistakes are enough to score within the abnormal range. Such a restricted range of scores is not a problem when dealing with patients who have brain injury that has resulted in auditory discrimination difficulties, but this same restricted range cannot be applied with respect to attention difficulties because of greater variability in functioning within the ADHD population. These same kinds of problems can be expected in other neuropsychological tests in which the deficits they are designed to identify are more defined and performance scores are usually found within a limited range.

It also is important to consider that neuropsychological instruments typically are standardized without screening out subjects with ADHD from the normalization group. Consequently, contamination can be a reasonable expectation. Even tests that are factor loaded for attention, concentration, and focus have this problem. For instance, the Wisconsin Card Sorting Test (Heaton, 1981) and the Stroop Color and Word Test (Golden, 1978) are often used as instruments of attention, but the normative groups were not screened for ADHD.

One can argue that the continuous-performance task should yield a wider range of scores, considering the distribution of attention-related performances in the normal population. However, this is not the case. The GDS, for instance, is plagued with a very high ceiling (a large percentage of the normative population that performs without any or very few errors), even more so than the child population. Of course, this increases the likelihood of false negatives, because the task is relatively easy to accomplish, and many ADHD adults can compensate for their attending problems during this brief period. Continuous-performance tasks do have an advantage over other neurological instruments because ADHD subjects have been screened away from the standardization groups.

In spite of all these problems, there are some possible advantages to including neuropsychological tests as part of the diagnostic process. First, the number of false positives on at least the continuous-performance tasks such as the GDS have been demonstrated to be very low. This means that a poor score is most likely reflective of real attention difficulties. If such an outcome is noted, it is a good way to arrive at a diagnosis with relative assurance.

Second, these tasks are relatively sterile. Thus, they sometimes can be helpful to differentiate attention problems that are due to real cerebral difficulties from attention problems mainly related to emotional difficulties. If time is spent to develop proper rapport to diffuse apprehensions and the patient still performs poorly, it may support the hypothesis that attention problems exist independent from emotional issues.

Third, and perhaps most important, test results that indicate attention problems can help provide concrete evidence to patients and the significant others around them that the problems are real, as opposed to some kind of perceived abstract finding. This last issue may be important enough to make a real difference with respect to treatment prognosis. Western society seems very much entrenched in the mechanical world. Even highly educated individuals need such concrete evidence to be convinced. This point cannot be emphasized enough. In fact, one can argue that the entire field of psychology did not make its mark until it started to introduce its "hardware." Before then, it was well embedded in its parent field of philosophy, and it received very little credit for practical use. Thus, results that come from concrete tasks such as interacting with a machine may carry extra weight with respect to acceptance of the diagnosis.

Although criticisms of the GDS are valid, it is worth considering this instrument as part of a comprehensive diagnostic battery. Certainly, Barkley's (1994) findings suggest that it has some potential value, at least greater than other neuropsychological instruments.

It is important to know that the GDS is one of a number of continuous-performance tasks that were initially developed for children, but claims have been recently made that they can be useful for adults. The continuous-performance tasks on the market today are often designed to use computer hardware. There are different forms of this test, but they all seem to claim to tap into the same cognitive functions. The subject is usually asked to pay attention to numbers or letters appearing on a screen, and some specific instructions are given to react (usually by pressing a button or the space bar on the computer keyboard) when a combination of numbers or another predirected stimulus appears. Thus, the patient is told beforehand what response to make under what conditions and, of course, the other stimuli conditions to which he or she should refrain from responding. Depending on the computerized system, the scores measure the number of hits (number of times the patient responded correctly to a response-required stimulus), the number of misses (the number of times the patient did not respond when the response-required stimulus appeared), and the number of commissions (the number of times the patient responded to a no-response stimulus). The number of hits usually reflects some measure of attention or vigilance; the number of commissions usually reflects a tendency to be impulsive. With different computerized systems, a number of other measures can be calculated. For instance, the time between stimulus and response, the variability of response times, and the variabilities of different scores with respect to response frequencies can be calculated for added information.

Also, the pattern of responses over the time period given for this task is considered. For instance, a patient may begin the task doing very well, but there may be deterioration over the course of the test; or the exact opposite pattern can happen, where the patient has difficulty settling down and focusing but eventually adapts and improves over time.

In an attempt to minimize liabilities and maximize potential advantages, I decided to develop new normative data with respect to the adult population for the GDS-Distractibility task (Triolo, 1994). The process in its development included the following: first, I chose a continuous-performance task, because it seemed to be the most promising single test as suggested in studies presented above; second, the distractibility task from the GDS seemed most appropriate because of its relatively high level of difficulty; third, this distractibility task was reprogrammed 3 min longer than the previous standard (12 min instead of 9 min). The reasoning for this change was to help correct the problem of a high ceiling. I hypothesized that the increased duration of the task would naturally increase the number of errors. The actual task, along with the original directions for administration and scoring, remains the same, however.

In the GDS-Distractibility task, the patient is asked to pay attention to a screen that flashes digits and to press a button whenever a 1, followed by a 9, appears. Meanwhile, on adjacent screens to the right and left of the target screen, digits are flashing to distract the patient. He or she is asked to not pay attention to the adjacent screens and to respond only to the digits flashing in the middle. With the extra time necessary to complete this task, the machine is programmed to display 1–9 combinations in the center screen 60 times.

A subset of 173 subjects out of 306 (norm group) used to develop the standardization for the ADSA scales was administered this reprogrammed distractibility task. The mean for this normative sample was 52.422, with a standard deviation of 10.592. Thus, in spite of the fact that the new program increased the probability of errors, a perfect score on this reprogrammed task was still within 1 SD; the problem with a high ceiling was obviously not eliminated. The number of commissions (the number of times the button is pressed when it should not have been pressed) for this sample group was 3.57, with a standard deviation of 7.68; again, a perfect score with no errors was still within the first standard deviation. In spite of a continued ceiling problem, a significant difference was found ($p = .012$) in the number of correct responses when this subset of 173 subjects was compared with the first 18 clinical subjects who were administered the reprogrammed distractibility task (see Table 4.4). The same analysis was done for the number of commissions, and no significant difference was found ($p = .478$) (Triolo, 1994).

Since the development of these new norms the TOVA has been advertised as providing fewer ceiling effect problems because the continous-performance

Table 4.4 Differences Between Groups with Respect to the Number of Correct Responses on the GDS Distractability Task

Group	N	M	SD	SE
Norm	173	52.4220	10.592	0.805
Clinical	18	45.6111	13.360	3.149

Note: $t(189) = 2.53$, $p < .012$.

task has a longer time limit. In this practice, the reprogrammed GDS distractibility task has been used to help make clinical diagnoses, but with very strict guidelines. The most important and perhaps strictest rule is that scores within the average range are never, by themselves, reason to rule out ADHD. On the other hand, scores within the abnormal range are considered very seriously as significant evidence of ADHD, especially if the patient presents no intellectual difficulties. Furthermore, abnormal scores have been very instrumental in teasing out comorbid conditions. For instance, in patients who show signs of depression as well as ADHD, it is sometimes difficult to know if many of the ADHD symptoms are due to the mood disorder. Patients who are depressed are also quite likely to become inattentive, lose their capacity to concentrate appropriately on tasks, and not be very organized with day-to-day responsibilities. Thus, it can be hypothesized that the mood disorder has been responsible for ADHD symptoms. However, an abnormal score on this reprogrammed distractibility task, unless the patient is acutely despondent and distressed during testing, could provide support for an ADHD diagnosis. It does not rule out a possible comorbid condition of depression, but it can help a clinician not overlook one dysfunction in the presence of another.

Finally, in reporting test results to ADHD patients, abnormal scores from this distractibility task have been very convincing to both patients and their significant others that the problem with attention is real. In fact, the report of these scores may sometimes be the motivating factor to make changes and address treatment seriously.

CONCLUSIONS

The diagnostic process presented in this chapter is far more extensive than the *DSM–IV* criteria. At first, the procedures presented may seem awkward and cumbersome, but they are not significantly different from many of the considerations necessary for other psychiatric disorders. For instance, good clinical practice involves close observations, and the notion of matching observed behaviors with test findings is not foreign to the study of other disorders.

Also, the diagnostician is presented with a number of options available with respect to testing instruments. This is most noteworthy in the analysis of the patient's psychological and emotional dispositions. In fact, in this area it is advised that the diagnostician rely on the testing instruments that are most familiar and provide the best comfort in making appropriate judgments.

This principle can be applied to the use of standardized measures of ADHD. However, only three standardized instruments have been identified, and it is recommended that the diagnostician not consider popular checklists, which may present endorsement of ADHD symptoms without the stable normative parameters necessary for proper diagnostic judgments. The diagnostician is free to choose from the three standardized instruments reviewed. Again, the diagnostician can apply personal preferences and judgments.

Perhaps the most confusing and overwhelming portion of the diagnostic process includes the use of neuropsychological testing. As explained earlier, the computer industry has opened the marketplace for numerous additional instruments. Fortunately, at this juncture of the diagnostic process, a fairly reliable diagnosis is expected. Of all the neuropsychological instruments available, only continuous-performance tests have been identified as having some diagnostic utility. However, extreme caution is advised, because none of these tests—including continuous performance tests—were originally designed to specifically address ADHD. One of the major flaws of neuropsychological testing stems from the fact that it is administered in a fairly sterile environment; ADHD may be neurologically based, but the problems are best identified in the nonsterile conditions of everyday life. In spite of this quite significant flaw, the computer industry will most likely continue to generate much research on new and different measures of "laboratory" ADHD (e.g., reaction time, reaction time ratios, detail selection tests, etc.). It is recommended, especially for the practitioner in private practice, that very practical and common-sense judgments be exercised.

It is reasonable to assume that the different steps of the diagnostic process are interrelated. Although there most likely exists some shared variance, the different components are seen as being somewhat orthogonal or independent from each other. For instance, information from clinical interviews should be independent from information gathered during the collateral interview phase. Consequently, it is hoped that each step along the diagnostic process reveals a new and reasonably different piece of the ADHD puzzle. Perhaps a stepwise statistical procedure, like that found in the analysis of the ADSA subscales (Triolo & Murphy, 1996), can offer some empirical support with respect to diagnostic utility. The objective is to discover which component—or combination of components—of the process best explains between-group (ADHD and non-ADHD) variance. Meanwhile, it is hoped that the above diagnostic process provides adequate and practical guidance.

REFERENCES

Amando, H., & Lustman, P. (1982). Attention deficit disorder persisting in adulthood: A review. *Comprehensive Psychiatry, 23,* 300–314.

American Psychiatric Association. (1980). *Diagnostic and statistical manual of mental disorders* (3rd ed.). Washington, DC: Author.

American Psychiatric Association. (1987). *Diagnostic and statistical manual of mental disorders* (3rd ed., rev.). Washington, DC: Author.

American Psychiatric Association. (1994). *Diagnostic and statistical manual of mental disorders* (4th ed.). Washington, DC: Author.

Baldessarini, R. J., Finklestein, S., & Arana, G. W. (1983). The predictive power of diagnostic testing and the effect of prevalence of illness. *Archives of General Psychiatry, 40,* 569–573.

Barkley, R. A. (1994). Can neuropsychological tests help diagnose ADD/ADHD? *The ADHD Report, 2*(1), 1–3.

Barkley, R. A., & Grodzinsky, G. M. (1994). Are tests of frontal lobe functions useful in the diagnosis of attention deficit disorders? *The Clinical Neuropsychologist, 8,* 121–139.

Benson, D. F. (1991). The role of frontal dysfunction in attention deficit hyperactivity disorder. *Journal of Clinical Neurology, 6,* 9–12.

Bhatara, V. S., Kumer, M., McMillin, J. M., & Bandettini, F. (1994). Screening for thyroid disease in ADHD. *The ADHD Report, 2*(4), 7–9.

Biggs, S. H. (1995). Neuropsychological and psychoeducational testing in the evaluation of the ADD adult. In K. G. Nadeau (Ed.), *A comprehensive guide to attention deficit disorder in adults: Research, diagnosis, and treatment* (pp. 109–131). New York: Brunner/Mazel.

Brown, T. E. (1996). *Brown Attention-Deficit Disorder Scales.* San Antonio, TX: The Psychological Corporation.

Brown, T. E., & Gammon, G. D. (1992). *Attention deficit disorder without hyperactivity in adults: Instruments for assessment.* Paper presented at the annual convention of the American Psychiatric Association, Washington, DC.

Carroll, K. M., & Rounsaville, B. J. (1993). History and significance of childhood attention deficit disorder treatment seeking cocaine abuser. *Comprehensive Psychiatry, 34,* 75–82.

Castellanos, F. X., Giedd, J. N., Eckburg, P., Marsh, W. L., Vaituzis, A. C., Kaysen, D., Hamburger, S. D., & Rapoport, J. L. (1994). Quantitative morphology of the caudate nucleus in attention deficit hyperactivity disorder. *American Journal of Psychiatry, 151,* 1791–1796.

Ciaranello, R. D. (1993). Attention deficit hyperactivity disorder in resistence to thyroid hormone—A new idea. *New England Journal of Medicine, 328,* 1038–1039.

Cunningham, C. E., Benness, B. B., & Siegel, L. S. (1988). Family functioning, time allocation and parental depression in families of normal and ADHD children. *Journal of Clinical Child Psychology, 17,* 169–177.

DeMilio, L. (1989). Psychiatric syndromes of adolescent substance abusers. *American Journal of Psychiatry, 146,* 1212–1224.

Duffy, F. H. (1982). Topographic display of evoked potentials: Clinical applications of brain electrical activity mapping (BEAM). *Annals of the New York Academy of Sciences: 388,* 183–193.

DuPaul, G. J., Anastopoulus, A. D., Shelton, T. L., Guevremont, D. C., & Metevia, L. (1992). Multimethod assessment of attention deficit hyperactivity disorder: The diagnostic utility of clinic based tests. *Journal of Clinical Child Psychology, 21,* 394–402.

Elwood, R. W. (1991). The Wechsler Memory Scale—Revised: Psychometric characteristics in clinical application. *Neuropsychology Review, 2,* 179–201.

Elwood, R. W. (1993). Clinical discriminations and neuropsychological tests: An appeal to Bayes' theorem. *The Clinical Neuropsychologist, 7,* 224–233.

Exner, J. E., Jr. (1986). *The Rorschach: A comprehensive system. Vol. 1: Basic Foundations* (2nd ed.,) New York: Wiley.

Eyestone, L. L., & Howell, R. J. (1994). The epidemiological study of attention deficit hyperactivity disorder and major depression in a male prison population. *Bulletin of the American Academy of Psychiatry Law, 22,* 181–183.

Fuster, J. M. (1989). *The prefrontal cortex: Anatomy, physiology, and neuropsychology of the frontal lobe* (2nd ed.). New York: Raven Press.

Gilliam, J. E. (1995). *Attention Deficit/Hyperactivity Disorder Test.* Austin, TX: Pro-Ed.

Golden, C. J. (1978). *Stroop Color and Word Test: A manual for clinical experimental users.* Chicago: Stoelting.

Goldman, R., Fristoe, M., & Woodcock, R. W. (1974). *G-F-W Auditory Selective Attention Test.* Circle Pines, MN: American Guidance Service.

Goldstein, S. (1993). Young children at risk: Recognizing the early signs of ADHD. *The ADHD Report, 1*(4), 7–8.

Gordon, M. (1983). *The Gordon Diagnostic System.* DeWitt, NY: Gordon Systems.

Greenberg, L. M., & Dupuy, T. R. (1993). *TOVA interpretation manual: Test of variable of attention continuous performance tests.* Los Alamitos, CA: Universal Attention Disorders.

Greenberg, L. M., & Waldman, I. D. (1993). Developmental normative data on the Test of Variables of Attention (TOVA). *Journal of Child Psychology and Psychiatry, 34,* 1019–1030.

Hallowell, E. M., & Ratey, J. J. (1994). *Driven to distractions.* New York: Pantheon Books.

Hartsough, C. S., & Lambert, M. N. (1985). Medical factors in hyperactive and normal children: Prenatal, developmental, and health history findings. *American Journal of Orthopsychiatry, 55,* 190–210.

Hathaway, S. R., & McKinley, J. C. (1989). *Minnesota Multiphasic Personality Inventory–2 (MMPI-2).* Minneapolis: University of Minnesota Press.

Hauser, P., Zametkin, A. J., Martinez, P., Vitiello, B., Matochik, J. A., Mixson, A. J., & Weintraub, B. D. (1993). Attention deficit-hyperactivity disorder in people with generalized resistence to thyroid hormone. *New England Journal of Medicine, 328,* 997–1001.

Heaton, R. K. (1981). *A manual for the Wisconsin Card Sorting Test.* Odessa, FL: Psychological Assessment Resources.

Herman, J. H., Roffwarge, H. P., & Becker, P. M. (1989). The evaluation of daytime vigilance: A new function of sleep disorders centers. *Journal of Sleep Research, 18,* 120.

Kaufman, A. S. (1990). *Assessing adolescent and adult intelligence.* Boston: Allyn & Bacon.

Lavenstein, B. (1995). Neurological comorbidity patterns/differential diagnosis in adult attention deficit disorder. In K. G. Nadeau & P. D. Anderson (Eds.), *A comprehensive guide to attention deficit disorder in adults: Research, diagnosis, and treatment* (pp. 74–92). New York: Brunner/Mazel.

McCarney, S. B., & Anderson, P. D. (1996). *Adult Attention Deficit Disorder Evaluation Scale (A-ADDES).* Columbia, MO: Hawthorne Educational Services.

Meehl, P. E. (1960). The cognitive activity of the clinician. *American Psychologist, 15,* 19–27.

Meehl, P. E., & Rosen, A. (1955). Antecedent probability and the efficiency of psychometric signs, patterns, or cutting scores. *Psychological Bulletin, 55,* 194–216.

Mitchell, E. A., Aman, M. G., Turbott, S. H., & Manku, M. (1987). Clinical characteristics in serum essential fatty acid levels in hyperactive children. *Clinical Pediatrics, 26,* 406–411.

Murphy, K. (1994). Guarding against overdiagnosis of ADHD in adults. *The ADHD Report, 2*(6), 3–4.

Murphy, K., & LeVert, S. (1995). *Out of the fog: Treatment options and coping strategies for adult attention deficit disorder.* New York: Skylight Press.

Murray, H. A. (1943). *Thematic Apperception Test: Manual.* Cambridge, MA: Harvard University Press.

Nadeau, K. G. (1995). *A comprehensive guide to attention-deficit disorder in adults: Research, diagnosis, and treatment.* New York: Brunner/Mazel.

O'Brien, J. D., Halperin, J. M., Newcorn, J. H., Sharma, V., Wolf, L., & Morganstein, A. (1992). Psychometric differentiation of conduct disorder in attention deficit disorder with hyperactivity. *Developmental and Behavioral Pediatrics, 13,* 274–277.

Owens, N. & Owens, B. W. (1993). *Adult Attention Deficit Disorder Behavior Rating Scales* [Unpublished instrument].

Palumbo, D., Como, P., Porter, J., Barbano, R., Giang, D., & Silverstein, S. (1995, November). *Discriminate validity of self-report measures and neuropsychological tests in diagnosing adult ADHD.* Paper presented at the annual conference of the National Academy of Neuropsychology, San Francisco.

Rorschach, H. (1921). *Psychodiagnostik.* Bern: Bircher. (English translation, Bern: Hans Huber, 1942).

Rosnow, R. L., & Rosenthal, R. (1989). Statistical procedures and the justification of knowledge in the psychological science. *American Psychologist, 44,* 1276–1284.

Rosvold, H. E., Mirsky, A. F., Sarason, I., Bransome, E. D., Jr., & Beck, L. H. (1956). A continuous performance test of brain damage. *Journal of Consulting Psychology, 20,* 343–350.

Sandford, J. A., & Turner, A. (1994). *Intermittent visual and auditory continuous performance task: Version 1.5.* Richmond, VA: BrainTrain.

Shemic, W. O., Asarnow, R. F., Hess, E., Zaucha, K., & Wheeler, N. (1990). A clinical and demographic profile of a sample of adults with attention deficit hyperactivity disorder, residual state. *Comprehensive Psychiatry, 31,* 412–416.

Shipley, W. W. (1940). A self-administered scale for measuring intellectual impairment and deterioration. *Journal of Psychology, 9,* 371–377.

Sleator, E. K., & Ullmann, R. I. (1981). Can the physician diagnose hyperactivity in the office? *Pediatrics, 67,* 13–17.

Szatmari, P., Offord, D. R., & Boyle, M. H. (1989). Correlates, associated impairments, and patterns of service utilization of children with attention deficit disorder: Findings from the Ontario Child Health Study. *Journal of Child Psychology and Psychiatry,30,* 205–217.

Triolo, S. J. (1994). *New GDS-Distractability norms for adults* (unpublished study).

Triolo, S. J., & Murphy, K. R. (1996). *Attention-Deficit Scales for Adults (ADSA) manual for scoring and interpretation.* New York: Brunner/Mazel.

Triolo, S. J., & Murphy, K. R. (1997). *Attention-Deficit Scales for Adults (ADSA): Windows Version* (Beta Version 1.0). New York: Brunner/Mazel.

Trites, R. L., Tryphonoas, H., & Ferguson, H. B. (1980). Diet treatment for hyperactive children with food allergies. In R. M. Knight & D. Bakker (Eds.), *Treatment of hyperactive and learning disordered children* (pp. 151–160). Baltimore: University Park Press.

Trommer, B. L., Hoeppner, J. B., Lorber, R., & Armstrong, K. (1988). Pitfalls in the use of a continuous performance test as a diagnostic tool in attention deficit disorder. *Developmental and Behavioral Pediatrics, 9,* 339–345.

Wechsler, D. (1981). *WAIS-R manual: Wechsler Adult Intelligence Scale–Revised.* San Antonio, TX: The Psychological Corporation.

Weiss, L. (1992). *Attention deficit disorder of adults.* Dallas, TX: Taylor.

Wender, P. H. (1995). *Attention-deficit hyperactivity disorder in adults.* New York: Oxford University Press.

Wood, D., Wendor, P., & Reimherr, F. W. (1983). The prevalence of attention deficit disorder, residual type, or minimal brain dysfunction, in a population of male alcoholic patients. *American Journal of Psychiatry, 140,* 195–198.

Zametkin, A. J., Nordhal, T. E., Gross, M., King, A. C., Semple, W. E., Rumsey, J., Hamburger, S., & Cohen, R. M. (1990). Cerebral glucose metabolism in adults with hyperactivity of childhood onset. *New England Journal of Medicine, 323,* 1361–1366.

Chapter 5

Case Studies

INTRODUCTION

The purpose of this chapter is to share with the reader past cases and to review some of the diagnostic processes with respect to reported ADHD symptoms and other possible comorbid conditions. For reference purposes, the first cases presented in this chapter will reflect rather classic ADHD conditions. Scores from different subscales and tests are usually not conflicting, and the diagnostic conclusions are considered quite valid. The majority of the cases in this chapter, however, will try to tackle diagnostic issues that may sometimes be confusing. This would include conflicting test results and, most often, unclear reported histories. I decided that it may more helpful to the practitioner if the majority of this chapter is spent in discussion of the more difficult cases rather than reviewing cases that practitioners may find obvious and relatively easy to diagnose. Most practitioners have felt the frustration of reading texts, especially those discussing psychotherapeutic techniques, in which all the data are lined up in a very neat and straightforward manner and brilliant conclusions are drawn, which are always correct. In real life such "textbook" cases are rare.

It is believed that most practitioners would prefer to learn about the cases that do not seem to fit neatly into their diagnostic categories. Thus, the consultation model was adopted in putting together this chapter. Practitioners do not engage in consultation on cases that are straightforward. It is far more likely that consult discussions are pursued on cases that are atypical or at least do not fit the usual textbook descriptions. These types of cases are presented here.

Case studies are inherently limited because of a lack of control measures and restricted sampling. The cases presented below all come from a private practice setting. The private practice is located in a middle-sized city surrounded by several rural communities in the southeastern region of the country. This location is approximately 100 miles from a major metropolitan city, and the private practice is professionally connected to a medical center that serves the surrounding regions, including out-of-state populations. Also, because a military facility is nearby, a sizable percentage of the patients are from other regions of the country. However, it is important to understand that their military background is reflective of a select group of Americans across the country.

Most of the patients tend to come from either a middle-class or working-class background. They are usually referred by the medical community; most of the time this is a family practitioner, but there have been occasional referrals from internists, endocrinologists, and other medical specialists. The second-most-frequent type of patient is the self-referred. These patients present themselves because they are encouraged by former patients, or they have had their child diagnosed as having ADHD and they have noted similar problems in themselves. Occasionally, patients refer themselves after reading about ADHD or listening to a local presentation on ADHD. The third major source of referrals is colleagues. These include counselors at the local university counseling center, other private practitioners, and personnel from the local psychiatric hospital or surrounding mental health agencies.

It is important to note that almost all of the patients seen in this private practice have been reasonably functional. A great majority have a high school diploma. Some have had at least some college experience, and there have been a number of patients who have completed their bachelor's degree and have gone further in their studies. Most of the patients are employed or are students. Those who are unemployed usually seem to have special support from their family.

The above conditions are very important to consider when reviewing the cases presented. There is a strong belief that most adult individuals who have ADHD are not seen by the proper professionals. Some are incarcerated, heavily involved in chemical abuses, or both. Also, a sizable portion of the ADHD population cannot take advantage of professional interventions for economic reasons; they do not have health insurance or are unemployed, just trying to survive with minimal basic resources. Consequently, practitioners may very well be exposed to a limited range of ADHD patients, and perhaps the more serious cases may not be represented here.

RELATIVELY UNCOMPLICATED ADHD CASES

The patients described in this section represent relatively uncomplicated conditions. The descriptions of symptoms are often very similar to textbook descriptions, and the test data fit neatly into the overall profile of the patient. Although these cases are relatively uncomplicated, they were specifically selected to represent the potential variety of dispositions. The theme that I hope will come across is that there is much variance within the ADHD population, even among patients who do not present major complications.

To this end, special attention is given to variations in lifestyles and test scores. Also, although none of these patients was diagnosed after the *DSM–IV* (American Psychiatric Association, 1994) was published, the cases will be reviewed with respect to the latest ADHD subcategories. Of all the patients described in this section, the first was the easiest to diagnose, because of the favorable combination between textbook descriptions of symptoms and her denial of problems. In spite of the fact that she did not want to come across as a person with attention problems, most of the data strongly suggested ADHD. The second case was chosen because it was quite typical of ADHD patients with inattentiveness as a predominant feature. For comparative purposes, the third case was chosen to represent typical patients who have both inattentive and hyperactive–impulsive features. The final case was chosen to demonstrate a special feature that is unique to adults with ADHD, as opposed to children with ADHD. These are adults who are bright enough to do well on neurological tests of attention but usually have high scores on the Consistency/Long-Term subscale of the Attention-Deficit Scales for Adults (ADSA; Triolo & Murphy, 1996). The important theme to consider is that looking at the patients' capacity to manage responsibilities or follow through with achievement goals over a long period of time is a far more reliable factor than performance on an artificial task of attention.

Denial of ADHD

This patient is a woman in her early 30s who was referred by her family physician because he suspected ADHD. She reported that she had complained to him about having memory lapses and, after a brief set of questions, her physician told her that she may have attention problems. The patient was very reluctant to talk to a psychologist, but she cooperated with all of the tasks presented. As she began to explain some of the consequences in her life of her memory difficulties, it was obvious that these problems dated back to her childhood years. She remembered that as a teenager she had had a habit of leaving her homework at home and that her school performance had suffered because she had problems remembering directions. As discussions continued, she admitted to other symptoms. For instance, she had always been annoyed by the fact that she can easily become distracted in the middle of a conversation. Attending to tasks such as reading has always been difficult.

As mentioned earlier, the patient was not pleased to have been referred to a psychologist and seemed very reluctant to admit to a number of the symptoms. In fact, for every symptom that she described, she went out of her way to explain how she had compensated. For example, she reported that she could manage quite well because she had developed a habit of writing notes to herself. The kinds of symptoms described, along with the compensatory strategies, reflected textbook descriptions of ADHD patients. The fact that she had no prior knowledge of attention problems and that she had an interest in not receiving a diagnosis of any kind of "deficit" validated her reports even further. Certainly, they seemed more valid than they would coming from someone who has already read the literature and has already been convinced that an ADHD diagnosis is valid.

Even before formal testing began, there was a relatively high degree of certainty that the patient did have attention problems. Testing in this case seemed to be necessary mainly to convince the patient that the diagnosis is valid. The ADSA profile was clearly indicative of someone with problems in attention. She scored at the 99th percentile on the Attention-Focus/Concentration subscale and at the 90th percentile on the Consistency/Long-Term subscale. The impression based on the ADSA profile was that of a woman who tended to have significant problems in attention but may not be described as having impulsive–hyperactive tendencies.

Scores on the Gordon Diagnostic System distractibility task (GDS; Gordon, 1993) were actually within the average range. However, observations during this task also provided evidence for an ADHD diagnosis. The patient complained that the task was a strain to her eyes. Regardless of normative scores, it was obvious she had to put forth extra effort, more so than most others. This experience seemed to support the theme that the attention problems were real.

During follow-up discussions of test results, special time and energy were put into explaining the diagnosis of ADHD. It was important to communicate to the patient that she was not brain damaged and that these problems are relatively common. Also, it was important to communicate to her that she seemed to have done a reasonably good job compensating for her problems. It was recognized that she had done well and that she had the power, independent of anyone else, to continue to manage with relatively few negative consequences. In line with this theme, bibliotherapy was recommended as the most appropriate primary intervention.

ADHD, Predominately Inattentive Type

This patient is a young woman in her early 20s who was referred for evaluation by a colleague because of academic difficulties. At the time of the evaluation, the patient was a college student who was having problems passing her courses. Initially, a learning disability was suspected; however, historical reports suggested that she may have attention-related problems. She literally described herself as someone who is simply unable to pay attention to the things that she does. She reported that her mind tended to wander off to other things, and daydreaming was described as a major "flaw" in her life. She gave the example that she had never been able to read more than a few dozen pages of a novel at a time. In school, she could not sit through a lecture without her mind wandering to other things. She could not sit for more than 30 minutes without becoming restless, and she described herself as someone who is very disorganized and scattered. These problems extended beyond her academic life; she reported that she tended to forget orders and other verbal directions while at work.

All these problems were considered chronic, dating back to her early childhood years. Although she received average to better-than-average grades in grammar school and in high school, she went on to explain that her mother became involved in her homework assignments to the point that she provided the external structures necessary for academic success. Also, the patient admitted that she could always talk to her high school teachers and manage to compensate for poor test grades by writing a report or simply substituting an extracurricular activity for the grade earned. An independent collateral interview with her mother confirmed many of the patient's descriptions, especially those of her early childhood years.

Also, during interview the patient had difficulties responding to questions. They often were repeated to her, and there were signs that she had problems organizing her thoughts well enough to provide comprehensive answers. Considering the initial suspicions that she may have a learning disability, notations were made during interview that she may have expressive difficulties.

The Wechsler Adult Intelligence Scale–Revised (WAIS-R; Wechsler, 1981) was administered, and indeed her Verbal IQ score was 19 points lower than her Performance IQ score. The Full Scale IQ score fell within the average range, but the Verbal IQ was below average. It was concluded that the patient did have some problems communicating verbally, and particular problems were noted in subtests that required concentration. These included the Arithmetic and Digit Span subtests. In spite of these problems, most of her achievement scores were within the average range. The only exception found was in her expressive writing score.

The patient's total score on the ADSA was almost 3 *SD* above the mean. Her subscale profile on the ADSA indicated that major problems existed with respect to attention and concentration. Also noteworthy was a relatively high score on the Consistency/Long-Term subscale. This profile is quite typical of someone who has predominant problems with attention but does not have hyperactive–impulsive tendencies. This theme was clearly reflected in her scores on the GDS distractibility task. She scored below average (41 out of 60) in the number of correct responses; this is usually an indication of poor attention skills. By contrast, she had only 4 commissions, which was within acceptable levels; thus, this score supported the theme that she did not seem to have impulsive tendencies.

Together, the test results seemed to fit the general theme presented during the interview of someone who has problems attending to the responsibilities of her life. Apparently, the patient had managed to compensate for these deficits during her early academic years by allowing her mother to maintain external structures and reinforcers and by convincing her teachers to consider alternatives to poor test scores. Unfortunately, she could not do this as a college student, and her attention-related difficulties kept her from maintaining passing grades. To some extent, verbal weaknesses could be considered a factor, and this issue was communicated in follow-up sessions. This patient did not technically qualify for a diagnosis of learning disability, but her diagnosis of ADHD did qualify her for special academic consideration.

The projective profile indicated that the patient experienced chronic anxiety and some depression. Also, there were some signs that the patient may ruminate over past mistakes and excessively worry over the possibility of future errors. She seemed to maintain a pessimistic view that was considered quite irrational. Her irrationalities also included a sense of inferiority that quite possibly interfered with her interactions with others and her general performance.

Psychotherapy was highly recommended. Given the extent of the patient's emotional troubles, it would be naive to believe that many of her psychological dispositions would improve if the problems with attention were managed. Although the psychological problems may have been a result of her history of undiagnosed ADHD, it was highly recommended that they be given special focus. This young lady had spent most of her life believing that she was not worthy and intellectually inferior to those around her. It was believed that this had become a stable personality trait that would be resistant to change unless special psychological intervention were given.

ADHD, Combined Type

This patient is a man in his early 30s who referred himself for evaluation because of concerns that he may have attention-related problems. The patient presented a long history of difficulties, including poor grades in school, chronic feelings of inadequacy, and a brief period during his teenage years of alcohol abuse.

The patient had dropped out of school, but later, during his adult years, passed his high school equivalency exam. At the time of this evaluation, he was employed in his family business, but he was not happy with his work. For instance, much of his work included repetitive tasks, and he found them incredibly boring. He went on to explain that he could not stand many of the work-related tasks and found himself in a very restless mood throughout most of the day. Although much of his work required attention to paperwork at a desk, he needed to walk away from his desk several times throughout the day in an effort to release excessive energy. The patient also went on to describe himself as being easily distracted. He reported that he wrote things down in an effort not to forget them and that this was a major inconvenience.

A collateral interview was conducted with the patient's wife, and she confirmed many of the symptoms reported by her husband. The impression given was that she had helped him compensate for his lack of concentration and focus. In many respects, he had become dependent on her to remind him of the day-to-day details and, at home, many of the routine tasks, including paying the bills and taking care of groceries, were performed by her. Developmental history seemed to be important in this case. As a very young child, the patient had to be rocked to sleep and, although he was not considered to have a conduct problem, he described himself as someone who had always had excessive energy.

These reports came from the patient's parents, but the parents were never interviewed directly.

Originally, there were some concerns that the problems described were due to intellectual difficulties rather than ADHD. The patient's Full Scale IQ score, according to the WAIS-R, was at the lower end of the average range. A subsequent subscale profile did suggest some problem areas, but they certainly could not explain all of the symptoms presented. The difference between the Verbal and Performance IQ scores was not significant and, with the exception of a relatively low score on the Digit Symbol subtest, the profile was suggestive of someone who should be able to perform reasonably well academically, if he applies himself. The poor score on Digit Symbol raised some suspicions that he may have difficulties scanning visually, and this could translate into some sluggishness in reading.

Multiple elevations were noted on the ADSA profile. His total score was approximately 3 *SD* beyond the mean, and the subscale profile was indicative of someone who tends to be restless and behaviorally disorganized as well as inattentive.

The scores from the GDS proved to be quite helpful in this case, factoring out performance-related problems due to psychological difficulties. As stated earlier, this is a relatively sterile task, and the patient's performance is typically independent of emotional dispositions. The patient's total correct score was 44 (out of a total 60); this was well below average. He had a total of 6 commissions, which was interpreted to be at the threshold of clinical significance. The overall impression was that attention-related difficulties did exist and that they were due to cognitive impairments rather than psychological problems.

A projective screening was administered to address emotional issues. Depression and anxiety were indicated. Also, the analyses seemed to be reflective of someone who did not give himself much benefit of the doubt. It was concluded that the patient may very well be hypersensitive, and this may distort his judgment. For this reason, the reverse scored items of the ADSA were reviewed and compared with the rest of the scale items. There was no indication of deliberate distortions.

ADHD, Inconsistency Over Time

This patient is a man in his early 30s who presented for evaluation because his wife strongly suspected ADHD. The patient's wife was a professional, and she was well educated and knowledgeable of ADHD. After some discussion, she encouraged the patient to have an evaluation. The patient came across as being very bright and articulate. The main problem reported was that he had a tendency to lose objects, including keys, hats, books, and other items. Although the patient described this tendency as the major frustration, other symptoms emerged during interview. For instance, the patient admitted that he could not study more than 30 minutes without taking a break and that he almost always needed to write down things the night before to follow through with them the next day. He went on to describe a very disorganized life with numerous distractions. Examples given included observations that it took him 2 hours to clean his desk, something that can be done by most others within 20 minutes. During his early academic years, these same kinds of problems existed, but he seemed to be bright enough to get at least average grades. He was also bright enough to do well in college and consider postgraduate work. All through his growing years and his present adult life he seemed to be very busy. He came across as someone who always had something going on and may be involved in more than one project at a time.

The patient's wife was interviewed for independent collateral information. She reported that she first noted problems when her husband seemed to have problems studying in school. However, she also reported that he had extraordinary discipline. While other students were procrastinating, he seemed to take extra time to prepare for classes and upcoming tests. The theme presented was that of someone who maintained rigid controls and perhaps rechecked his work more than the typical college student.

The patient's wife complained that, outside of his academics, he did not seem to have a concept of time. Consequently, he was consistently late meeting obligations. She also went on to explain that her husband always seemed to have many things to do, and he would often go from one thing to another. She believed that her husband would be very restless without something do to and that it was important to him to keep busy. On the ADSA profile, his total score fell between the first and second standard deviations. Most notably, his highest subscale score was on Consistency/Long-Term. The second and third highest elevations were on the Behavior-Disorganized Activities and the Attention-Focus/Concentration subscales. The overall ADSA profile was reflective of an individual who may have numerous internal resources to compensate and do well over a short period of time. However, problems may arise in tasks that require long-term focus and an ability to follow through over time. The patient's GDS distractibility score was well within the average range. He seemed to be able to settle down and focus on this task, even though he was challenged with distractions.

A brief screening was conducted to address possible emotional issues. The ADSA did not suggest major problems in this area, and the subsequent Minnesota Multiphasic Personality Inventory–2 (MMPI-2; Hathaway & McKinley, 1989) profile was not reflective of major psychopathological issues. In fact, the general impression was that of an individual who had a relatively healthy, nondefensive posture. He came across as someone with the capacity to share and be open about feelings. Some mild elevations were noted in indicators of depression and anxiety, but they were not suggestive of major problems that could be considered clinically significant. In fact, it was imagined that the patient did not let any of his frustrations due to ADHD symptoms get in the way of his overall happiness and psychological well-being. Interpersonal relationships seemed to be strong, and he came across as someone who was rich in psychological and intellectual resources, certainly enough to compensate for limitations and weaknesses. Minimal interventions were indicated in this case.

MILD ADHD

The main purpose of this section is to present cases that can demonstrate that the diagnosis of ADHD is often a matter of degree of symptoms and, indeed, ADHD should be seen as a condition that is toward the extreme end of a set of normative cognitive functions.

The two cases presented in this section were purposely chosen to demonstrate how the same conclusion can be drawn from two completely different sets of data. Both cases presented ample data to make a diagnosis of ADHD, but each case presented a rather unique set of findings, certainly different from each other. In the first case, history, collateral interview, and test results all indicated significant problems with attention. However, the patient presented no major psychological problems, and her adjustments were so functional that ADHD presented minimal impairment. In the second case, help was requested in making adjustments although objective test scores were statistically elevated only slightly.

These cases were also chosen to demonstrate how varied patients view their problems. In the first case, although the patient's scores were significantly elevated, she did not see her problems as being major. In the second case, the opposite was true: Mild elevations on standardized instruments were considered major problems by the patient.

Mild ADHD With Appropriate Psychological Adjustments

This patient is a woman in her mid-30s who was referred for evaluation by her family physician because of suspected ADHD. At the time of her evaluation, she was a part-time college student and reported that she had been in and out of college for more than 10 years. She reported that she had accumulated many college credits and consistently earned As and Bs in school. However, she had switched majors numerous times and did not have enough of the credits necessary in any field of study to receive a degree. At one point, she was very interested in nursing but quickly became bored with it. It was interesting that the main motivation for this evaluation was to consider the possibility that her "scattered" lifestyle—as she described it—may be due to ADHD, and she agreed with her family and physician that perhaps she was getting too old to continue life as a college student. This was an afterthought on the part of the patient; in essence, she simply agreed with the observations of others.

During the initial interview the patient reported a number of attention-related problems. She admitted that she did not read very much because her mind wanders. In class, she "half" listened to the professor, even when she made an effort to pay attention. Also, in areas beyond her academics, she had a tendency to be distracted from ongoing projects and responsibilities, including her art and crafts projects, which she enjoyed immensely.

The patient did have a history of experimenting with hallucinogenics, but she reported that she had stopped this practice. The patient did report that her tendency to not attend in school and in other areas dated back to her childhood years well before any experimentation with drugs.

During the independent collateral interview with the patient's mother, a number of examples were given of a child who tended not to pay attention as well as her classmates did. The major complaint was that she has always been late and never had really developed a concept of time. These behaviors were observed even when the activity was something that she enjoyed. For instance, she would be sluggish getting her things together to meet with her friends for an organized play activity.

Both the GDS distractibility task and the ADSA profile yielded scores in the abnormal range, greater than 2 *SD* beyond the mean. The theme presented by the objective data was that of an individual who had significant problems with attention. In particular, the ADSA profile suggested major problems with long-term goals and consistency.

This case was somewhat unusual because many of the patient's ADHD symptoms seemed to be ego syntonic; it seemed that she was very happy with herself and accepted her tendency to be inattentive with no frustrations or special concerns. In fact, there were signs that she somewhat enjoyed her scattered lifestyle and did not see it as a major liability.

According to the projective analyses, the patient seemed to be adjusting quite well, and there were even signs that she was fully enjoying her life. She came across as having a very easygoing personality with much acceptance of her tendency to not be as efficient as others. Perhaps the best evidence was found in her behavior during testing. The day of the scheduled testing, it was discovered that the GDS instrument was at another office. When this was communicated to her, along with apologies, she simply smiled and dismissed it as no major problem. She even offered to come back on another day rather than inconvenience the staff. It was clear that these kinds of problems were considered part of a typical everyday life for her rather than an intolerable frustration. Thus, although the objective scores indicated rather significant problems, the patient was seen as being unusually adaptable, and the problems were interpreted by her as being minor.

There was a temptation is this case to describe this patient as someone with ADHD symptoms, but not fulfilling the criteria of impairment. She was so good at adapting and, unlike any other ADHD patient before her, there were no signs that she was suffering psychological consequences. In fact, one could argue that her casual and free-flowing personality fully accepted and even welcomed the distractions and interruptions in her life. Thus, it would be difficult to defend the argument that her day-to-day life is impaired by the ADHD symptoms.

On the other hand, it would be difficult to make the same argument if the patient's entire adult life is considered as a whole. Although the patient's family first brought it to her attention, she did realize that time had passed her by and goals she had hoped to achieve have not been completed. Perhaps the best example would be her many years in college without a degree. It was therefore concluded that the ADHD symptoms have impaired her life, but only if a lifelong perspective is considered. Again, consistency over time and the management of long-term goals seem to be extremely important factors to consider for the adult population.

Mild ADHD With Adjustments Specific to Lifestyle Changes

This patient is a man in his early 20s who was diagnosed as having ADHD during his childhood years. Although no formal testing was conducted, the diagnostician took the time to review school records and consulted with both parent and teacher to validate clinical impressions.

The patient reported that he was placed on stimulant medication, and he remembered major improvements in his academics due to medication effects. By the time he reached his senior year of high school the patient felt confident he would graduate and decided to complete his last year without the use of stimulant medication. This decision was his, but it was endorsed by his parents and his physician. The patient went on to report that he was quite satisfied with the cognitive adjustments he had made and, on completing high school, he continued with technical training and employment in a paraprofessional field. After several years of employment and advancements, he began to think about going to college. Concerned that the demands in college would be greater than those of his employment, he began to suspect that he may need special assistance, perhaps going back on stimulant medication. To this end, he asked his friends and colleagues to recommend a therapist, and he was eventually referred through a colleague. The patient came across as a very reasonable and intelligent young man. He was very interested in following through with objective testing, and he was very willing to follow up with specific recommendations regarding his decision to return to school. He seemed very motivated and wanted to take the appropriate steps to increase the probability of success.

Mild but definite problems in attention were noted on the ADSA profile. He scored between the first and second standard deviations on the total score and the two subscale scores usually associated with inattentiveness: lack of concentration and inconsistent focus. Scores on the GDS were within the normal range, although they approached statistical significance.

In addition, a WAIS-R was administered because the patient had some concerns regarding possible learning difficulties. No major problems were found, and he was told there were no signs to indicate that he would not be successful managing college academics.

In the follow-up interview he was told that there was certainly enough evidence to suggest mild but definite ADHD. He was given the feedback that his motivation to do well in college was perhaps the single most important factor related to his success. However, it would seem reasonable to turn to stimulant medication to help him. No psychotherapeutic interventions were indicated, but he was told that he was free to contact the office should any problems arise.

This case is presented, in particular, because it seemed as though some theoretical and criteria rules were violated. The patient's problems with attention seemed to be associated with academic responsibilities only. This would violate the rule of multiple settings. However, the patient did report attending difficulties outside of his academic life. The difference was that the consequences were considered relatively minor. By contrast, the patient was not about to risk similar consequences, such as doing poorly on a final exam and jeopardizing his grade point average. Also, on the surface it appears as though the diagnosis of ADHD is very much dependent on environmental circumstances rather than stable cognitive dispositions. However, at a closer look, it was clear that the inner cognitive dispositions remained stable throughout his childhood and adult years. It is important to keep in mind that the objective scores were indicative of someone who did indeed have problems with attention, although the patient was not in school at the time of testing. This case is a good concrete example of the limitations of a pure neurogenic theory of ADHD.

ADHD WAS RULED OUT

All of the cases in this section are patients who were specifically referred because ADHD was suspected, but it was eventually ruled out. These cases were purposely selected because the alternative diagnosis given is usually cited in the literature as a comorbid condition to ADHD (e.g., Lavenstein, 1995; Tzelepis et al., 1995). These include anxiety, depression, personality disorder, neurological disorder, and problems with respect to temperament. Unlike patients who are diagnosed as having ADHD with additional psychological problems secondary to the ADHD dispositions, these patients' psychological and neurological problems were the primary issues and were not not due to ADHD.

Anxiety Disorder, With ADHD Ruled Out

This patient is a male in his mid-50s who presented himself for evaluation because his teenage son was diagnosed as having ADHD and he was experiencing similar problems. During interview, he reported that he seems to jump from one project to the next. He had a tendency to scan reading material rather than take the time to read it completely. Also, he had a tendency to be forgetful and often worried about leaving the door unlocked to his house or forgetting to pick up the children on special practice days. During his early academic years he remembered having to study extra hard to keep pace with those around him.

However, he always received better-than-average grades. In fact, he attended college, graduated with honors, and successfully completed professional school. In spite of all of these successes, he seemed to always concern himself with the next round of performance, worried that he might fail the next test or that some other inadequacies would be discovered. In spite of an objective assessment that he was well liked in school, shyness and fears of rejections were constant during his growing years.

Extra time was given to interview both the patient and his wife independently and then together. Through interview discussions, it was discovered that his forgetfulness rarely resulted in major negative consequences. For example, he had never forgotten to pick up the children from football practice or any other after-school activities. Professionally, he had gone into business for himself after years working for a local consulting firm. In the more recent months he became a partner to several related companies and, according to his own reports, all of his professional activities had become rather successful. Still, the patient had a belief that success came only after extra hard work, and recently he had caught himself being somewhat scattered in thought. He agreed that he may have spread himself somewhat thin with all his duties, although his list of successes continued to grow. Special time was spent suggesting to him that he may have very high standards for himself and that a state of anxiety may have contributed to his ADHD-related symptoms.

Each of the ADHD-related symptoms presented was reviewed and, again, minimal consequences were noted. For example, although it may be true that the patient tended to jump from one project to the next, it is also true that he has many projects that need almost simultaneous attention, and he almost always eventually gets back to finishing what he started.

Minimal testing was administered in this case. The purpose for the testing seemed to be more to give the patient reassurance rather than help in making a diagnosis. On the MMPI-2 profile, the classical 2–7 profile (depression and psychasthenia) was presented. The ADSA also was administered, and the total score was somewhat elevated. Mild elevations were found on several of the ADSA subscales, including the ones that represent the classical indicators of ADHD, such as Attention-Focus/Concentration, Behavior-Disorganized Activities, and Consistency/Long-Term, along with other subscales, such as Emotive, Interpersonal, and Negative Social. It was not surprising to see the elevated Emotive subscale, but it was very surprising to see that the Interpersonal and the Negative Social subscale scores were elevated. A brief item analysis took place during a follow-up interview and, as suspected, the patient had problems giving himself the benefit of the doubt. It was concluded that his perception of himself was negatively biased. For instance, he reported that others never see him as a patient person when in reality his patience and tolerance of others are seen by those around him as one of his dominant personality traits.

It was concluded that the patient did not suffer from ADHD. Instead, his problems were due to an almost constant state of anxiety. During a brief intervention with this patient, it was suggested that he had reached an age in his life when he can cash in on some of his achievements. Rather than adding on to the stressors of his life, he may want to consider selling off some of his partnerships in companies and use the extra time and funds to enjoy himself. Most of the focus during the follow-up therapy sessions was spent addressing the need to continually prove himself.

Major Depression and Medical Problems, With ADHD Ruled Out

This patient was a woman in her mid-40s who was referred for evaluation by both her psychotherapists; she was attending individual and family counseling at the time of this evaluation. After presenting numerous ADHD-related symptoms to her psychotherapists, a formal evaluation was recommended.

The ADHD-related symptoms included a long history of restlessness and agitation, a very disorganized lifestyle, forgetfulness, and an inability to initiate and follow through with tasks. All of the symptoms reported were limited to domestic duties. The patient worked part time taking care of children with special needs, and she had absolutely no problems attending to these responsibilities. This was the first sign that the reported symptoms were not due to ADHD. The impression given was that taking care of children with special needs made her feel good and, although the responsibilities were numerous, she managed them quite well because of her feelings of well-being.

The patient reported that she had had problems in school during her childhood years. She went on to explain that she could not sit very long in class, and she had had to repeat two grades. She had no conduct problems. Eventually, she decided to drop out of school altogether when she found herself failing in junior high. According to the reports from the psychotherapist, the history of academic failure was not due to intellectual limitations.

The patient reported that her ADHD-related symptoms had increased in number and in intensity as she had gotten older. This is somewhat unusual; it is more typical to receive reports that symptoms have been better managed over the years because of maturation and trial-and-error development of strategies to overcome the problems.

In addition, the patient reported a long history of medical difficulties. She was under the care of an internist to attend to what was described as "hormonal imbalances," and her physician had her on antidepressants in order to attend to mood-related symptoms. Also noteworthy was the report that family-related problems had increased over the years. Marriage problems had been chronic, and she was having difficulties managing her teenage stepchildren.

Even before formal testing began, there was some confidence that ADHD-related symptoms were due to emotional issues rather than to attention-related deficits. A series of projective analyses supported this hypothesis. On the MMPI-2, several clinical scales were elevated. Her highest score was on the Depression scale. Other elevations included Schizophrenia and Paranoia. Although there were no overt signs of psychosis during the interview, irrational–delusional thought processes could not be ruled out in this case, and these problems over-shadowed any possible problems with attention. Other projective testing suggested fragile ego controls, and it may have been appropriate to at least describe the patient as being emotionally impulsive and reactionary to the external stressors in her life. It was difficult to predict, but she seemed to be at the threshold of a psychotic break, and the psychotherapist was advised that ADHD would be the least of the patient's problems, if she suffered from it at all. The overriding theme presented was that of an individual who was miserable and had been very unhappy for a long time. It was recommended that special sensitivity be given to the patient's medical conditions and that she continue to receive intense psychotherapeutic interventions.

Antisocial Personality Disorder, With ADHD Ruled Out

This patient was a man in his early 20s who was referred by his parents because of suspected ADHD. The patient had a long history of behavioral problems. He was not aggressive and did not engage in overt confrontive behaviors; however, he was described as being untrustworthy. Tendencies to lie, steal, and cheat others were relatively frequent, and attempts to change his ways during his growing years had been very unsuccessful. By the time he was seen for evaluation he had been incarcerated by the juvenile authorities several times, and he had already accumulated several adult criminal charges, such as auto theft and dealing drugs.

At one point, the patient's parents admitted him into a local psychiatric hospital. They had suspected that he was suffering from depression and that his acting-out behaviors were immature ways by which to express unwanted feelings. The patient had been prescribed several antidepressants over the past 10 years both as an inpatient and outpatient. Compliance with the medical regimen had been minimal.

During the past few months the patient had been incarcerated for a theft charge, and his parents suspected that this may have been due to impulse control problems. They had been reading about ADHD and requested an evaluation. Right from the beginning interview interactions, it was evident that the patient's parents were more concerned for him than he was for himself. Both of his parents had been working feverishly for years trying to find the answers to his misbehaviors. He had dropped out of school and spent most of his time at home, unemployed. Each problem that had involved law enforcement was immediately countered by a parental hypothesis that there must be some psychological issue that is undetected. This had been a defense tactic during previous incarcerations, and it was a major motivation for an ADHD evaluation, at least on the part of the patient's parents. The patient also seemed motivated to "try Ritalin," but it was difficult to believe he was thinking in terms of therapeutic use.

In regard to ADHD symptomatology, there were reports that the patient may be impulsive. His parents reported that he might be easily led by others and that he tended to act without thinking about the long-term consequences. Later it was discovered that he was more of a leader than a follower and that many of his misbehaviors were well planned. Another area presented by the patient's parents was his lack of appropriate social sensitivity. They had read how people with ADHD seem to lack social skills and do not have the social sensitivities to maintain good friendship ties. This was later explained as a secondary condition to ADHD, and there were suspicions that the patient simply could not be bothered with normal social interactions, unless it was to his advantage. The patient did not seem to have any problems with social skills when it came to getting his needs met.

The patient came across as being a very bright young man and, on the basis of a review of past report cards, it seemed that he had the intellectual talents to do well in school, in spite of numerous absences. For someone who had dropped out of school, he came across as being extremely articulate and cognitively aware of present environmental circumstances. For instance, he recognized how his parents worried about his incarcerations, and in a written report from one of his former therapists there were strong suspicions that he used his parent's worried state to his advantage

On the MMPI-2 profile, there was a slight elevation on the F scale, with the suggestion that he may exaggerate problems. The clinical profile had three elevations. The first was Hypomania (Scale 9), followed by Psychopathic Deviant (Scale 4) and Paranoia (Scale 6). This seemed to be a rather classical profile of an individual who tends to act out and may have little regard for social norms and expectations. Also noteworthy was the patient's lack of emotional distress. There were no indications that he was as worried as his parents, and there were no findings to suggest a mood disorder, as was once suspected by his parents.

Other tests supported the MMPI-2 profile. In particular, the Rorschach was unable to pick out any signs of underlying distress. This was considered significant, considering the recent legal charges against the patient. As expected, he did show signs of anger, and he may have had a tendency to become passive–aggressive when interacting with others. From a human standpoint, he seemed to have a capacity to disengage. He was simply not the type of person who would offer sympathy and care to others who may be in need.

Although no formal intellectual test was conducted, there were ample signs to suggest that the patient had adequate cognitive faculties. His memory seemed to be intact, and all cognitive indicators suggested a person who is well organized and capable of long-term planning. On the basis of a reported family history, it seemed the patient used his intellectual skills to manipulate family members. This included strategies that require patience and attention to long-term consequences.

At the follow-up interview, special time was given to report all of the findings that challenged the theme of ADHD. The diagnosis of antisocial personality disorder was given because it best explained all of the data. Subsequent family sessions dealt with emotional issues brought forth by the patient's parents rather than the patient himself. A mourning process took place in which the parents came to accept the reality of a poor prognosis. Support was given to help the parents deal with feelings of helplessness and guilt. The patient disengaged from professional services as soon as he learned that Ritalin would not be recommended.

Neurological Disorder, With ADHD Ruled Out

After this patient's parents saw a television program on ADHD, they referred their teenage son for evaluation. He had already been under the care of a neurologist because of a rather long history of seizures. At the time of the evaluation, the seizures had been under control with medication. The patient had also had a history of repeated abnormal EEG readings under strobe conditions. Against the advice of his parents and his physician, the patient used a friend's motorcycle for a joyride, which ended in an accident. On the basis of descriptions by the patient, it was concluded that the accident was due to poor judgment rather than a seizure. The patient insisted that he "hardly ever" had seizures anymore. The patient also insisted that he never lost consciousness. Emergency room reports indicated that he had suffered a concussion.

During the interview, the patient admitted that he had problems focusing on written material and that he became frustrated very easily. His frustrations caused him to have angry outbursts during which he became destructive of property (i.e., kicking the wall), but a point was made that he had never been aggressive toward other people. His parents, during collateral interview, provided a list of symptoms that they suspected were due to ADHD. It is important to note that many of the items on their list—temper tantrums, low self-esteem, mood swings, and so on—were secondary symptoms of ADHD. With the exception of problems following through with responsibilities and restlessness, no core ADHD symptoms were reported. More important, many of these symptoms had emerged during the teenage years. It was difficult to know if the symptoms had emerged after the accident. The impression given was that they certainly had increased in frequency and intensity; however, the choice of defying recommendations from medical personnel by getting on a motorcycle in the first place may have been indicative of the patient's frustrations, mood, and other symptoms. Also, a scan of the patient's academic reports was suggestive of a child who may have had cognitive difficulties and emotional liabilities related to these difficulties throughout his adolescent years. With the exception of problems in reading, minimal difficulties were noted during the grammar school years.

In this case, ADHD was not diagnosed because onset of symptoms had occurred during the adolescent years and the symptoms themselves did not reflect core deficits usually associated with ADHD.

The patient was referred back to the neurologist in consideration of additional injury due to his motorcycle accident. It was decided to address this first before engaging in psychological interventions. Consequently, no testing was administered.

Temperament Problems, With ADHD Ruled Out

This patient is a man in his mid-30s who presented for evaluation because of suspected ADHD. The patient was referred by a former ADHD patient. As a child, the patient was diagnosed as having ADHD and was placed on medication by a pediatrician. The patient admitted that he had a long history of behavior problems in school. He passed all his grades but consistently received below-average marks. This pattern did not change very much while on stimulant medication; after approximately 3 years, the medication was stopped.

History was somewhat sketchy, and the patient's parents were not available for collateral interview. It was difficult to know if the behavior problems the patient reported were due to ADHD or to oppositional–conduct problems. The pediatrician who made the diagnosis of ADHD had not tested the patient, and the impression given was that the patient's parents were supplied with a prescription to see if misbehaviors subside. It is difficult to speculate, but the medication probably did help somewhat, because the patient was on it for so long. Still, this could not validate a diagnosis of ADHD, because behavioral improvements while a patient is on stimulant medication are often observed regardless of whether he or she has ADHD. Regardless, behavior problems obviously did not subside completely, and difficulties were reported through the high school years. The patient could not remember any other problems outside of academics. He did report that he did have some peer conflicts, but it was difficult to know if these were beyond normal parameters.

The patient's main concern was his temper. He admitted that he became angry very easily, and he went on to explain that this was affecting his marriage. The patient's wife was interviewed to gather independent collateral information. She reported that he could lose his temper very easily and that his angry outbursts had escalated to physical violence. Later, it was noted that husband and wife became aggressive toward each other.

Regarding other symptoms related to ADHD, there were differences of opinion between husband and wife. The patient's wife reported that he was extremely disorganized and messy. The patient later explained that he may appear to be disorganized and that he does not keep a very tidy household, but he can find everything that he needs. When the patient's wife gave specific examples of him losing some household items and turning to her for help, he quickly responded that this was because she moved his things. These kinds of differences and viewpoints were expressed consistently as different ADHD-related symptoms were reviewed. It was noteworthy that the patient seemed to be relatively satisfied with his daily life and considered his temper the only problem.

The patient was employed and reported that there had been no problems in this area. It was interesting to note, however, that he worked outdoors, where much physical activity is necessary. The patient reported that he preferred such jobs, but only because they made him feel industrious. When questioned further, he seemed to describe a lifestyle that was quite active and energetic. There were some suggestions that his wife was left out of many of his activities; this may have been another marital issue.

Before testing began, the only certainties were that the patient had a tendency to lose his temper and that his angry outbursts included violent behaviors. The patient's explosiveness was not limited to conflicts between him and his wife. The problems never escalated to the point where legal authorities became involved.

Intellectual testing was administered to rule out possible cognitive troubles. During interview, the patient tended to respond with one-word answers or very short sentences. He also seemed to be somewhat concrete in his thinking. Although below-average scores were expected, all of the testing yielded scores within the average range of intelligence. There were no significant differences between the verbal and nonverbal subtests, and that also was somewhat of a surprise.

On the GDS distractbility task, the patient scored well within the normal range. In fact, he seemed to be able to attend to the requirements of this task much better than the average adult. No significant elevations were noted on the MMPI-2 and or the ADSA profile. The internal consistency score of the ADSA was somewhat elevated, which suggested some inconsistency in response style; it was interesting that the items that lacked consistency were associated with issues of temperament. These were as follows: "I do not have much patience with people" (response: "often") and "Others see me as a patient person" (response: "often"). One of those two items had reversed scoring so that the same response (often) yielded different scores. Finally, the patient's raw score on the lie scale was one point away from reaching significance. Many of the clinical subscales scores were below the average. This was certainly curious considering the patient did admit to angry outbursts.

At this point of the evaluation, there was enough evidence to feel certain that ADHD was not an issue. Childhood reports suggested oppositional troubles rather than ADHD. The judgment made by the patient's pediatrician was questionable, especially considering the facts that problems were not solved and that they were found only in the patient's academic world. Finally, he did not present any objective data to confirm ADHD, and there did not seem to be enough evidence to suggest significant impairment in his daily life, although his wife considered this point quite debatable.

Antisocial personality traits could be ruled out in this case. Special attention was given during the follow-up interview to the perceptions of others regarding the patient's behaviors. Although the patient's wife had complaints about her husband, she felt secure that he genuinely cared for her and did present numerous examples of warmth and affection. More important, she was able to describe how caring he had been to others in his family. Also, the violent behaviors were all associated with feelings of frustration. Although inappropriate, the patient always had been responding to external stressors, and the inappropriate behaviors were considered ego dystonic. Although the patient may tend to deny problems, he readily admitted that his temper was a problem, and he clearly perceived it as an unwanted trait, separate from who he really is as a person. The patient did not fit the criteria for ADHD but did seem to fit the criteria for intermittent explosive disorder.

ADHD WITH SEVERE MULTIPLE COMORBID CONDITIONS

Discussions of comorbid pathologies are usually presented one at a time in the literature (Nadeau, 1995). Depression, personality disorders, drug abuse problems, anxiety disorders, and other pathologies are typically discussed separately in relation to ADHD. However, it is often the case that multiple problems exist and that ADHD patients are found with a long history of multiple difficulties. In this section, cases are reviewed to discuss the complexities associated with multiple pathologies. In a general clinical practice, it is usually accepted that patients will not present themselves in textbook fashion. Quite often, layers of pathologies will present themselves, especially if they are usually associated with adult conditions (i.e., personality disorder), and these can sometimes disguise or perhaps overshadow problems in attention.

The following case studies were purposely chosen to cover this issue of multiple comorbid conditions. In some cases, ADHD was not presented as an initial complaint; for this reason, this section may be most helpful for the practitioner who typically deals with problems that are usually associated with the adult population (marital problems, substance abuse, etc.) but may not be as familiar with ADHD symptomatology. It is also designed to share some of the difficult cases that do not easily fit into the sterile textbook categories. For this reason, many readers may disagree with some of the assessments and conclusions.

ADHD, Depression, Alcohol Abuse, and Personality Disorder

This patient is a man in his early 50s who reported that he had suffered from depression for at least two decades and that most of the time he had been fighting suicidal thoughts. His family physician had been treating him with antidepressants for approximately 2 years, but minimal changes in mood had been noted. He first presented for psychotherapeutic interventions because of depression, but psychological interventions were pursued mainly because of marital conflicts; he had recently been asked to move out of his home, and he may have been motivated to seek help to prove to his wife that he was willing to change his ways.

The patient reported having been unhappy all of his adult life, and there were reports of struggles dating back to his grade school years. He reported that he had done well in math but struggled with reading and writing. He admitted to having conduct problems but added that his teachers had misunderstood him because he had always been conscientious enough to try to do well in school. The patient went on to explain how none of his teachers during his school days believed that he was trying the best that he could, and his demeanor when presenting this issue seemed as though he was reliving this frustration. He finished his report by stating that he still had problems reading and that he could not write as fluently as he would like.

Suicidal episodes coincided with major losses in his family, including the death of a sibling. Although no overt action toward killing himself had ever taken place, he was prone to abusing alcohol. Most noteworthy, he had some problems because of drunk driving episodes, and there were the usual suspicions of abusing alcohol to fulfill inner suicidal tendencies.

The first consideration of ADHD took place when the patient described his desperate wish to reunite with his wife. He described himself as being lost without her, and the specific examples given were reflective of ADHD symptoms. He reported that he was very disorganized and often procrastinated when a job needed to be done. His disorganization included a tendency to be forgetful and to lose items around the house. Even when he managed to overcome tendencies to procrastinate and he took on tasks, he tended to become distracted and did not follow through. Some time was spent asking him about his reading difficulties and, among other things, he reported that his mind tended to wander off and that he simply could not pay attention long enough to remember what he had read. According to the history presented, these problems had been constant throughout his childhood. Apparently, his mother compensated for him and, after his marriage, his wife took over his mother's role. The patient's symptoms seemed to be robust in that they existed across numerous situations. For instance, he reported some brief times when he felt motivated to pursue a long-time hobby; however, his initial motivation was short lived, and he found himself unable to follow through. The patient reported this as one of his many regrets in life.

Testing for this patient did not take place for several weeks because of his despondent mood when he first presented for psychological interventions. Over the first few weeks the patient came across as someone who genuinely tried to do well for himself but always fell short. At this stage of his life, he seemed helpless and totally dependent on others for support. Although an ADHD diagnosis was still not certain, the patient presented a history in which classical ADHD symptoms were present early in childhood and the mood-related problems became more intense and more prominent with age. Thus, the impression given was that of an ADHD child who was never diagnosed and even mislabeled negatively. As time passed, it seemed that the patient decided to not rely on himself and eventually convinced himself that he could not survive without constant support and attention. Separation from his wife led him not only to intense feelings of depression but also to feelings of panic much like a young child experiencing acute separation anxiety.

Testing took place over two separate times. The first and primary testings focused on emotional issues and were projective in nature. Depression was certainly confirmed, and there were additional signs that the patient harbored inner hostilities and cognitive confusions. In fact, delusional thinking could not be ruled out, especially during times of severe mood disturbances. The MMPI-2 profile was considered valid, and multiple elevations were noted. Findings from the Thematic Apperception Test (TAT; Murray, 1943) and the Rorschach (Exner, 1986) were suggestive of someone who relies on fantasy to the point of significant cognitive distortions. It was also hypothesized that the patient oscillated from one extreme to the next with different emotions. Acting out impulsively was certainly not ruled out, and he could become agitated to the point of being aggressive. At this point in his life, perhaps the most aggressive act was his tendency to drive under the influence of alcohol. This very same acting-out personality can also become very dependent. To this end, he may have been somewhat submissive, and it was suspected that this was so he could win over and secure the support of others.

The problems seen in this case were certainly considered chronic, and tests pertinent to ADHD were administered after several sessions and the acute distressors had subsided. The patient's ADSA profile was highly elevated, and the three major subscales reflecting ADHD symptoms were the highest scores. These included Attention-Focus/Concentration, Consistency/Long-Term, and Behavior-Disorganized Activities. It was somewhat surprising to find the Interpersonal, Negative Social, and Childhood subscale scores within the normal range. Originally, the patient presented because of difficulties with his wife, and there were certainly numerous reports of childhood difficulties, especially in school.

For this case, the most helpful testing was the GDS distractibility task. The patient could capture only 2 out of 60 combinations, and 10 commissions were recorded. During this testing, the patient was relaxed and in a reasonably good mood. He recognized that he had problems with this task and complained that the flashing digits were moving too fast. The indication was that he felt overwhelmed. The findings of this test, especially because it was a mechanical task, suggested that the patient did indeed have a problem with attention.

The direction of psychotherapeutic intervention, in addition to continued emotional support, moved toward helping the patient learn more about ADHD and validating his criticisms of his teachers. As time passed, the patient was encouraged to take charge of himself and address the symptoms by developing his own compensatory strategies. A combination of stimulant and antidepressant medications also was considered.

ADHD and Paranoid and Obsessive–Compulsive Personality Features

This patient is a man in his mid-30s who had been attending psychotherapy because of marital difficulties. The therapist referred him for evaluation because she suspected attention-related difficulties. The patient reported that he had always had trouble focusing his attention on tasks. He reported that his wife has always accused him of not listening during conversations with her, and he admitted that his mind tended to wander off. He also admitted that he tended to cut people off in conversation, although he did try not to do so.

The patient's history included many of the same symptoms. The patient reported that he managed to do well enough to pass in school but never really learned anything. Tasks that were easy for others, such as writing down sentences from the blackboard, were impossible for him.

The patient's wife was available for interview, and she independently endorsed many of the symptoms reported by him. She also went on to give specific examples. She expressed much frustration as she reported that even everyday routine tasks are forgotten and she needs to remind her husband repeatedly. She also reported that he hardly ever follows through with tasks to their completion. It was particularly frustrating for her to see tasks that are "99 percent" done left hanging.

These symptoms were not the main cause of marital conflicts. Both husband and wife presented rather significant personality dysfunctions. On the MMPI-2 profile, for instance, the patient had numerous elevations on the clinical scales and the supplemental scales. There was clear evidence of chronic emotional instability with very poor reality testing capacity. Paranoia was the dominant personality feature, with associated feelings of isolation and depression. It seemed that feelings of paranoia focused mainly on the patient's wife, but general feelings of being persecuted could not be ruled out. For someone who presented feelings of impulsivity, it seemed he spent much time and energy focusing on the motivations of others. Unfortunately, the patient did not engage in reality-checking practices. Most of the time, the patient would keep irrational thoughts to himself, and they tended to develop into major delusions.

No testing was administered to the patient's wife, but there were indications that she used the patient's negative feelings for secondary gain. She seemed to feed into his paranoia by refusing to talk about issues such as fidelity and loyalty. It seemed that his intensity for securing her love was a maladaptive validation for her own sense of worthiness. Both husband and wife seemed to lack the inner warmth and mutual respect necessary to move past their conflicts. On the contrary, typical of severe personality dispositions, conflicts seemed to be maintained as a necessary component of their relationship.

With respect to ADHD testing, the GDS distractibility task provided the best evidence in support of attention-related problems. The ADSA profile was elevated, but the subscale configuration presented a theme of a mixture of emotion and attention-related problems. It was difficult to tease out one from the other. On the other hand, the patient's abnormal scores on the GDS task, a relatively sterile neuropsychological measure that is somewhat independent from emotional contamination, supported the diagnosis of ADHD.

For this patient, problems related to ADHD were considered minimal compared to the personality issues. There were some concerns that treatment with a stimulant medication may only add to his tendency to ruminate: It would be like giving him a greater capacity to attend to his paranoid ideations. This viewpoint was passed along to the psychotherapist, and it was suggested that husband and wife engage in individual psychotherapy before moving on to marital therapy. As a final note, the patient's wife seemed to want to use ADHD as evidence to blame her husband for all of the marital difficulties. It was strongly recommended that this viewpoint be challenged at some point during the psychotherapeutic process.

ADHD, Alcohol Abuse, Depression, and History of Hormonal Problems

This patient is a woman in her late 30s who was referred for psychological interventions by her gynecologist. She had had a history of physical problems related to her menstrual cycle, but her physician was convinced that additional problems existed beyond physical pathologies. At last consult, her physician described her as being in good health. In this case, history revealed that ADHD symptoms existed long before physical ailments, and they persisted after successful medical treatments.

During the interview, the patient was highly agitated and restless. She described herself as being "hyper inside" but seemed to provide ample observational evidence that this condition also existed behaviorally. She became quite tangential in explaining her symptoms, going from one topic to another. Often she would lose her place, become more agitated, and then impulsively move on to a new topic. She managed to report that she had no patience, especially when dealing with her three children. She would go from yelling at them to feeling guilty and overindulging them. She reported that at home she was having problems staying on task and apparently had developed a system by which she had several things going on at the same time. She went on to explain that this is her way of getting things finished; she would jump from one task to the next, and eventually something would be accomplished. She reported having excessive internal energy but lacked the focus and direction necessary to use it efficiently.

Over the years, the patient turned to drinking alcohol as her way to calm herself. She recognized that she had not acted responsibly by turning to alcohol, especially when interacting with her children. However, she insisted that it was quite effective in calming her "nerves." Over the last year or so she had attended Alcoholics Anonymous (AA) meetings to stop drinking. However, in subsequent sessions, it was noted that the patient had been drinking.

The patient reported that the memory of her childhood years are was blurred, but she did remember struggling in high school. She went on to explain that she had received average grades although she always had the habit of passing in assignments late. She reported that she tended to daydream in the classroom and then remembered that she was always the last to finish a test during her grade school years. This kind of memory seemed to come forth suddenly, and it also seemed to be associated with intense emotions. She explained how much she had felt embarrassed by being the last to finish.

A collateral interview was conducted with the patient's husband. He reported that the patient could not manage time well and gave examples of his wife being late and always in a rush. He went on to explain that she had problems with long-term planning and often did not fully appreciate the long-term consequences of her actions. Her choice to use alcohol as a way of calming herself was presented as an example. According to the patient's husband, her alcohol consumption was far more excessive than she initially reported, and there had been some physical symptoms that eventually led her to seek help.

Regarding the marriage, the patient's husband reported that he was at the threshold of asking for a separation. Particular attention was given to the patient's capacity to manage the children. Her husband recognized that she loved the children but that she was totally inconsistent and often irrational in regard to proper discipline. He insisted that the problem was constant and not related to her menstrual cycle, although there were times in the past few years when her impulsivity and lack of patience became too intense to manage around the time of her menses. The impression given was that there was a cyclical change for the worse, but the typical behaviors were still abnormal.

The patient's total ADSA score was one of the highest recorded. She endorsed numerous items related to ADHD behaviors, such as "I get restless easily," "I tend to daydream," "I easily lose interest in tasks," and "Tasks which need persistence frustrate me." Almost all of the items on the two major subscales of the ADSA, which reflect inattention and impulsivity, were endorsed by the patient. By contrast, she performed reasonably well on the GDS distractibility task. In both the number of correct responses and the number of commissions, the patient scored very close to the average for adults. However, behavioral observations during this testing seemed quite significant. She began to feel excessive agitation and stated at the end of the task that she was finished for the day. It was clear that it took everything she had to stay focused. Although other tests were scheduled, the patient went home as soon as she finished the GDS.

Results from the patient's projective profile were suggestive of someone who has feelings of desperation. Depression and anxiety seemed to be the most prominent symptoms. The impression was that of a woman who has a very negative view of herself, and this may lead to some distortions in interpretations. Even neutral comments about her may sometimes be perceived as being critical and harsh. The patient came across as being hypersensitive and unable to control her emotions. Pathological personality features were certainly suggested.

A diagnosis of ADHD was made with the recommendation to help the patient find some relief through a trial of stimulant medication. Although antidepressants were considered and certainly not ruled out, it was decided that she needed a fast-acting medication that could provide her with some hope that her problems can be managed.

ADHD, Learning Disabilities, Drug Abuse, Temperament Problems, and Possible Adjustment to Neurogenic Anomalies

This patient is a man in his mid-40s who was referred for evaluation by his physician because of suspected ADHD. At the time of the interview, he had separated from his wife, and he described himself as being emotionally in crisis.

A very long list of problem areas was presented in this case. The patient reported that he had suffered a mild stroke approximately 2 years prior to this evaluation. Brain scans found no major anomalies but did note a decreased attenuation adjacent to the anterior horn of the right lateral ventricle. It was described by the neurologist as not being of major consequence, considering no other abnormal findings. Other medical issues dealt with reported chest pains, but subsequent EKG studies were normal. Reports indicated that the patient's chest pains were not due to cardiac conditions, and the reported complaints were considered to be related to stress.

The patient's history included the use of cocaine, but he insisted that he had stopped this practice on his own more than 5 years ago. A history of multiple maladjustments was clearly presented, and it dated back to his childhood years. He reported that in school he had not been able to express himself verbally as well as the other children. Some ADHD-related symptoms were reported during his early childhood years; they included a tendency to procrastinate and difficulty in following directions because of a lack of proper concentration and attention. Problems were noted the most in areas where he had to perform, either on tests or in school projects. He noted that the work was often sloppy and not a good representation of his knowledge. The patient did excel in the creative arts and even secured a scholarship for college studies. However, he continued to struggle in college and eventually had to give it up altogether. He reported that he had problems passing the core curriculum because of ADHD kinds of problems. These included a lack of concentration to complete the readings, a tendency to daydream in lectures, and a lack of organization, mainly due to an inability to remember the details of day-to-day life.

An interview with the patient and an independent interview with his wife provided a rather long list of current symptoms. He reported that he was very forgetful and often lost things such as keys and important papers. He often overlooked errands that need attention, and he still had problems communicating verbally. Emotional difficulties included a self-proclaimed temper through which he would become angry and verbally assault others. This often was followed by a period of remorse. The patient also described himself as being a chronic worrier and reported that his constant anxious state kept him from enjoying life. Inner tensions were clearly noted during interview and, in fact, he seemed rather desperate to find answers to his problems. Part of this pressure came from his perception that his wife would dissolve the marriage unless problems were solved.

After a medical consult, it was decided that many of the patient's ADHD-related symptoms were not due to medical conditions. The best supportive evidence was that the symptoms were certainly present during the childhood years, long before signs of medical problems emerged. The effects of a lifestyle with drugs were considered major factors, however. It was difficult to tease out ADHD-related symptoms from symptoms that reflected emotional difficulties. Also, it seemed that the patient had to deal with a learning disability that had never been diagnosed and addressed during his early school years.

In spite of all of the problems, it is important to note that the patient had done well for himself working as a very creative artist. However, the patient did describe a dilemma in which the free style of living associated with his creative duties cost him because of a lack of structure and organization necessary for a stable domestic life.

The first focus of testing was on the patient's intellectual profile. His Full Scale IQ fell within the average range and, ironically, he scored higher on the Verbal subtest than he did on the Performance subtest. At a closer look, however, some struggles were noted on verbal subtests requiring abstract thinking and logical judgments. Even relatively simple logical questions were difficult for him.

There was a difference between the GDS distractibility scores and the ADSA scores. The patient scored relatively well on the former. By contrast, he presented a profile on the ADSA that was indicative of numerous ADHD-related symptoms. The ADSA profile seemed to support historical reports and descriptions presented by his wife during collateral interview. To a lesser extent subscale scores on the ADSA also indicated emotional liabilities.

Projective analysis also supported the theme of multiple psychological difficulties. The MMPI-2 and Rorschach results were suggestive of an individual who had been depressed for much of his life and at risk of suicide. There were also some strong suspicions that the patient has been plagued by anxieties and worries for so long that he now accepted them as part of his identity. In a very unhealthy way the patient's emotional problems have had a secondary purpose in that they validated him. At the very least, there were signs that his maladaptive tendencies had stabilized and become imbedded in his personality.

Putting the historical pieces together in a meaningful sequence was difficult, but it was determined that ADHD and perhaps some verbal limitations set this patient toward maladaptive functioning. It was also determined that this patient needed special emotional support and psychological interventions immediately. Thus, it seemed more prudent to address the ADHD issues after the acute emotional problems received appropriate attention, especially considering the risk of suicide.

UNDETERMINED DIAGNOSES

The cases presented below represent the most difficult to diagnose. The data on these cases usually provide some evidence that attention problems exist, but there is not evidence to completely rule out alternative explanations confidently. The major difficulties in arriving at a definitive diagnosis stem from the fact that multiple disorders exist in these cases.

These cases represent the greatest challenge to practitioners willing to work with adult ADHD patients. Unlike in the child population, the multilayer of pathologies that can accumulate over the years can cloud the clinical picture. In all of these cases, a diagnosis of ADHD was deferred. However, it is extremely important to understand that a lack of a definitive diagnosis does not necessarily paralyze the practitioner in terms of providing appropriate interventions and recommendations. In many of these cases the needs of the patient dictated that some intervention action take place and, given the multiple problems presented, it is certainly advised to not wait until definitive diagnostic conclusions are made.

ADHD, Multiple Disorders, or Both?

This patient was a man in his late 30s who originally referred both of his children for intervention. These children were previously diagnosed as having ADHD by a pediatrician and were placed on stimulant medication. They continued to have behavioral problems, which included academic failures. Their father was convinced that they both suffered from ADHD and severe learning problems, in spite of some doubts based on objective data that did not support presented themes.

After attending a special local seminar on adult ADHD, the patient decided to refer himself for testing. The patient described himself as a recovering alcoholic who attended AA meetings regularly. He also reported that he had been depressed throughout most of his life and that he had experimented with street drugs to self-medicate.

In addition to these problems, after the adult ADHD presentation the patient began to recognize problems in his everyday life that could be attributed to ADHD. He reported seeing his life as being totally disorganized and unfulfilled. Although he saw himself as a reasonably bright man, he could never do well in school, and he had problems following through with even simple tasks. By the time the initial interview ended, this patient endorsed every symptom related to ADHD. It was noteworthy, however, that the most prominent symptom reported was a sense of inadequacy.

The patient's history included physical abuse by his biological father and later by his stepfather. He dropped out of school before finishing tenth grade and entered a pattern of moving from one job to another. Most of the time, he did not last more than 6 months, and he was repeatedly released because of poor performance. He did complete military service but was discharged for medical reasons. His interpersonal life was also somewhat checkered as he moved from one relationship to the next very quickly. At the time of this evaluation, he was divorced and unemployed. Although still young, he reported that he felt as though he had the body of a much older man and had declared himself disabled. In fact, he was in the process of applying for Social Security disability.

A brief intellectual assessment was conducted, and the patient scored in the low average range of intelligence. Verbal scores were somewhat higher than nonverbal scores, but the difference was not statistically significant. A series of memory tasks was administered, and patterns presented were somewhat typical of an individual who has had a long history of alcohol abuse. A forced-choice memory task was also included in this assessment to check for possible issues of malingering; none were indicated.

The validity configuration of the MMPI-2 was suggestive of someone who either exaggerated problems or was crying for help. He had a very high F scale score (T score of 90) combined with low scores on the Lie and K scales. Not surprisingly, all of the clinical scales were elevated, and the Schizophrenia scale headed the list. Likewise, high T scores were noted across all of the ADSA subscales. Some time was spent looking at the items of this instrument that are reverse scored, and it was interesting to note that he scored lower on those items.

On the GDS distractibility task the patient scored a total of 36 out of a possible 60; this was certainly well below the average range. In addition, he had 25 total commissions, which usually indicates impulsivity. Thirteen of these commissions took place by responding to the machine before the designated sequence was complete. Behaviorally, it was noteworthy that the patient complained that the flashing digits were moving along too fast. He genuinely seemed overwhelmed by this task, although he did not seem concerned about his performance. At the time, a notation was made that he may not expect much out of himself.

There seemed to be enough clinical and projective evidence to describe this patient as being alcohol dependent and significantly depressed. However, in spite of data indicating that he may have ADHD, there were still some questions regarding his motivation for such a diagnosis. Certainly, the high F score on the MMPI-2 along with the relatively low scores on the reversed items of the ADSA raised some questions. Perhaps the most suspicious evidence was observed in the beginning interview, when it was believed that he had been highly influenced by the local ADHD presentation. Certainly, there were some concerns raised when he endorsed all of the textbook symptoms.

As time passed, however, there were numerous observations to indicate a personality who lacked organization and consistency. He would often come late to his appointments or not show up at all. This behavioral pattern was also seen in other circumstances, even those that may be financially advantageous to him. For instance, he was once offered the opportunity to receive free transportation but missed this opportunity because of his own neglect. Of course, it was not known if this pattern was due to problems with attention or to self-defeating personality traits.

ADHD or Obsessive–Compulsive Disorder/Anxiety?

This patient was a woman in her mid-30s who presented for evaluation because one of her children had recently been diagnosed as having ADHD and she began to suspect that she had the same problem. She was referred through several therapists; apparently, she spent some time interviewing professionals within the area before coming for an official evaluation. Right from the first interview interactions, it was apparent that this patient was very bright and very well read. She described herself as acting on impulse much of her life, but her method of choosing the evaluator, along with several examples of how she thoroughly investigates situations before acting, did not support her impression of herself as being impulsive. When this was reflected back to her, she became annoyed and somewhat irritated.

The patient's history was rather impressive, with a number of major accomplishments. She had completed college and successfully completed two master's programs. At the time of the evaluation, she owned her own business and, although her business was still in the building stage, major successes had already been achieved.

In spite of a very industrious history, the patient described herself as someone who is prone to procrastinate. She went on to explain that she was often overwhelmed by all of the responsibilities in her life, and it takes everything she has to not let things go. She went on to explain that she had had periods in her life when she had become behaviorally paralyzed and had to give up some of her duties. It was later noted that these episodes were few in number, the time periods were short, and the consequences were relatively minor. In fact, during a subsequent therapy session, it was suggested to her that these periods of procrastination may actually be functional because they were her way of regrouping and recharging her batteries. Unfortunately, this was not accepted by her.

At any rate, there seemed to be a pattern in which her interpretation of ADHD symptoms was not matched by her presented history. In fact, the exact opposite theme seemed to be more accurate. Still, other symptoms were presented, and they were supported by independent collateral interview. These included a tendency to become distracted. The patient's husband confirmed that unexpected events during the day could easily derail her from completing her tasks. Also, she seemed to have classical problems paying attention to information she received verbally. Multiple directions were difficult for her to follow, and her mind tended to wander in the middle of conversations. During the initial interview, the patient talked very quickly and expressed an urgency that she may forget all the things she had to say if she did not get them out quickly enough. Both the patient and her husband reported that she tended to become forgetful. However, she seemed to compensate for this problem by making special efforts to write things down or asking others to remind her. The patient's husband was often used as someone who would remind her of specific errands throughout the day.

Emotionally, it was clear that this patient maintained a high level of anxiety and tension. She admitted that she was often worried about one thing or another and that this sometimes predisposed her to having a quick temper. She was certainly frustrated and perhaps angry that she could not live her life as smoothly as others seem to do. On the other hand, her standards seemed to be quite high; errors that usually are tolerable for the average person would most likely frustrate and perhaps anger her. There were impressions that she had high demands for herself and, in turn, may have high demands of others. It was interesting to note that she made it a point to communicate that she had researched extensively before choosing the evaluator and that she would tolerate nothing less than infallible results.

The patient's childhood history was certainly indicative of ADHD. Not surprisingly, she reported getting A's and B's in school. However, she also reported that she had had to work harder than the other children to keep pace. This included spending 2–3 hours per night with her studies. She remembered that much of that time was wasted as she kept finding herself off task because of external distractions. She also noted that many of her poor grades were due to misdirections or inefficient use of time. For instance, she remembered studying excessively for a social studies test and failing the test because she spent so much time with one essay question that she could not finish most of the other questions. Similar problems were also reported outside of her academic life. The intensity noted during the initial interview seemed to have existed during her childhood years. The patient admitted that she had problems developing and maintaining friendship ties due to her high demands and angry moods.

On the ADSA profile, her total score was between three and four standard deviations beyond the mean. However, she scored the highest on the Interpersonal and Emotive subscales. The classical Attention-Focus/Concentration and Behavior-Disorganized Activities also were elevated, but to a lesser degree. The overall profile is that of someone who may have attention deficit, but it was difficult to rule out the alternative theme that many of her attending problems are due to emotional dispositions.

The GDS distractibility scores were not very helpful. The patient scored correctly 50 out of 60 possible times and made only 4 commissions. Both of these scores were within the normal range. However, it must be kept in mind that many ADHD patients, especially those who are relatively bright, do well on continuous-performance tasks as well as other neurological tasks.

Projective findings were certainly reflective of emotional problems. The MMPI-2 profile was considered significant, and multiple problems were noted. Rather classical signs of obsessive–compulsive disorder were suggested. Also, other nonstandardized tests suggested that this patient actively defended against inner feelings of insecurity or inadequacy. She may have been driven to achieve to compensate for these inner feelings of inferiority. Both the MMPI-2 as well as other projective indicators were suggestive of someone who tends to distort reality. The unrealistic expectations first noted during interview seemed to be supported by test findings. Although the Schizophrenia scale of the MMPI-2 was elevated, the Harris Lingoe breakdown of this scale, as well other indicators, was suggestive of someone who was not psychotic. She was best described as someone who often engages in irrational thinking and perhaps ruminates and becomes self-absorbed without exercising proper reality checks. This may very well be indicative of someone who has not paid attention adequately to the outside world.

Finally, there were other projective signs to suggest a personality who indeed is angry and perhaps overly controlling. In spite of her obvious capacity to achieve, the patient was not considered to be a very happy person. Unfortunately, the personality style projected was that of someone who sees psychological problems as a sign of weakness, something that cannot possibly be tolerated. Emotionally, this patient was somewhat reminiscent of a defiant adolescent who may see authority figures as being threatening and may be hypersensitive to criticism.

This case was difficult, because it was uncertain if the personality traits developed secondary to ADHD symptoms. Certainly, the patient presented a childhood history that would seem to suggest ADHD; it was unfortunate that no collateral interview regarding the patient's childhood was available. Follow-up with respect to ADHD was allowed by the patient, but she was not interested in addressing any other emotional issues. She hypothesized that taking care of the attention-related problems would automatically rectify any other psychological problems. This hypothesis was unrealistic, but it was not challenged because it would have been futile to do so.

ADHD or Temperament Problems?

This patient is a man in his early 20s who was referred for evaluation and intervention by his family physician. The patient's parents encouraged him to seek help. At the time of the evaluation, the patient was newly married and had a very young infant. Although he was living away from his parents, they provided much financial support.

The patient presented a long history of behavioral problems that could classically be described as ADHD symptoms. These included an inability to follow through with tasks, a tendency to become distracted easily, and a lack of energy to start projects that usually take some time to accomplish. The patient labeled his problem procrastination, and he gave examples of projects such as putting a resume together, painting the trim of his parents' house, and cleaning out the garage. The most consistent and troublesome problem was the patient's inability to get along with others. He would become angry when things did not go his way and often would get into conflicts with schoolmates. On reflection, the patient admitted that he had never really had friends in school. This problem with anger continued to present problems as he entered his adult years. He candidly reported that he had never had a job lasting more than 6 or 8 weeks. Usually, he would have problems with his supervisor, coworkers, or both. He reported that, rather than becoming physical, he thought it best to just simply quit the job. Although his parents maintained him financially, he did recognize that this is not a healthy pattern, especially with a wife and new child.

An independent collateral interview was conducted with the patient's parents that included a developmental history. Developmental milestones were reached within normal limits, but it was interesting to note that the patient did not sleep through the night until he was 4 years old. As a toddler he was prone to ear infections that included fevers of 104° or higher. Overall, however, he was considered a healthy child, and no other health problems were presented throughout any of the historical data collected.

The patient's parents reported that he did pass every grade but managed only to squeeze by with C's and D's. He was tested by the school system twice because of suspected learning disabilities, but none were found.

On the basis of parental report, there were suspicions that the patient may have been socially immature. Specifically, it seems that he did not have the skills necessary to make the appropriate social connections, and his parents reported that he was "picked on" as a young child. This included being singled out by the entire class and teased to the point of physical harassment. As time passed, the patient became more and more aggressive, and the parents concluded that he must have been very frustrated and acted out angrily to rebel against mistreatment. However, they also reported that he had always had a temper and was easily frustrated when things did not go his way.

The patient did not like the idea of going through psychological testing. He made some comments about being "poked at," and he had clear apprehensions regarding the entire process. It was interesting to note that he went ahead with the testing when told that he was an adult and, regardless of the wishes of his parents (and perhaps his wife), the final decision would be his. In spite of his negative attitude toward testing, it seemed he recognized problems, and there was a part of him that was eager to find answers.

The WAIS-R was administered to look at subtest patterns. Also, although no learning disabilities were indicated by previous school testing—the state in which the testing was conducted requires a difference between IQ and achievement greater than or equal to two standard deviations—significant intellectual patterns have often been discounted by the school system because the scores did not meet the two-standard-deviation criterion. All of the patient's IQ scores fell within the average range of intellectual functioning, and there was no significant difference between verbal and performance IQ scores. The subtest patterns did not suggest any major problems with learning as the scatter was still within normal limits. However, it was noteworthy that the classical third-factor subtest scores were at the lower end (Digit Span, Arithmetic, and Digit Symbol for adults). Also, the patient scored lower in Comprehension and Picture Arrangement, tests usually associated with social judgment and general social awareness. By contrast, the patient's highest scores were in Similarities and Block Design. The spread between high and low scores was no more than 5 points; considering the history, however, the patterns seem to be worth noting clinically.

The ADSA total score was elevated, but mildly so. A breakdown of the subtest scores suggested that the patient may have had more acute problems earlier in his life (his highest scores were on Childhood and Academic Theme), but he also had a high score on the Attention-Focus/Concentration subscale. By contrast, scores on the Interpersonal and Emotive subscales were within the average range. This pattern of average scores was also reflected on his MMPI-2 profile. The validity configuration as well as clinical scales all yielded scores within the average range. Perhaps this is reflective of the patient's view that he did not have major problems. It was important to keep in mind that he went ahead with this evaluation on the insistence of others.

All of the GDS distractibility scores fell within the average range. In this case, this test was administered to help with the diagnosis only if scores were beyond the average range. The test is good in ruling in favor of ADHD if scores are positive. However, the high frequency of false negatives prevented any definitive conclusion from being drawn on the basis of his average scores.

It was clear that the problems described were real. The intensity of the patient's personality could not be dismissed, especially with reports that he did not start sleeping through the night until he was 4 years old. Therefore, temperamental issues were considered. However, there were also some cognitive issues regarding social development. Specifically, the patient had a long history of weak social skills, which cost him in peer relations earlier in his life and in coworker–employer relations later in his life. History also was indicative of ADHD symptoms. However, neither history nor test results were conclusive.

It was decided to begin psychotherapeutic interventions and to use the time week by week to monitor and keep an open mind regarding diagnoses. What was learned was how much control the patient's parents had over the patient and how much he was struggling to gain independence. Although in his 20s, married, and with a baby, many of the issues were reminiscent of adolescent development. With respect to his need for independence, there was a therapeutic shift away from family engagement. Less time was spent with family members and the patient, and more time was spent in individual sessions. Family issues remained quite prominent in discussion; however, as the patient felt freer to express himself and gain insight into the dynamics of his growing years and present family situation, focus shifted toward future plans independent of life with his parents.

Eventually, the patient terminated therapy on his own. Although there were numerous issues that would ideally be best discussed in a therapeutic setting, some major positive changes were worth noting. First, the patient was making some long-term plans for his life and his immediate family; as he noted himself, this was the first time in his life that he addressed long-term plans and consequences. Second, and perhaps most important, he made a decision to join the military. Although he reported that his parents were against this move, he concluded that it would be the best way to make a break. He correctly assessed the financial leverage his parents had over him and decided that he was not strong enough to resist the temptation offered by his parents. The patient was also very much aware of his wandering lifestyle, going from job to job, and decided that the structure of the military might provide the external reinforcers necessary to settle down and maintain a consistent positive direction. In fact, he was thinking of continuing on with his education through the military programs available.

To date, it is still uncertain if a diagnosis of ADHD fits this case, or what the correct diagnostic mixture is. However, although no definitive diagnostic conclusion was made, positive changes seemed to take place.

CONCLUSIONS

In the conclusions of the previous chapter, future study of the proposed diagnostic process was suggested. Specifically, empirical support for the diagnostic process could possibly be achieved by a stepwise statistical procedure that can weigh the individual phases of the diagnostic process with respect to how much between-group (ADHD and non-ADHD) variance is explained. Meanwhile, patients will continue to ask for assistance, and it is hoped that the gaps of empirical proof are filled with sound clinical judgments. This chapter was specifically written to share some of the most difficult clinical judgments with respect to the diagnosis of ADHD. For the pure empiricist, these case studies may appear to be quite messy. However, it is hoped that the general practitioner can find the discussions of these case studies useful, especially when dealing with the most difficult diagnostic situations.

These cases come from a single private-practice setting that attends to a variety of psychological problems, in addition to ADHD. Consequently, many of the ADHD patients originally presented other problems and, in turn, many patients who were eventually not diagnosed as having ADHD originally presented problems related to ADHD. Although the diagnostic process outlined in the previous chapter was used in all of these patients, each patient presented very unique features and needed special individual attention, aside from the mechanics of the diagnostic process.

One of the major themes is the vast variety of individual circumstances and lifestyles among ADHD patients. Although, as stated earlier in this chapter, most of the patients tend to come from middle-class or working-class backgrounds, and it has been recognized that a vast patient pool of ADHD patients—prison population, homeless people, and so on—may have been untapped because of the self-selection processes of a typical private practice, it is still amazing how individual and different ADHD patients can be.

For practical purposes, most of the cases in this chapter dealt with very challenging complexities. They were selected on purpose, because the aim was to share with the reader the clinical thought process involved in coming to a diagnostic conclusion. In most of these difficult cases, the thought process did not eliminate all of the uncertainty. In fact, most of the cases were selected for this chapter because much uncertainty remained. Consequently, decisions and directions presented in these case studies were not intended to be received as "the absolute correct" choices without any other reasonable alternatives. They were simply presented the way a colleague would share information about a particularly difficult case to increase awareness and activate thinking toward more refined clinical judgments.

REFERENCES

American Psychiatric Association. (1994). *Diagnostic and statistical manual of mental disorders* (4th ed.). Washington, DC: Author.

Exner, J. E., Jr. (1986). *The Rorschach: A comprehensive system. Volume 1: Basic foundations* (2nd ed.). New York: Wiley.

Gordon, M. (1993). *The Gordon Diagnostic System.* DeWitt, NY: Gordon Systems.

Hathaway, S. R., & McKinley, J. C. (1989). *Minnesota Multiphasic Personality Inventory–2* (MMPI-2). Minneapolis: University of Minnesota Press.

Lavenstein, B. (1995). Neurological comorbidity patterns/differential diagnosis in adult attention deficit disorder. In K. G. Nadeau (Ed.), *A comprehensive guide to attention deficit disorder in adults: Research, diagnosis, and treatment.* (pp. 74–93). New York: Brunner/Mazel.

Murray, H. A. (1943). *Thematic Apperception Test: Manual.* Cambridge, MA: Harvard University Press.

Nadeau, K. G. (1995). *A comprehensive guide to attention-deficit disorder in adults: Research, diagnosis, and treatment.* New York: Brunner/Mazel.

Triolo, S. J., & Murphy, K. R. (1996). *Attention-Deficit Scales for Adults (ADSA) manual for scoring and interpretation.* New York: Brunner/Mazel.

Tzelepis, A., Schubiner, H., & Warbasse, L. H. (1995). Differential diagnosis and psychiatric comorbidity patterns in adult attention deficit disorder. In K. G. Nadeau (Ed.), *A comprehensive guide to attention deficit disorder in adults: Research, diagnosis and treatment* (pp. 35–57). New York: Brunner/Mazel.

Wechsler, D. (1981). *WAIS-R manual: Wechsler Adult Intelligence Scale–Revised.* San Antonio, TX: The Psychological Corporation.

Chapter 6

Psychotherapeutic Treatment
of ADHD Adults

With an increase in the popularity of a particular subject matter, an abundance of written material is provided to the practitioner with respect to treatment. In this area of study, however, much scientific investigation is still needed. Consequently, most of what is written is not supported by rigorous scientific testing. The clinician is therefore advised to be cautious of communicated information.

To date, there has been no controlled—or even semicontrolled—study to demonstrate the benefits of psychotherapeutic interventions in treating ADHD adults. There are, however, numerous well-respected authors (e.g., Murphy & LeVert, 1995; Nadeau, 1995; Solden, 1995; G. Weiss & Hechtman, 1993) who have written extensively on the multiple benefits of psychotherapeutic interventions. Even Wender (1995), who does not see much benefit in treating the symptoms of ADHD with psychotherapeutic interventions, believes that psychotherapeutic treatments can be quite useful in the management of secondary symptoms such as low self-esteem, relationship problems, and so on. Perhaps the strongest evidence of psychotherapeutic benefits was provided by G. Weiss and Hechtman (1993) in their prospective reports of hyperactive adults managing their lives through their growing and young adulthood years. In fact, reports from the patients themselves indicated that they wished for even more psychotherapeutic involvement than they had received. The authors reported that "they would have liked to have had available when needed: adequate remedial education; tutoring; cognitive therapy (some had this therapy for some months); individual psychotherapy; and family counseling" (p. 300).

G. Weiss and Hechtman (1993) went on to add that a multimodality type of therapy for the adult hyperactives in their study seemed to have been helpful, considering that they had a condition that has so many multiple associated deficits. G. Weiss and Hechtman's extensive work basically stands alone in providing a 15- and 20-year prospective study of hyperactive children growing into adulthood. Although the research lacks the more rigorous control measures, some control conditions were implemented for comparative purposes, and this provides invaluable insights into the progress of hyperactive children as they grow into adulthood.

The overall impression regarding treatment is that medication is effective in providing relief of ADHD symptoms and that it has an advantage in its ability to deliver acute remedy. However, long-term maintenance and sensitivity to changing environments throughout the patient's life require psychotherapeutic forms of treatment (Weiss & Hechtman, 1993). It is interesting to note that findings of emotional struggles, both within the hyperactive subjects and within the families, persisted throughout the years and, in some cases, deterioration in functioning took place. This finding has greater meaning when one considers the subject pool. This sample of hyperactive subjects has certainly received more attention throughout the years of testing and retesting than most other ADHD individuals have. It may be reasonable to theorize, therefore, that most ADHD individuals and their families have a most difficult time coping with this chronic condition and associated disability features.

PSYCHOTHERAPEUTIC PRINCIPLES

Individual Differences

Magic Moment

Maybe looking out a window
will evoke a magic moment
my mist shrouded mind will clear
and I think I hear the call of the wind
and I am not there
but near.
I am on top of a rocky pinnacle
facing a fire lit dawn
looking down on breezy plains
and something ageless will stir within,
I am light and filled with light
all the mysteries have been solved
and I feel as if I shall take flight
as the hawk soars above.
And as I sit
staring out of the window,
I long to be on horseback
and feel his muscles ripple
as we surge away in salty air.
Sitting here

in such sweet torture
aching to answer the call,
to run, to fly, to leap,
to dance, to love . . .
I'm held there spellbound
knowing that
the mystic beaconing
of the wind
is just a parting of dust in my mind
that reveals to me
the wonder, the ecstasy,
the splendor of life.
I sip my coffee
and resume my staring.
In those rare magic moments
when I hear the wind call,
I know that every tear
I ever spent is worth it all.

The Knowledge of MANKIND . . .
or the lack of!!!

I've traveled many places
I've met many things
I've met many people
still none know human beings
many were so peaceful
others more discreet
some were out of control
most seem elite
some were so harsh
yet, more were kind
numerous had religion
still so many appear blind
I can feel their emotions
some most profound
some unsettled as the ocean
others firm as solid ground
it's such a strange manage
I do not understand
I do not seem to get it
I just may need a hand
to grasp hold the concepts
of the human mind
and to truly believe in
what's known as . . . MANKIND!!!!

The first poem was presented by a female patient in her mid-30s with multiple diagnoses of ADHD, drug abuse, chronic depression, and personality–borderline and histrionic–defects. She tested well above average in intelligence yet presented with rather classic struggles leading to unfulfilled potentials. During her treatment she was still struggling to complete college. Academically, she performed well, but she struggled, going from one major to the next, and she often dropped out of classes because she felt overwhelmed and stressed. True to form of borderline features, she had very intense relationships that seemed to drain her emotionally rather than provide lasting fulfillment. Resolutions to interpersonal problems, as well as life stressors, were always products of impulsive decisions and emotional irrationalities. She was often trapped between the two extremes of feeling intense dependence and attachment and having feelings of anger and disengagement. Regardless of mood, there was often a sense of emptiness in her life.

The second poem was written by a man in his early 20s who was diagnosed with ADHD during his middle childhood years. He had a history of being emotionally and physically abused by his father, who may have been hyperactive himself and treated his dysfunction by abusing alcohol. As a child, he was also diagnosed as having leukemia and, although he was currently in remission, the trauma of his treatment experiences lingered. His ADHD symptoms included kinetic disorganization and procrastination. He had much difficulty getting started with the day-to-day responsibilities of life. This had been so much of a problem that he has yet to graduate from high school, although he is now on track to do so. Along with his high intelligence, this young man's capacity for intimacy is considered a major strength. Emotional involvements run deep, and he is often seen by those around him as a true, loyal friend. In fact, he may prefer to help others rather than help himself. Family ties are conflictual but strong. Regardless of the problems, there is always a sense of commitment, which is a healthy source of much strength.

These two cases are presented to bring across two main points. First, it is important to fully appreciate the vast variability among individuals with ADHD. Although they have similar symptoms of ADHD, they often come from different backgrounds, and sometimes they share nothing but their ADHD diagnosis. Thus, the psychotherapeutic intervention must adjust to the particular needs of each ADHD patient. Second, it is important to keep in mind that psychotherapeutic efforts need to be holistic in nature. It would be a major error to focus on the ADHD symptoms without considering the entire personality. In some cases, the primary problems may be pathological personality features that are now somewhat independent from the ADHD symptoms. In other cases, interpersonal ego strengths and other external resources (family, community, etc.) are extremely helpful in helping to address the ADHD symptoms. Thus, not only is each patient different with respect to interpersonal features, but differences exist with respect to the milieu of each patient. It is always important to move beyond the ADHD symptoms, because the patient's life as a whole must be considered.

Systemic Conditions

It is important to keep in mind that ADHD is a neurobiological condition that presents itself as being problematic when the patient interacts with the environment. Consequently, environmental factors should be a consideration in psychotherapy. Whenever possible, for instance, it is often beneficial if the patient's significant other is included in treatment. Therapists who have background in systemic forms of interventions may have an advantage. Barkley, Guevremont, Anastopoulos, and Fletcher (1992) demonstrated positive outcomes of family therapy programs directed toward treating families with ADHD adolescents. Similar sensitivity to adult ADHD patients has been suggested by other authors (e.g., Hallowell & Ratey, 1994; Murphy & LeVert, 1995; G. Weiss & Hechtman, 1993). Certainly, considering that ADHD runs in families (Barkley, 1990), it is quite possible that more than one member of the household is afflicted, and therapy issues would certainly include interpersonal issues within family members.

Also, experience has dictated that many of the most efficient intervention strategies can be implemented with the support of the patient's significant other. A systemic approach to presenting problems can help facilitate such efficiency. This often entails a wider scope of analyses into personalities, the structures they have interpersonally, and the range of interactions in the community (i.e., church activities, social clubs, etc.). Perhaps the most successful case was that of a previously described young man who, consciously or unconsciously, fell in love with a woman who did not mind dealing with the tedious day-to-day details of life. This young man did well for himself as an entrepreneur. He stayed active, working long hours to build his own business, and left all of the detail work to his wife, who coincidentally enjoyed attending to the schedules and other details of the business. The coordination between husband and wife and the apparent matching that took place prior to any professional intervention earned the respect of the therapist and spoke volumes regarding issues of inner strength and human capacities to adapt and adjust. Insights into the system in which the patient is embedded can help dictate and influence directions in psychotherapy. It can also provide insights into prognosis.

Interdisciplinary Perspective

It is always important to keep in mind that ADHD is a problem that affects numerous facets of the patient's life. Also, given its chronic nature, the changes in circumstances over the span of a person's life require special sensitivity. A multidisciplinary approach seems prudent. Perhaps the most common example is the use of medication to help patients with their symptoms. Psychotherapeutic processes are very slow and, as suggested in the earlier section, patients may not get on with the mechanics of changing their lives behaviorally until they settle some emotional issues. Meanwhile, medication treatment can be very effective in providing immediate relief of ADHD symptoms.

Other disciplines also can be involved. For instance, Quinn (1994) discussed the special needs of the college student with ADHD. It has been most helpful to refer to college counselors when patients think about going to college or wish some practical advice regarding career choices. Most colleges and universities have advisory offices in place for such purposes.

Thus, a good working relationship with professionals from other disciplines is highly recommended. The hope is that members of the community of professionals have mutual respect and some understanding of what other disciplines can offer. The best results seem to come when professionals from different disciplines are able to respectfully work in concert for the best interest of the patient. Without question, knowing that an entire support team is available makes a difference to a patient.

PROCESS IN PSYCHOTHERAPY

From Diagnosis to Psychotherapy

Murphy and LeVert (1995) suggested that therapy is initiated with the empowerment of knowledge that comes from the diagnostic evaluation. One could argue that therapy actually begins at first contact and that the diagnostic process itself is embedded in a healthy therapeutic atmosphere. Even patients who have their own therapist and were referred only for evaluation purposes should be treated with this same therapeutic perspective. For these referred patients, it is assumed that their psychotherapist trusts the diagnostician, and the assessment process is, in some way, part of a holistic path to a healthier life.

There are a few concrete markers, other than subtle communication given to the patient, that the diagnostician is working in partnership for the same goal as that of the therapist, in service of the patient. Ideally, when the patient is referred back to the psychotherapist, the diagnostic process, as well as the diagnosis itself, is viewed by the patient as a step further in achieving the therapeutic goals. With this theme in mind, all contact with patients, whether it is giving directions for a psychological test or listening to them describe the lifelong effects of presenting symptoms, are embedded in a therapeutic atmosphere.

The general rule of empowerment, according to Murphy and LeVert (1995), should involve the patient receiving feedback on all of the diagnostic findings as well as their interpretations. However, considering the therapeutic atmosphere, it is most important to be sensitive to the patient's disposition. Some of the most powerful emotional times experienced during a session take place when test results are first given to a patient. It is not uncommon for patients to become overwhelmed with emotions, and it makes sense to allow—or even give permission—the patient to express his or her intense feelings. The diagnostic impression may be the first time in the patient's life that inner beliefs and feelings have been validated. If patients in their histories have experienced severe negative feedback, such as being told they were stupid or bad, the validation of an alternative explanation for their past behaviors may very well result in a catharsis that can be totally overwhelming. It is certainly prudent at this juncture to not be so concerned about giving back all of the test details before the session is finished; two or three sessions may be needed before all the details of test results are addressed. Obviously, the role of a therapist is to be there in support and to continue to provide an atmosphere of comfort so that emotional expression continues.

A client-centered modality (Rogers, 1951) should be most prominent in the psychotherapist's mind. In plain terms, it is important to simply listen to the patient, even if the circumstances involve giving feedback on test results. This is a relatively simple rule, but it may be difficult to follow, especially when patients are in denial and may not be accepting of test findings. Rather than engage in argument, it is recommended that the therapist take the extra time necessary to understand the patient's perspective. It may very well be that the patient is not refuting the findings but has extensive concerns about the ADHD label. There may still be a distorted interpretation that includes images of twisted brains, going crazy, and rejection from mainstream life. None of these thoughts or feelings are likely to be expressed voluntarily. It is up to the psychotherapist to listen carefully, ask the appropriate questions, and empathize with the patient's needs. As suggested earlier, the most common worry seems to stem from descriptions such as " a chemical imbalance," which unfortunately brings forth science-fiction–like images. It must be kept in mind that ADHD patients can have vivid imaginations and may make associations that most others do not. One patient thought that this "chemical imbalance" can lead eventually to another, and then another; so how long would it be before everything falls apart? These types of interpretations will most likely remain secret, and it is up to the psychotherapist to provide the atmosphere and then the opportunity for disclosure of these silent worries.

Solden (1995) described a grief cycle in which denial is part of a normative process expected of all patients, or at least the women that she treats. Although this may not be universal, it is certainly important to attend to denial issues. Even among the more educated and accepting patients, it is a difficult task to receive and accept a diagnosis of a dysfunction that has no known cure. It is sometimes quite obvious to see that patients' intellectual acceptance may not be matched by their emotions. Moving on to the more intellectual task of addressing the symptoms, without taking care of the emotional issues inside, may compromise prognosis. For many patients, it is most important to communicate that, although there is no cure, it is reasonable to expect very positive results from treatment and that it is equally reasonable to expect that treatment will improve in the future as scientific knowledge accumulates.

From Client-Centered to Cognitive Strategies

The therapeutic techniques implemented should change with respect to the changing needs of the patient. As a general rule, patients have initially responded well to client-centered modalities and, when a good trusting relationship has been established, there is a gradual move toward the more directive therapies with the use of cognitive strategies. Again, latitude must be considered for the variations encountered in therapy, but this general sequence seems to be most effective.

After a diagnosis is made, it is important to consider the numerous bits of information that the patient must digest. It is important at this stage to be very supportive and responsive to the individual needs of the patient. Thus, in a very Rogerian style (Rogers, 1951), it may be important to allow the patient to express feelings and attitudes. Even in some cases when patients are demanding some specific recommendations in a way to "get on with it," it is important to understand that they may be simply working through some inner emotional turmoils. At times, one or two directions are given, but that may be enough to trigger other emotional facets. Obviously, at that point, the client-centered style comes into play again.

As the adjustment to the diagnosis and other needs dealing with the interpersonal processes settle, patients may be open to the kinds of directive information that can help them cope and manage ADHD symptoms. At this point, they may be more open to the cognitive techniques used to make day-to-day changes in life. The popular literature is saturated with numerous behavioral and cognitive management techniques to help the ADHD adult. For instance, Hallowell and Ratey (1994) provided "Fifty Tips on the Management of Adult Attention Deficit Disorder" (pp. 245–253). They covered everything from strategies to being a better parent, to the use of humor, to help deal with potentially stressful situations. Other authors have covered a rather extensive variety of potentially difficult situations—everything from coping strategies for a college student (Quinn, 1994) to mechanical strategies to overcome the demands of day-to-day life (Murphy & LeVert, 1995; Solden, 1995; L. Weiss, 1992).

Caution is advised to the user of these publications. There are innumerable behavioral strategies to help ADHD adults cope, but there are no guarantees that they can significantly change patients' lives. To date, no control study exists that has measured the effects of these suggestions found in the popular literature on ADHD adults. Consequently, it is recommended that the therapist spend some time with the ADHD patient to make some comments and judgments regarding the different behavioral strategies published. A spirit of experimentation is sometimes helpful with the communication to the patient that these are things that can be tried just to see if they are helpful. Certainly, the patient is in command and can disregard suggestions that do not seem to be very practical. This advice may seem obvious, but the patient may need explicit permission to disregard anything suggested by the "experts."

From a strictly clinical perspective, implemented cognitive strategies are conceptualized into two components. The first is based on internal thought processes. The second is external and deals with behavioral techniques and environmental structures. Murphy and LeVert (1995) provided helpful insights into the cognitive preparations necessary to help ADHD patients. They discussed extensively the need to prepare the "self" for success. The aim is to identify and change negative thought processes that could get in the way or even sabotage positive changes. On the basis of clinical observations, many ADHD adults need to work through old self-damaging scripts. The aim is to achieve the personal inner balance and harmony necessary to eventually reach a position of self-acceptance and an inner sense of self-worth (see **Self-Esteem** section).

This cognitive shift is necessary to tackle some of the behavioral components of ADHD. Murphy and LeVert (1995) described it as the "the first step toward taking control" (p. 142) in their chapter entitled "Taming the Organizational Devil" (an interesting choice of words).

The second component deals with the actual mechanics of managing day-to-day life. As stated earlier, there are numerous behavioral strategies offered in the popular literature, and it is difficult to know how successful these strategies are with respect to improving the lives of ADHD individuals. However, in clinical practice there are a number of behavioral strategies that have been helpful to ADHD patients. Likewise, there have been many that have not been very useful; in fact, even some very popular strategies found in the literature have been found to be counterproductive.

For many patients, it has been helpful to break down major projects into smaller ones. Helping patients divide and conquer seems to work best when a self-reward system is built in. ADHD patients do not delay gratification as well as others. Thus, the grand reward (e.g., the big check after a construction job is completed) may not be enough to keep them on track. Therapists should work with their patients to develop a reward system that is simple, relatively inexpensive, and available as frequently as possible. The therapist should also be on guard for self-defeating reward systems; for instance, a patient who has had a history of spending impulsively should not include going to the mall as a reward.

Children with ADHD have been instrumental in developing the simplest and perhaps the most effective reward systems. It has been interesting to note how well the adult patients have responded to the systems learned from children. For example, there have been a number of adult patients who have enjoyed the "hug attack" system of reward. An entire task, which might take a full day to complete, is broken down into many tasks that can be rewarded with hugs (or variations thereof). One patient actually reported that he regretted running out of projects to do in the home. He subsequently developed a token system to use at work. He placed poker chips in a glass jar so that the accumulation could be seen readily, and he cashed in the poker chips at the end of the day when he arrived at home. Given the proper structure and guidance, ADHD patients can be very creative in developing a reward system that is simple, relatively inexpensive, frequent, and therapeutically constructive.

Another set of behavioral strategies is to devise ways in which symptoms can work with the patient rather than against him or her. For years, patients have been reading that it is bad to start a task and then jump to another before the first is finished. For many patients this is difficult to overcome, even with the help of medication. Some success has been noted by the implementation of a paradoxical technique in which the patient is asked to start several tasks at the same time. Either at the office or at home, the patient is instructed to have four or five places or stations and a job for each. For instance, bills to be paid could be placed in one area, paperwork from the office in another, a woodworking project in another, and so on. While paying the bills, as the mind starts to wander off and feelings of boredom emerge, the patient is instructed to switch to a new station and begin work there. In turn, as boredom and a lack of attention are experienced again, another switch is made. The idea is to take a symptom of ADHD that is normally perceived as being negative and make it work more constructively. One patient noted that the problem may not have been so much the fact that she wandered off task as much as she had no place else to go but to drift away aimlessly once she did lose concentration. The fact that she had a concrete place to go helped her become more productive.

The best behavioral strategies seem to be those that require minimal attention and provide maximum reinforcers. Patients have reported some success with programmable watches that are set to beep every 10 or 15 minutes as a way to remind them of, or reinforce them for, their task-oriented activities. The strategy is simple because, once the watch is programmed to beep every 15 minutes or so, no other maintenance is necessary until the battery runs down. The watch provides a built-in interval reinforcer to remind the patient to stay on target. When the watch beeps, the patient silently checks to see if he or she is on task. If not, the patient simply switches back to the target behavior. Patients seem to like these strategies because of the built-in privacy. Even in public places, no one but the patient needs to know the meaning of the periodic reinforcers.

Computers may eventually eradicate numerous ADHD symptoms by providing sophisticated programs that help eliminate errors. A woman reported that she has found much relief with her new computer at work because programs are set to help her remember the details of her responsibilities. Apparently, the sequence of tasks is now incorporated in the program. In fact, in one of the program procedures, she is guided step by step, and it has totally alleviated her worries of missing procedural steps because the program does not allow her to move on unless the previous steps are completed. She reported she no longer needs to worry about missing details.

Murphy and LeVert (1995) provided excellent practical advice in managing all of the items of everyday life. For instance, many ADHD adults struggle with the paperwork in their lives. Complaints include losing bills and important documents, adding clutter by keeping outdated paperwork, and so on. Murphy and LeVert advised ADHD patients to consider three special categories for the items in their lives. The first is marked "To Do," and a particular place is designated for just those items; this place could be a corner of a desk at work or a box at home. It is literally marked "To Do," and it contains nothing but items that must be completed. These might include telephone bills at home or notes to review for an upcoming meeting at work. Brochures on an aerobics class, last month's sports magazine, and other nonessential items are forbidden from this special place.

The second category is marked "To File," and it includes material that is needed on a daily and weekly basis at home and at work. For example, daily logs, inventory sheets, budget worksheets, and so on, would all fit into this category. The category includes any item that the individual may need to retrieve on a daily, weekly, or monthly basis. A filing system is obviously essential and, for ADHD individuals, it may be best to have a master sheet that is readily available for reference purposes. Also, it may be wise to have several of these master sheets in different locations, and it may be even wiser to give copies to coworkers and family members.

The final category is marked "To Store," and this includes a set of designated places (or boxes) that are clearly marked and labeled so that the individual knows each item inside. At home, this category might include insurance policies, receipts, birth certificates for the children, and warranties. At work the same category could include contracts, inventories, and sales receipts. Murphy and LeVert (1995) described a detailed system of labeling. Hallowell and Ratey (1994) suggested that ADHD individuals use a color-coding system to take advantage of their tendency to be visually oriented.

In this organizational process, some important decisions need to be made. Many ADHD individuals complain of clutter, and there may be a tendency to keep nonessential material because of some fears that it may someday be needed. This applies to clothes and other personal items as well as paperwork. Murphy and LeVert (1995) discussed the application of the "1-year" rule. With the exception of sentimental items and important documents (e.g., birth certificates, insurance policies, etc.), if the item has not been used for 1 year, it is likely that it will not be missed if it is gone. At home, the biggest challenges may be closets packed with old clothes and cabinets and drawers that have not been opened for fear of everything spilling out. For those who may have feelings of guilt when throwing away unbroken material, it might be easier to give away some of this unused material. For instance, it is not unusual to rediscover an old camera, which is still quite functional, that had been placed in the closet to collect dust after it was replaced by a newer model. At work, obsolete tools, first drafts of reports, useless computer printouts, and other material may be competing for valuable space. With the goal of having clear and easy access to essential items such as sales receipts, quarterly tax forms, and so on, the task of clearing away the clutter must be considered major, and most ADHD patients may need help from others to complete it. Once it is accomplished, patients report that the management of daily life seems easier.

Hallowell and Ratey (1994) suggested that ADHD patients seek out a "coach" to help them with their daily responsibilities. This is an excellent suggestion and, from clinical observations, it seems to be most helpful to ADHD patients. In fact, ADHD patients are almost always encouraged to consider several "coaches" in their lives. The term *coach*, however, reflects a personal relationship that is not equitable. A subordinate status may be perceived by the ADHD patient, and others around him or her. Consequently, many ADHD patients are directed to view interpersonal relationships through a potentially complementary system. With coworkers, team work structures are advised. The ADHD individual may need external structures and other supports, but the same individual may have much to offer in return, such as creativity, energy, and problem-solving skills. For every ADHD adult who is too bored with the details and prefers to look at the big picture, there may be another person who is not very interested in grand schemes and finds comfort in detailed repetitive tasks. The high-energy need to jump from one job to the next may work best in a community of coworkers where production flow varies because of machinery breakdown, supplies, absenteeism, and so on. A community of workers with two or three who are happy to move about the plant as needed allows others to stay on their job with minimal disruptions.

One highly creative individual, who has learned to deal with his hyperactivity well, managed to get a raise from his company by volunteering to do much of the traveling for his consulting team. He works as a computer programmer, and his associates are quite pleased to let him go on trips while they stay home. In turn, they have been extremely helpful in the provision of external structures. Most notably, they provide reminders and help organize his schedule. His coworkers have been instrumental and, in time, he has learned to prioritize his tasks. Improvements have been noted with respect to efficiency of expended time on jobs. Although he has had many who have coached him, he has never been viewed as a subordinate.

Although there are no objective measures to assess the advantage of positive human involvements, clinical observations suggest that they may be an essential ingredient to the management of ADHD symptoms. By contrast, behavioral suggestions may actually be quite cumbersome and difficult to follow without guidance and support from others. In fact, some of these behavioral suggestions have turned out to be detrimental in the long term. Numerous patients have reported that they have found no use, for instance, in making out lists. It is more likely that the list itself becomes a burden, because it is one more thing to which the patient must give attention. It is more likely that the list is lost or forgotten some time during the busy activities of the day. Organizers that are often advertised also seem to be somewhat useless to ADHD patients or, for that matter, for anyone else. People who are organized do not seem to need them, and people who are disorganized may lose things in them. However, lists, organizers, daily schedules, and other aids can be quite useful if they are also attended by the significant others in the life of an ADHD individual. As one patient explained, "I just kept losing that stupid list. So my wife decided to keep the original and just keep giving me copies."

Perhaps the best help ADHD patients can receive in alleviating some of their symptoms comes from the people around them. The significant people in the patients' lives, whether they are parents, siblings, spouses, or just close friends, can go a long way in either making life difficult or easy. It has been interesting to observe how patients describe the significant others in their lives. They are described as either a major burden and source of constant stress or saviors without whom life would be unbearable. If the people around the patient are seen as a source of support, it is strongly recommended that they be included as part of the planning and strategy process of managing day-to-day life. In fact, there may be no substitute for the caring significant other who is both understanding and forgiving. The greatest success stories in psychotherapy with ADHD patients come from patients who have the human resources available to them. These very special people are able to move beyond the daily frustrations and not lose sight of the more important issues of human regard and respect.

The shift from patient-centered to more directive cognitive treatments is not totally clear. Some therapists talk in terms of percentage of time in therapy sessions, making statements such as

> It used to be that 90% of the session was taken up just reflecting back and validating inner hurts and negative feelings; only 10% would be left to actually make some plans to turn things around. Now it seems that 90% of the session is taken up getting on with the nuts and bolts of coping with life; the emotions are still there, of course, but there seems to be more constructive energy available toward actual change.

This perspective can also apply to patients who present multiple troubles. In the midst of learning more efficient coping strategies, one woman with ADHD came to a session to report that her husband may be involved with someone else. Obviously, it would be wrong to conduct the session "business as usual" under such circumstances. However, attention to the emotional issues of this new circumstance for this woman was much shorter in duration than it would have been when she started therapy. It was clear that she had done much to strengthen her inner self since first starting psychotherapy. This allowed her to address the new challenge in her life—and there have been many—from a position of strength.

In all of the strategies presented, it is often helpful to see how well patients receive advice and suggestions. Patients who seem to do best are those who are surrounded by support and have a healthy perspective to their problems. Humor, or a sense of playfulness and enjoyment, as opposed to the perspective that these strategies are cumbersome and burdens, are positive signs. After reading Murphy and LeVert's (1995) chapter on organizing paperwork for the office, a patient reported on the tedious work of having to label folders, color code everything, and place them neatly in her drawers. It is obvious that she gave up in midstream. However, rather than acting discouraged, she simply shook her head with a smile and reported back the following week "Life is what happens while you are organizing." She had no desire to continue with this project, and she accepted her responsibility for this choice.

Therapists can be quite instrumental in developing an atmosphere of enjoyment. For instance, a patient who complained that a list is useless because he never gets to check anything off was asked to put "make a list" as the first item—that way he would have something to check off immediately. Whenever someone brings a schedule to a session to be reviewed, usually to receive approval, it is immediately rejected if it does not have enough times marked off "do nothing." Hallowell and Ratey (1994) advised the patient to have "blow off" times; taking it one step further, patients are encouraged to have at least some time during the day when they can be as ADHD as they want to be.

Self-Education and Termination of Psychotherapy

Although ADHD is a lifelong condition, psychotherapeutic treatment need not be so. The theme of empowering the patient is an important goal in psychotherapy because it will eventually allow the patient to feel the inner confidence necessary for self-management. Just as psychotherapy begins at first contact, even before the diagnostic process is complete, the process of termination begins at the beginning of formal therapy. Thus, the theme of empowerment through sharing is already presented as the patient is given feedback of test results and other diagnostic information. The underlying message is that the patient is respected and, with this respect, the patient must ultimately take responsibility for his or her own life.

The theme of empowerment also includes the possibility of bibliotherapy. Again, the patient is asked to take on responsibility by learning more about the diagnosis and treatment of ADHD. Toward the end of the therapeutic process, it is not unusual for patients not only to discuss popular articles but also to effectively critique reports and other written materials. Some very bright patients have reached the same level of understanding as that of many experts in the field. This is often a very positive sign that much progress has been made, but the most important signs are those of emotional stability and an inner sense of self acceptance. These issues are discussed later in the chapter, when comorbid conditions such as depression and self-esteem are reviewed.

Some patients may no longer need the psychotherapeutic environment but may find continued assistance and help through local support groups. This not only is a healthy transition but also is a natural progression toward reaching the goal of empowerment. Patients are often directed toward support organizations early in the treatment process. ADHD organizations can be a major source of information on dealing with other issues outside of the therapeutic arena. For instance, these organizations tend to keep up to date with respect to the legal rights of patients, and some can even provide referral sources for legal assistance.

From a therapeutic standpoint, it is often helpful for ADHD patients to be able to share and discuss problems with others who have had similar experiences. Although support group experiences are generally very positive, there are some cautions that need to be communicated to the patient, especially within the context of termination. ADHD has enjoyed the popular spotlight for quite some time now and, though this is generally positive, it may present a risk for ADHD patients. The risk is that patients may start to see themselves as having an ADHD personality that is central to their personal self-identities. As presented in the **PSYCHOTHERAPEUTIC PRINCIPLES** section, it is essential to reinforce the theme that the patient is a unique individual, beyond the symptoms of ADHD. The termination process therefore includes the perspective that problems related to ADHD are well controlled and that the individual is free to move on with life, wherever it may lead.

Patients who show signs of obsession with respect to their diagnosis may need special consideration before termination is complete. Some indulging is considered normal, especially if the patient has endured years of neglect. However, this must be considered one of several steps toward a healthy and well-integrated life. It is easy for patients to use the energy found in support group settings to become entrapped in a lifestyle that is never free of any ADHD issues. Termination at this stage may be premature, and consideration should be given to the possibility of underlying personality defects. It is quite possible that an all-consuming involvement in ADHD-related activities may be a sign of inner emptiness, for instance. The main message for psychotherapists is to always understand that the psychotherapy is for the whole complex human being rather than for a set of symptoms.

TREATMENT OF MULTIPLE DYSFUNCTIONS

During my early experiences at a psychiatric hospital, it was not unusual to find patients enrolled in multiple concurrent treatments. Patient schedules were packed with individual therapy, group therapy, recreation or activities therapy, family therapy, and so on. Depending on the presenting problems, patients may be required to attend AA meetings, a women's awareness group and, when their turn came to be discharged, a termination group. All of these efforts were well intended and were aimed at addressing all of the problems of the patient. Unfortunately, it was not unusual to have patients become overwhelmed and, as one bright young patient jokingly stated, "I have family therapy tonight, so it must be Tuesday."

The literature is saturated with discussions of comorbid dysfunctions among ADHD patients (Barkley, 1990; Hallowell & Ratey, 1994; Murphy & LeVert, 1995; Nadeau, 1995; L. Weiss, 1992; Wender, 1995). It is, therefore, not unusual to present an argument for concurrent therapies addressing all the facets patients present—everything from managing ADHD symptoms, to learning difficulties, to family dysfunctions, to drug abuse. It is common for ADHD patients to be overwhelmed, but it may be equally easy to recognize how a therapist, faced with multiple presenting problems, also could become overwhelmed. In the previous section, emphasis was given to having a team approach in which multiple professionals are involved in managing the needs of patients. This may help the psychotherapist, but it may not be sensitive to the patient's feelings of being overwhelmed. It would certainly be counterproductive if the patient started to feel as though the treatment itself is an extra burden, in addition to all the other things that need attention. This point is especially important for the ADHD patient who has never felt as though life has been organized and manageable.

It may be prudent to prioritize problems and attend to the more immediate issues first. Again, listening to the patient is paramount to understanding the priorities. A man once presented for assessment and intervention for the sole reason that his wife had reached her limit and was about to leave the marriage; consequently, special attention to the marital relationship quickly became the central issue. There have been a number of patients who were diagnosed ADHD and were also diagnosed as having specific reading problems. Now that they were out of school and had managed to cope with the learning disability, addressing reading problems was not a priority. However, their impulsivity and inattentiveness had caused them to reach a level of frustration that had become intolerable. For these patients, discussing the use of medication for relief of symptoms and gearing psychotherapy sessions toward that direction may be a primary focus. By contrast, patients with a dual diagnosis of ADHD and drug dependency may present a different set of priorities. For these patients, it is often necessary to address the chemical dependency issues first, especially if they are life threatening.

It is most important to understand that the priority of problems is dependent on the patient's needs, and there may be some paradoxical components to the actual procedures involved. For instance, prioritizing needs does not necessarily mean that a rigid rank-ordered list must be followed for every patient. There may be a few patients who find comfort receiving this kind of external structure, but most patients may have difficulty with this kind of mechanical approach. The paradox is that these are ADHD patients who are normally disorganized; thus, following the priorities of their needs may mean that the list may change from session to session or even moment to moment. Flexibility is advised, although the psychotherapist sometimes feels as though all the problems are being addressed concurrently and that the patient is again at risk of becoming overwhelmed. The difference here is that the patient is in charge. For instance, one young lady began a session talking about her need to organize a schedule for her daughter, fearing that her tendency to become disorganized would hurt her daughter's academics. The session started innocently enough, with patient and therapist looking at possible times in the evening for the patient to look over her daughter's homework and other academic-related activities. The discussion very quickly shifted to the patient's own childhood and the lack of academic support she had received. From there the patient revealed that she had been experiencing acute symptoms of depression and, coming full circle, her feelings of depression included a negative view of herself as a parent with a need to do better, at least in regard to attending to the academics of her daughter. For this particular patient, it may first appear that the priorities stemmed from the need to attend to ADHD-related symptoms, but in fact her true priorities were with her feelings of depression and working through the numerous experiences of neglect during her own childhood. Her verbally impulsive nature of jumping from one topic to the next is quite typical of ADHD adults. Fluidity and flexibility are highly recommended for the psychotherapist to keep pace. In the midst of all of the problems presented by patients, it is also important to be very attentive and sensitive to the central underlying issues. It is not uncommon to find that they are not at all related to ADHD symptoms.

The above discussions refer to the use of efficacy in providing psychotheraputic services. Chambless and Hollon (1998) reported on the importance of efficient psychotheraputic techniques and they present empirical support for this theme. These guidelines have been implemented to assess psychological treatments for a number of adult mental disorders (DeRubeis & Crits-Christoph, 1998). With the appropriate sensitivity, the psychotherapist can be a steady beacon of consistency and encouragement, guiding the patients through a seemingly overwhelming set of problems.

Therapeutic Considerations of Comorbid Conditions

There are numerous comorbid conditions that are presented in the literature. Tzelepis, Schubiner, and Warbasse (1995) provided a comprehensive review of the research in this area. Discussion in this section will be on some of the more common comorbid conditions. Emphasis, of course, will be on the psychotherapeutic interventions, but some time will be spent discussing the etiology and associative properties with ADHD.

The comorbid conditions discussed in this section have numerous overlapping features. They are categorized and discussed separately for the purpose of organization. However, the reader should understand that the actual therapeutic experiences may be more fluid as the different issues presented intertwine. Also for the purpose of organization, the comorbid conditions are discussed in a sequence that parallels the psychotherapeutic process discussed earlier. Thus, conditions reflecting interpersonal issues are presented first, and the more interpersonally related issues are discussed last.

Depression One of the most common comorbid conditions of ADHD is depression (Barkley, 1990; Murphy & LeVert, 1995; Nadeau, 1995; Ratey et al., 1992; G. Weiss & Hechtman, 1993). There may even be a preference by some clinicians toward treating ADHD with antidepressants instead of stimulant medication because antidepressants have been seen by a number of clinicians as being helpful in managing both ADHD and mood-related symptoms (Wender, 1995). However, C. S. Brown and Cooke (1995), in their review of medication effects, did not find antidepressants to be superior to stimulant medication. More extensive discussions regarding the use of medication are presented in Chapter 7; the discussion in this section focuses on the use of psychotherapeutic techniques to help ADHD patients with mood disturbances.

The trend for several years now seems to have been toward the use of pharmacological interventions to take care of depression (Bielski & Friedel, 1976; Joyce & Paykel, 1989; Schatzberg & Cole, 1991). The use of a combination of pharmacological and psychotherapy treatment is talked about, but the popularity of drugs may have placed the importance of psychotherapy into the background. This is a major mistake, and it does not do justice to the patients. Unfortunately, the new trend toward managed-care companies taking over the health insurance industry has pushed away many of the traditional long-term psychotherapies as primary interventions for depression.

Before continuing on, it may be worthwhile to put into perspective this changing trend, especially in regard to patients with diagnosed mood disorders. The use of antidepressants has been supported by neurotransmitter theories that have suggested that many patients are predisposed to depression with respect to their biochemistry, instead of environmental influences. Earlier studies of individuals afflicted with bipolar disorder (previously called *manic depression*) strongly suggested that mood swings were due to destabilization of neurotransmitter systems (Schou, 1979). The original theories of bipolar disorder observed that the onset of mood swings was very gradual and usually went undetected as a problem until the individual was well into adulthood. In fact, advancing age was considering a contributing factor to this destabilization, which was usually treated with lithium (Johnson & Johnson, 1978; Winokur et al., 1969), and it was virtually unheard of to diagnose adolescents or even younger patients with this affliction.

A second major area of investigation supporting the biochemical disposition theory came from observations of the chronically depressed who seemed to be afflicted regardless of environmental influences (Burrows, 1977; Cole, Schatzbergaf Frasier, 1976). Today, these patients are often diagnosed as having major depression with chronic and sometimes psychotic features. Symptoms of mood disturbances seem to be independent of environmental influences. For instance, patients from upper-class families with minimal environmental stressors experience the same debilitating symptoms as those from poorer families with fewer environmental resources.

On the basis of these early findings, there has been a push toward treating mood disorders with medication. This form of treatment is now not limited to bipolar disorder or chronic depression. It is not unusual today for patients with clear acute reactions that are due to a well-defined negative life event to still be prescribed antidepressants. For instance, a patient with no previous history of depression, who loses his job because of company downsizing after 20 years of service, may today most likely be treated with medication rather than be afforded the opportunity to re-evaluate and reorganize his life directions through psycho-therapy.

Perhaps another way to look at present trends and some concerning issues related to depression is to compare the use of antidepressants in treating depression with the use of antibiotics in treating infectious diseases. Before the introduction of antibiotics, it was not unusual for patients to succumb to diseases such as pneumonia, tuberculosis, and other infections. With the advent of antibiotics and their widespread use, the incidents of death due to infectious diseases decreased dramatically. In fact, worldwide statistics on deaths due to infectious diseases are highly correlated with the inaccessibility of these medications. This same pattern has not been found with respect to depression. Over the last few decades, the number of antidepressants available has increased dramatically (Schatzberg & Cole, 1991). Unfortunately, there are no corresponding statistics to suggest that depression has been eradicated, and one could easily argue that depression is more prevalent than ever before. The argument here is not to discount the advantages of having these new medications but to place their use and importance in proper perspective. This is particularly true of ADHD patients who have gone undiagnosed for decades and have had to endure numerous embarrassments and other negative environmental conditions. To not properly address all of these issues or, much worse, to reduce lifelong struggles in fighting off negative feedback from parents, teachers, and other significant individuals to the amount of serotonin reuptake—one of the major neurotransmitter theories—is simply an injustice.

One of the best models to explain depression within the ADHD population may be the learned helplessness model (Seligman, 1975), which suggests that depression is an outcome of reinforced cognitive perspectives. In consideration of the number of negative experiences ADHD adults have had throughout their lifetimes, it may be worth reviewing this theoretical perspective to best appreciate and properly treat these patients.

The learned helplessness model of explaining depression was developed on the basis of a series of experiments with dogs (Overmier & Seligman, 1967; Seligman & Maier, 1967). A dog was placed in a pen with a divider in the middle. The dog was then trained to jump over the divider when a light was turned on. This learning process was relatively quick, because the grid under the side of the divider in which the dog was standing would be charged enough to provide an electrical shock to the dog after the light would come on. Thus, the dog would learn very quickly to jump over the divider to avoid electric shock. Once over the divider, the same process could be repeated by electrically charging that side of the divider after the visual stimulus (light) was turned on. Again, the dog successfully jumped over the divider to avoid shock and, with a minimal learning period, the dog could be trained to continuously jump from one side to the next with respect to the visual stimulus.

The next step of the experiment was to see what would happen if both sides of the divider were charged when the stimulus light turned on. Initially, the dogs in the experiment jumped back and forth feverishly, trying to avoid shock. No other alternatives were provided, and the dogs were left to this learned behavior to avoid the shock. Eventually, the dogs learned that shock was unavoidable and, rather than continuing to jump back and forth, they settled with the acceptance that shock was inevitable.

The most important aspect of the experiment took place next. The experimenters went back to the first system of stimulus light and opportunity to avoid shock by jumping over the divider. In essence, they kept the other side of the divider uncharged, as done originally. The aim was to see how quickly the dogs could relearn the old system and apply the behaviors of avoiding shock. The experimenters found that the dogs had difficulty relearning. By this stage in the experiment, the dogs seemed to have developed a "what's the use" attitude and were reluctant to try again. In essence, the dogs had learned that their efforts would be futile and that it would be useless to try further. It seemed as though they accepted a helpless position, and this predisposed them to no longer be active in finding solutions to problems. The striking observation here is that the new opportunity to escape an adverse condition was never realized.

The findings of these experiments led to observation of human behavior, and it was hypothesized that individuals who have experienced numerous negative experiences, especially those who have struggled for a long time to find solutions but have not been successful, eventually reach a point where they believe that nothing will make things better, no matter how hard they try or what efforts are used (Gotlib, 1981; Raps, Peterson, Reinhard, & Seligman, 1982). Even when circumstances change to their advantage, or at least the obstacles are not there as before, many people find it difficult to shift gears and develop a sense of optimism. Researchers have been able to present evidence of a cognitive selective bias toward the negative among depressed patients (Bellack & Hersen, 1979; Teasdale & Fennell, 1982; Rehm, Fuchs, Roth, Kornblith, & Romano, 1979).

For many adult ADHD patients the critical parent or teacher (or both) is no longer in their lives, but their messages of not being smart enough, or good enough, echo in the recesses of their minds and may even be amplified through the reinforcement of self-fulfilling prophecies. Even positive experiences offered as proof that life has really changed are often not enough to overcome the negative inertia. It is not uncommon for these patients to report feelings that positive outcomes are due to some unusual "luck" and that it will be only a matter of time before they face disaster once again. Some patients seem to have become accustomed to a pessimistic lifestyle, and giving up this pessimistic personality feature may translate into giving up a piece of themselves.

All of the above issues must be considered in treatment. Initially, support for the emotional states of patients may include a special sensitivity to not discount feelings, regardless of whether they are irrational. The process of change should be anticipated as being very slow, with the patient's pace kept in mind. A patient-centered modality demands that no set timetable into which the patient must fit should be enforced.

In the early stages of therapy it is not unusual for patients to feel an emotional catharsis. Most of the session may be taken up by re-experiencing past failures, and the psychotherapist's responsibility is to provide ongoing support and permission to express some feelings that perhaps have been held inside for many years. There may be an urgency for many psychoherapists to get to work in solving these problems by presenting the usual cognitive restructuring modalities. However, the patient may not be ready to receive this at the initial stages of psychotherapy. For the less experienced therapist, it may not seem as though much progress is made in therapy initially; it is important to keep in mind the adult patient's long history of pathological reinforcers and that it is unlikely that all of them will be addressed in a short period of time. For instance, the psychotherapist may be the first person the patient has ever experienced who is not seen as an antagonist. The therapist may be perceived by the patient as the first ally he or she has ever had.

Another perspective to consider is that the introduction of cognitive strategies with homework assignments and other restructuring activities may be perceived by the patient as just another burden. The psychotherapist may also be perceived as just another person in the patient's life who is critical and demanding. From the patient's perspective of helplessness, the psychotherapist's encouragement to try something new may be just a setup for another experience of failure; so, "what's the use" of trying in the first place. Thus, the theme to adopt to address feelings of depression in psychotherapy is to progress slowly (Rogers, 1961; Sahakian, 1974). Client-centered forms of psychotherapy are highly recommended, with special attention to Rogerian techniques in establishing empathy and understanding (Rogers, 1951). This slower pace includes a special effort to not challenge the perceptions of the patient, even if clear irrationalities are apparent. Opportunities to challenge and redirect will be plentiful once the patient feels secure that the therapist is an ally. Although it may be difficult to believe, the experience of having an ally may be totally new for the patient, and it may take much time for him or her to accept.

As mentioned in the **PROCESS IN PSYCHOTHERAPY** section of this chapter, there is no concrete switch from client-centered to more directive approaches in psychotherapy. Castonguay, Goldfried, Wiser, Raue, and Hayes (1996) provided empirical data with respect to this transition. They noted that outcome of cognitive therapy—at least for depression—is most positive when a proper therapeutical alliance is established. Also, the authors found empirical support for the value of the patient's emotional involvement in cognitive therapy. The theme is that a positive therapeutic atmosphere must be established first, before psychotherapy moves toward a directive approach. In fact, it is quite possible that a premature engagement in the cognitive mechanics of psychotherapy may place prognosis in jeopardy. Every case will present its own set of challenges and unique needs. The psychotherapist should be attentive to the patient's capacity to receive information. The transition toward more directive approaches may be slow, but the psychotherapist may find an increase in opportunities for more cognitive approaches as trust and rapport develop within the psychotherapeutic setting.

Of all the possible directive approaches, cognitive–behavioral psychotherapy seems to have provided the most promising outcomes in the treatment of depression (Beck, 1993; Brewin, 1989; Dobson, 1989; Williams, 1984). A meta-analysis of 27 research investigations that compared cognitive therapy with some other form of treatment or with a waiting list control found that cognitive therapy was a superior treatment for depression (Dobson, 1989). Most notably, cognitive therapy seemed to have the most long-lasting effect. Beck (1993) reported that cognitive therapy has been found to be superior to pharmacotherapy, and he suggested that this was mainly due to the long-term benefits.

It can be expected that the ADHD patient will provide the psychotherapist with numerous irrational assumptions. As discussed earlier, the ADHD adult will quite likely present much data that can easily fit into the learned helplessness model. The task for the psychotherapist is to first identify these irrational assumptions and then challenge the patient to consider them as irrational. In essence, the patient must not only recognize these underlying assumptions but also must recognize that they do not stand up to objective analysis (Ellis, 1962). This form of psychotherapeutic intervention need not be excessively confrontive. The psychotherapist, from a helping position, can often challenge the patient's irrational thinking in a nonthreatening manner. It may be helpful to provide alternative explanations to the patient's rationale. Techniques involving reframing and redefining statements are often helpful because they do not discount the patient's beliefs entirely and, at the same time, they can open the door to an alternative rationale. Hollon, Shelton, and Davis (1993) and Hollon, DeRubeis, and Evans (1987) have reported numerous causal connections between cognition and mood. Their discussion also included the specific treatment approaches in shifting pathological rationalities to effectively help the depressed patient.

Self-Esteem   The topic of self-esteem is very popular in the media. Just about every negative condition, from poverty to sexual abuse, reportedly affects self-esteem. It may be worthwhile to take a break from the popular rhetoric to briefly consider the theoretical origins of this concept. Maslow (1968) outlined a hierarchy of needs, from the basics of life toward a unique human yearning to self-actualize. On the road to fulfilling these needs there is an interim need to reflect on the self as a worthwhile person. Impediments to getting these needs fulfilled, in his view, lead to psychological problems and maladjusted behaviors. Positive self-esteem is a need that must be met to continue human development and reach the full potential that life has to offer.

Implied are some conditions to help define self-esteem. First, it presents itself as a new challenge to human growth and development, once the more basic needs of shelter, care, and nurturance are fulfilled. The argument is made that people who are struggling to survive physically because of a lack of food or shelter are not likely to be very concerned about self-esteem issues. Second, once the basic needs are fulfilled, the complex human being will not be satisfied to simply exist and must therefore push on to find further challenges. Thus, issues dealing with self-esteem, once the basic needs are satisfied, are inevitable.

The popular topic of self-esteem actually dates back several decades under a different name. Many readers may remember people being described as having "an inferiority complex" years before the term *self-esteem* became popular. Alfred Adler believed that feelings of inferiority may be core characteristics of personality (Maddi, 1980). There may be some minor differences in definition, but both terms basically reflect the same human disposition of reflecting on oneself as not being worthy or good enough. Erikson (1950) presented a developmental hierarchy in which the task of industry (vs. inferiority) is inevitably encountered through the process of psychological maturity and growth. Erikson proposed that a sense of inferiority may be experienced if this normative stage of life is not managed well.

A comprehensive discussion of the etiology of self-esteem is beyond the scope of this book, but it is important to at least be knowledgeable of the fundamentals of its development, because much of the popular literature has misinformed the general population. For instance, self-esteem is usually formed during the childhood years and, once it is established, it is fairly robust and not easily changed by environmental influences. Around the age of 6 or 7, a child makes a psychological shift. Before this time, the act of doing, by itself, is of central focus. Most parents of 4- and 5-year-olds have experienced their children engaged in the busy work of doing. Often they imitate adults. The important notation here is that the children are perfectly happy in the activity itself without much concern about the quality of work. For example, a child who sees his or her parent painting the house may be interested in "helping" by grabbing a brush and slapping on paint. At the age of 4 or 5 there is little interest or concern about missing the wall and hitting the windowpane; just doing the activity seems fulfilling enough.

By the time a child is 7 years old, doing is still important, but doing the job well is more important. By this stage in life the child is able to understand the standards and expectations of others. Also, the child has a keen capacity to compare his or her work with that of others. By this time in life it is not unusual for parents to hear statements such as "Hey, I can do it better than _____," or "I'm not very good at this." What most parents do not know is that it does not take long for children to recognize hollow praises such as a compliment for finishing last in a race.

Thus, self-esteem is developed early in life, and there is evidence that it is not easily influenced by environmental experiences—positive or negative—later in adulthood. There have been people who have been recognized by winning prestigious awards, such as the Nobel Prize, but still express feelings of self-doubt. There are numerous individuals with prestigious positions such as presidents of large companies, medical directors, owners of successful law practices, and revered professional athletes, who still question their self-worth.

On the other hand, there are people in jail, who have contributed very little in their lives, with feelings of grandiosity. In spite of the negative feedback provided by their environment, they maintain a delusional belief that they are invaluable to those around them and that any negative feedback is only proof that the world is cruel and unappreciative of all that they have done. These cases are exclusionary of those who act confidently to cover up inner feelings of insecurity. The focus here is on individuals with no feelings of insecurity. If anything, they are frustrated that others have not discovered their great talents, and they become angry when they are not considered over others.

Another indication of the robust nature of self-esteem can be found in everyday life. Most people know of some acquaintances who seem to need special attention and praise. Sometimes they set up circumstances to receive this praise. Usually, the conversation starts with them appraising themselves in a negative manner with statements such as "I'm not very smart . . .," or "I'm not good enough to_____." The normal social response would therefore be something like "Oh, of course, you are." This small reinforcement to gain self-assurance, of course, does not last very long. These people may walk away initially feeling a little better about themselves, but it may not take very long before another booster of praise is needed. For many people with low self-esteem, much time can go by without feeling negatively about themselves, but one or two minor mistakes may be enough to unravel very fragile feelings of self-confidence. Again, the theme is that of a very fragile self that needs much maintenance, and often the positive feelings that come from environmental reinforcers quickly evaporate.

Treatments for patients who have problems with self-esteem seems to be as variant as there are psychotherapy theories. In this country, one of the oldest forms of intervention involved psychoanalytic processes. Not long after this initial introduction, a number of neo-Freudians came forth with their own blend of psychotherapeutic processes. A full discussion of their contribution to the treatment process is presented elsewhere (Menninger, 1964).

There are, however, some important conditions that need to take place to help people with low self-esteem begin to feel good about themselves. These are best seen in individuals who have a very healthy and confident feeling of themselves. First, they seem to have a natural stability that is independent of the changing whims of the environment. Criticism or praise do not seem to affect these individuals significantly. When faced with criticisms, they are least likely to take personal issue and are most likely to objectively re-evaluate. Likewise, these individuals seem to accept praise with simple gratitude and minimal self-indulgence. Second, it seems that individuals with a healthy self-esteem face obstacles in their lives with a sense of challenge rather than fear of a catastrophe. It is not that they approach the obstacles of their lives with great enthusiasm; facing disastrous situations with all smiles and confidence would certainly be artificial. However, they do seem to be resistant to much emotional fatigue, and they are often observed in a busy state of assessing the problems and making appropriate adjustments. Negative emotional reactions may very well exist, but they are clearly part of a necessary process and are seen as being constructive rather than pathological. Third, individuals with positive self-esteem are often able to separate themselves and their inner senses of self-worth from the deeds and circumstances around them. These individuals also may make statements such as "I am not as good as . . ''; however, such statements are not a reflection of their own feelings of themselves, only their levels of talent. The self-assessment is usually very objective, and there is no intention of soliciting hollow praise from others. There seems to be a sense of peace about their abilities and their limitations.

These individuals are motivated to do well and to take the responsibility of doing what is necessary to improve their performance, but they are often not obsessively driven as if they have something to prove. For example, a young college student expressed gratitude for being invited to participate in a special chess tournament after completing a very productive season. He entered knowing that he was now out of his league; he turned to a friend and jokingly stated "These guys (referring to the competition) sleep with chess books under their pillows." When asked how many books he had read on chess, he reported that he had not read any and added that he is interested in other things in life. It was interesting to note that this student made it through the first two rounds of the tournament, well above the 50th percentile of this elite group of players.

The goal in therapy is to help the patient move from a fragile sense of self, subject to changing environmental reinforcers, to a more robust sense of well-being that is stable enough to resist the changing environmental influences, whether they may be positive or negative. With reference to the above descriptions, it is unlikely that strict behavioral strategies are helpful. Classical behavioral theorists are actually not interested in terms such as *self esteem* and tend to be more concrete, asking for observable behaviors such as a reluctance to express opinions, willingness to accept criticism, or even more concrete behaviors, such as fingernail biting. Although it may be possible that a change in behaviors that is due to a reinforcement schedule may eventually change underlying feelings, it may be more efficient to address the issue of self-esteem through more cognitive strategies.

From a cognitive perspective, the array of different behaviors is not as important as the underlying cognitive assumptions. The task in psychotherapy is to challenge these assumptions and to reflect back some related irrationalities. For instance, a patient who reports "I am not very good at" may receive the response from the therapist "Perhaps you are not; so what do you need to do in order to get better at it?" A patient's report that it was terrible when a recent effort went sour could be challenged by asking what exactly happened that made things so terrible. The aim is to diffuse the intense emotionality related to a negative experience by challenging the "terrible" interpretation of the event. Most negative outcomes are annoying and perhaps exact some costs in terms of extra time, effort and, on occasion, money. But they are not usually the cause of lifelong impediments, and they are rarely in the same category of life-threatening consequences.

Of course, the therapist's job is not simply to point out possible underlying irrationalities but to explore these irrational assumptions. Usually, negative feelings associated with poor performances are due to underlying assumptions that the patient is not worthy, and the negative outcome is proof of such an assumption. Thus, while the irrationalities are challenged, a greater challenge is given to the therapist to communicate to the patient the interest and empathic regard that all humans deserve, regardless of deeds. Perhaps through some nonverbal expression, or the style involved in the therapist–patient dialogue, the patient slowly receives the communication that all deeds, whether positive or negative, are separate from the basic self. Moreover, although the consequences that are due to the deeds, again positive or negative, must be addressed, there is no need to punish the "self" and, in fact, the basic human being retains proper respect and regard.

It is important that this special regard is not artificial. Most patients are quite sensitive to hollow praises, especially if self-esteem issues are central in psychotherapy. Some patients may even voice this sensitivity making statements such as "You're a therapist; you have to accept me." This is a very common rebuttal, and it has much validity, unless two extremely important themes are addressed throughout the psychotherapeutic process. First, unlike others who may give the hollow praise that the patient is a very special person, it is important to communicate that respect and human regard are universal entities. The therapist is not placing the patient on any special pedestal of admiration. The psychotherapist is interested only in communicating the basic human respect that, ideally, all people should exercise. Patients with a low opinion of themselves are better prepared to accept this universal theme than the belief that they are special and separate from all others.

The second related theme presented by the patient's statement suggests that the psychotherapist is unique in being able to separate deeds from perceptions of self-worth. The rest of the world does not seem to do this, and often patients are very quick to present this observation in session. This is a very important pivotal time within the psychotherapeutic process. The patient is absolutely correct. A colleague, Jacqueline Lemme Cunningham, pointed out a subtle but important difference between American and French terminology with respect to the discipline of children. It is common for Americans to respond to misbehaviors by telling children to "be good." The French usually respond to children's misbehaviors with the saying "sois sage," meaning "be wise." She went on to explain that children are assumed to be good, regardless of their behaviors. Regardless of whether the French are better than Americans in the separation of deeds from the perception of self, the central focus of psychotherapy is to develop a self-acceptance of worthiness as a human being, regardless of the fact that the rest of the world may not be up to speed. This pivotal point in the therapeutic process is also important for termination purposes. In the beginning sessions, the communication that the therapist has accepted the patient is important for the patient to receive and experience. However, the patient must reach a point where the acceptance by the therapist is secondary to the patient's acceptance of the ''self'' as a fallible but respectable person. This takes much practice, and the patient is warned of the hard work ahead. The patient is also told that much of the process from this point on is dependent on what goes on outside of the sessionrather than in discussions during session.

A paradoxical therapeutic condition is sometimes helpful in therapy. The psychotherapist agrees with the patient that the outside world often makes judgments of people with respect to deeds. The psychotherapist also agrees that the outside world may be very punishing; one or two misdeeds sometimes can label people for life. Consequently, the patient has an ideal setting in which to test self-acceptance. Intelligent patients are most at risk of self-deception with reports to the psychotherapist aligned with what they perceive the psychotherapist would like to hear. Therefore, it is crucial that the therapist at this stage of the process assess the patients' feelings as they report interactions between themselves and others. Feelings of hurt and rejection may be a sign that the patient has not yet fully separated the inner ''self'' from deeds, accomplishments, or other behaviors. On the other hand, feelings of frustration, and perhaps some sense of puzzlement toward activities that have not gone well, are more in line with emotions related to the activity but separate from the sense of self. In essence, the feelings do not include self-degradation.

Obsessive–Compulsive Tendencies During my undergraduate school days, years before it was established that children do not outgrow hyperkineses (the terminology of the day), there was a belief that hyperkinetic children are relatively free from anxious tendencies. This belief was somewhat supported by empirical studies. Barkley (1981), in his earlier handbook for the diagnosis and treatment of hyperactive children, reported that these children do not seem to have the same dispositions of anxiety and worry that are found in other children, especially those who tend to be overly vigilant and reflective in thought. Objective data continue to reveal a relative independence between ADHD and obsessive–compulsive personality disorder (Tzelepis et al., 1995); however, these same authors have found through clinical observations that a number of ADHD patients (adults) possess the traits of the obsessive–compulsive personality. They went on to explain that many of the obsessive–compulsive traits seem to have developed early in life as a way to compensate for a lack of proper attention and organization. Other authors, on their review of cases, have supported this argument (Murphy & LeVert, 1995; Quinn, 1994; Solden, 1995).

The difference between clinical observations and a lack of empirical support may be due to the operational definitions used. Millon (1981) described obsessive–compulsive dysfunctions as a pervasive personality style in which the patient is consumed with uncensored thoughts and compelling actions that are both inefficient and emotionally debilitating. The patterns described are all consuming and seem to infiltrate all aspects of life. It is quite noteworthy that the *DSM–IV* (American Psychiatric Association, 1994) distinguishes this disorder as a separate personality disposition, but earlier writings of personality suggest varying degrees of obsessive–compulsive traits with respect to level of personality integration and development (e.g., Hartmann, 1958; Menninger, 1964; Rapaport, 1951; Sullivan, 1947). Millon (1981), although dedicating an entire chapter to the compulsive personality, eloquently described traits of obsessive–compulsive disorder in a number of other personality pathologies and certainly suggested that traits can be found in varying degrees and intensity levels.

Clinically, a number of ADHD adults have presented traits of obsessive–compulsive disorder. Unlike the rigid definitions of contemporary nosology, it is noteworthy that these patients actively adopt obsessive–compulsive tendencies to compensate for tendencies to lose focus and concentration. It is noteworthy, however, that these patients may have problems sustaining this level of attention and, quite often, they oscillate from one extreme to the other. Thus, they may present periods of excessive concentration driven by the classical intense–anxious dispositions found in obsessive–compulsive personalities, followed by a period of total disorganization and loss of focus. This cycle can be observed over days or over a couple of hours while engaged in an activity. A patient, for instance, once admitted that he exhausted his entire family preparing for a major remodeling of one of his bathrooms. All details were written, and several lists were made. Plans were checked and rechecked, and an excessive amount of time was spent comparing costs. Sleep was lost, and much strain existed between him and his wife during this period. Before the project was started, however, the patient began to run out of steam. He began to neglect phone messages, and he proceeded with some aspects of the project without first getting proper estimates. Eventually, the entire project was abandoned for several months.

In another case, obsessive–compulsive tendencies were seen in one aspect of the patient's life but not in others. This patient was a college student, and she spent extensive energy preparing for tests, term papers, and other academic requirements. Checking and rechecking notes, making outlines of her outlines, and other obsessive–compulsive activities drove her to near exhaustion. Social appointments for this particular patient, however, were often forgotten, and she sometimes put herself at risk by leaving the electric stove burner on. Although professors and classmates would perhaps see her as an obsessive–compulsive personality, her housemate, who watched the patient mix her dirty and clean laundry mistakenly for the third time in less than a month, would never draw the same conclusion.

Treatment for obsessive–compulsive traits, and any other tension- or anxiety-related problems, must take into account the underlying ADHD disposition. It makes a difference if the obsessive–compulsive traits are secondary to ADHD. Thus, the initial focus should be in providing relief of ADHD symptoms. Medication treatment is often quite helpful in providing this quick relief, and it is not unusual to see many of the obsessive–compulsive tendencies subside once the

ADHD symptoms are addressed successfully. Lingering anxieties, however, may very well exist even after ADHD symptoms subside, and this could be due to apprehensions that old patterns will eventually re-emerge. Consequently, a few patients may be reluctant to let go of the obsessive–compulsive controls they have developed over the years. Also, it is important to keep in mind that old habits are hard to break; even if they have produced much tension and anxiety, at least they have provided a sense of familiarity and predictability. Understanding the need for a safe and predictable world is a central factor addressing all obsessive–compulsive tendencies.

Again, cognitive psychotherapeutic efforts, with the precautions and processes presented earlier (e.g., Castonguay et al., 1996), can be helpful in easing anxieties and inner tensions. Most patients who have developed appropriate rapport and feel they have a trusting alliance with their psychotherapist will be open to suggestions to let go and try new methods. With a proper positive atmosphere, patients may sometimes respond well to verbal humor. One patient once asked "What if you're wrong?," referring to a behavioral suggestion and possible negative consequences. The therapist answered, "Then we all die," referring to the patient's exaggerated anxiety and the obvious minimal negative consequences related to the situation. Humor can be a very powerful component in psychotherapy, as long as it is nested in the correct therapeutic atmosphere. For instance, this particular woman was able to laugh at herself; this exchange took place after several weeks of therapy. By this time, she knew that no personal disrespect was intended, and she was certainly able to separate herself as a worthwhile human being from the neurotic content of her statement.

Directive approaches have traditionally included behavioral strategies. It may be helpful for patients to receive assignments so they can practice. For example, one patient was asked to stop all activity with respect to work by a given hour in the evening. From that designated time on, time would be spent with the family with no activity related to the office. The assignment was introduced as a way to reinstate some quality time with his family, but it was also necessary to give him a chance to release some inner tensions. With some initial apprehensions, the patient followed the prescribed suggestions and found that the time spent at home without engagement in office duties allowed him to feel fresher during the day and use the available work time more efficiently. It was interesting to note that, in spite of some encouraging changes, this man continued to be apprehensive and often reverted to old pathological behaviors. In fact, he terminated psychotherapy prematurely, and it was suspected that he felt bad because he was not following through with given assignments. In truth, the error was in the psychotherapist's judgment, because the patient may not have been ready for such directives.

It must always be kept in mind that obsessive–compulsive tendencies, along with other anxieties, represent reasonable responses to ADHD symptoms. For instance, it makes sense that someone who has had a history of leaving the burners on when leaving the house develops a pattern of checking and recheck-ing before moving on to other activities. A number of patients will literally report that their obsessive–compulsive tendencies have been very functional and have allowed them to graduate college and achieve successes in their career. For some patients, their anxiety and apprehension make up for what is weak cognitively. Thus, the psychotherapist must understand the balance and principal of exchange. The aim is to provide an avenue of relief from neurotic symptoms without sacrificing function. At present, there are no empirical studies that can provide adequate advice; however, the psychotherapist does have an expert avail-able: the patient.

Marriage and Family Conflicts   G. Weiss and Hechtman (1993) provided ample evidence that the family of the ADHD patient is faced with much enduring struggle. Their prospective findings suggest chronic difficulties—everything from depression and anxiety in parents of ADHD children to intimacy and communication conflicts for adult ADHD patients and their family members. Solden (1995) quite eloquently described the special relationship problems women with ADHD face. She reported how women are expected to maintain and manage the details of day-to-day family needs more so than men and, given the societal expectations, they may experience greater stress in relationships.

A shift in psychotherapeutic treatment to include marriage, family, or both should not be taken lightly. This shift means taking on new responsibilities and different therapeutic alliances. There must be a shift from seeing the individual with ADHD as the patient to a systemic view of the marital dyad or entire family as the patient. It is advisable to consider weighing the cost and benefits. One of the major costs involved would be the risk of disrupting the therapeutic alliance, if it has already been established, with the individual ADHD patient. This risk is especially important because of the theoretical shift from individual to a systemic gestalt.

In a systemic process, the theoretical approach is to change the whole system rather than one individual (Gurman & Kniskern, 1981, 1991). Approaches to accomplishing this task are radically different from those encountered in individ-ual psychotherapy. It is therefore strongly advisable to not engage in these forms of psychotherapy unless one is properly trained. Many of the state licenses and certifications allow for psychotherapists to engage in these approaches, although their discipline (e.g., clinical psychology, psychiatry) provided minimal training or no training at all in this area.

In many respects, marriage and family therapy can be seen as a discipline all by itself. The differences in philosophies between individual psychotherapy and the systems approach have often spawned much debate. Some family thera-pists (e.g., Minuchin, 1974; Satir, 1972) have argued that significant positive change cannot be expected unless the psychotherapeutic interventions involve a systemic approach. At the time, the field of marriage and family therapy was fairly young, and the pioneers advancing it may have been biased in their eagerness to place their new field among the ranks of the established. However, in the *Handbook of Family Therapy,* by Gurman and Kniskern (1981), an important shift took place in which the different systemic approaches were more objectively evaluated and some critical analyses were made with respect to which approaches best suited the variety of problems presented. It was considered an important shift because of the objective nature of the reports and the acceptance of limitations within the field.

Within the field of systemic approaches, there are several diverse theories and techniques involved with psychotherapy. Full analysis of all of the different theories is certainly beyond the scope of the present discussions. The reader is referred to Gurman and Kniskern (1981, 1991) for a more comprehensive discussion of the different theories in family therapy. However, it may be worth the presentation of a few to show the wide spectrum involved in this area of study.

The work of Framo (1992), for instance, addresses the systemic connections between generations, and theoretical perspectives are based on psychoanalytic thought. At the other end of the spectrum, Satir's (1972) work with families stems from theories of sociology, and her background is in social work. Unlike the more psychoanalytic perspective, her view of family systems takes into account the social milieu and its influence on family systems. Ascribed roles and interactions, according to her system, are associated with cultural expectations and the infiltration of social norms.

Psychotherapeutic procedures also include a wide spectrum of techniques. With Minuchin's (1974) work, for instance, there is a tendency to focus on techniques that address the pathological structures within the family. The concept of structuralism, which perhaps has been borrowed from the natural sciences, is adopted to understand systemic functioning of people (Lane, 1970). The psychotherapist sees the dysfunctional family as a structure that somehow perpetuates pathological functioning. The role of the therapist is that of someone who slowly enters into the pathological structure as another member of the system (family) and gradually effects change from within by more adaptive communication and management of problems. The process is very deliberate and slow, to be sensitive to the structural balance of the family system.

By contrast, Haley's (1963, 1976) work adopts a more directive approach. The aim through his perspective is to disrupt the pathological system through a process that perhaps stems from bioenergetic principles. Haley's direct approach can sometimes be seen as being extremely intrusive, but itis hypothesized that significant and enduring change can happen almost immediately.

Although there are no empirical data addressing the effects of family therapy on ADHD adults, Barkley et al. (1992) found some modest positive effects of family therapy on families with ADHD adolescents. Significant reductions were measured in negative communication, conflicts stemming from anger, and school adjustments. Also, family therapy helped by reducing marital depressive symptoms. In this study, three family programs were compared; these included structural family therapy, problem solving and communication training, and behavior management training. No one therapy program was considered superior to any other. Although the improvements were considered quite modest, follow-up findings did not suggest regression and, in some cases, improvements continued. Clearly, further empirical work is necessary in this field, especially with respect to ADHD adults, but the initial findings are positive.

Clinical observations of ADHD adults with respect to systemic interventions have been positive. Over the years, some basic principles have been applied to treatment quality. First, if a therapeutic alliance has been established with the individual ADHD patient, it is important to not compromise this therapeutic position by switching toward a more systemic approach. Patients sometimes ask to include their spouses in some of their psychotherapy sessions. This can be advantageous, but special time and energy may need to be given to reassure that the focus on the individual goals already established are not discounted.

Second, there are numerous occasions when family issues are brought up in individual sessions and the patient requests specific assistance. Assistance should not be denied, but efforts should be made to establish clear psychotherapeutic boundaries. Ideally, referrals can be made to qualified marriage and family therapists who are willing to consult and work as members of a psychotherapeutic team. On these occasions, it is important to be sensitive to the practical needs of the patient. As discussed earlier, it would be counterproductive if the patient felt overwhelmed with individual and family sessions taking place concurrently. This is particularly so for an ADHD patient, who may be prone to feelings of being overwhelmed and may also need periodic medical follow-ups, an additional responsibility that needs attention.

Third, as much as possible, shifts between individual and systemic approaches should be made with respect to psychotherapeutic needs. For instance, a man in his early 20s received several individual psychotherapeutic sessions after his diagnosis of ADHD. Individual adjustments in this case were made quickly, and improvements in emotional well-being were noted right from the beginning of psychotherapy. At one point, this young man made a decision to move out of his parents' home, a decision that seemed natural, based on his developing maturity and sense of independence. However, his choice to move out of the home was met with some resistance by his parents, and it seemed that there was a systemic investment in keeping him in the family. The patient was the youngest of four children and the only boy. According to the patient's accounts, the father had a tendency to abuse alcohol and, although no formal diagnosis was given, he too seemed to have ADHD. Perhaps because of the alcoholic behavior of her husband, this patient's mother possibly felt alienated from her husband and turned to her children to find fulfillment and interpersonal reward. By the time the patient was seen in psychotherapy, the other three siblings were all married and living away from home. The patient may have been the mother's favorite or, at least, he seemed to received special privileges from her. Certainly, he lived a life in which someone like his mother had to rescue him. Especially during his academic years, he struggled in school, and his mother expended much energy attending to his homework and other academic activities. Just to complicate matters further, the patient's mother had a history of cardiac problems, and she had been advised by her physician to avoid stressful conditions. Of course, the patient clearly recognized that moving out of the home would be quite stressful for her, and much time and effort had to be expended to deal with the feelings of obligation, especially in consideration of his mother's involvement in getting him through school.

In this case, the sequence of psychotherapeutic interventions started with the usual individual issues related to ADHD. In a very short period of time, this young man was able to work through issues of self-esteem and rectify some pathological dependent traits. As the individual sessions progressed, it became apparent that another underlying pathological pattern was in place, as the parents began to resist his wish for independence. Discussions during sessions turned toward this systemic view and, to the patient's credit, he gained much insight into his position in the family and the special script he played as the dependent child who will always need special guidance and attention. He correctly assessed that moving toward independence would be healthy for him personally, but he also realized that the disruption in the family may instigate life-threatening medical problems for his mother. Family psychotherapy was clearly indicated, but there was some resistance from the family. Referral options were provided, and the feedback given was that his mother did not see any need for psychotherapeutic help because she saw herself as the "strong" member of the family. The father was reportedly not interested in paying money to hear someone describe him as being "crazy." A special contract was eventually established with the patient, based on this feedback. The patient was asked to continue to improve by making healthy decisions for himself, in spite of the fact that he may see his mother deteriorate physically.

In another case, a 25-year-old man was presented for diagnosis and treatment by his family. Some impulsive behaviors had resulted in law enforcement involvement, and this was the motivation for the family to seek help. Much time was spent initially dealing with the conflictual relationships within the family. A structural approach was adopted to attend to the systemic dysfunctions. As time passed, improvements were noted and, with positive behavioral changes due to mediation treatment, family involvement in psychotherapy terminated. Some time later, the patient contacted the therapist for individual psychotherapy. By this time he was no longer living in the home, and some identity-related issues had begun to surface. The young man candidly reported that he had always seen himself as being a "loser" and, in essence, was asking permission if it would be wise for him to try college. The *main* question, of course, was whether he was seen by the therapist as worthy of such a venture. After a few psychotherapy sessions, the obvious decision was made to try out the local college. He was then referred to the counseling center at the college, and there he continued with both college life and individual psychotherapy.

Fourth, in the ADHD population, there is a special consideration, when dealing with family therapy, between function and pathology. In an earlier discussion of a patient, minimal problems arose with respect to his ADHD disposition. This was because he somehow had managed to find a very caring and attentive woman who enjoyed attending to details and taking care of the day-to-day responsibilities of life. She was involved in her husband's business as well as the management of the household. Among some marriage and family therapists, this mutually dependent relationship may be considered pathological. They might point out that there are similar stable systems in place in alcoholic families, where the alcoholic is free to indulge in irresponsible behaviors and the insecure spouse finds self-worth and satisfaction by taking on extra responsibilities. The point is well taken, and it is the therapist's responsibility to see through the stable structure of the family to detect signs of dysfunction. For instance, the insecure spouse may be quite resentful, although he or she outwardly plays the part of the understanding and caring person. Of course, the alcoholic will pay the price through physical deterioration, if not psychological deterioration. However, there are some cases in which individuals are open about their feelings and do not harbor inner resentments. Also, they do not seem to be locked into a system that will eventually cause them to deteriorate psychologically. Framo (1981) offered a special caution against being quick to describe families as being pathological. He stated

> Little is known about the self corrective mechanisms that all families have. Since family therapists usually see families and couples when they are under stress and behaving at their worst, therapists often get distorted views of the positive sides of the relationships. Besides, most people think of therapy as the place where one talks about what goes wrong rather than what goes right. (I have observed couples being intensely hostile to each other during treatment sessions, and then, as soon as they leave the office, walking away arm-in-arm.) Finally, under the intense scrutiny of the therapy microscope almost every individual, family, or couple can look sick. I believe that nearly every person, family, and marriage, over the course of a lifetime, go through periods of turmoil and disorganization that at the time appear pathological. (p. 139)

It is most difficult to operationally define the criteria necessary for a well-functioning family. However, some guiding principless have been developed, and the reader is referred to publications from the National Council on Family Relations (3989 Central Avenue NE, Suite 550, Minneapolis, Minnesota 55421) for more comprehensive discussions regarding this issue. The principal journals—*Family Relations* and *Journal of Marriage and the Family*—have been very helpful in providing some objective parameters to best define well-functioning families. The journals have been quite helpful in developing an appreciation of the multiple variables and complex processes involved in families, covering normative issues from child development to death and loss. Although a comprehensive discussion is certainly beyond the scope of this text, there are some principles that can be helpful to psychotherapists engaged in work with families. These principles are quite general and can certainly be applicable to families with ADHD adults.

The first principle is that the family is a source of resource and strength rather than a source of stress and emotional strain. The individuals in families should be able to draw on others in the family for nonpossessive warmth and affection. Usually this is reflective in a number of important family variables. For instance, communication within the family is usually open, honest, and constructive.

The second principle focuses on the boundaries within and around the family. All boundaries should be well differentiated but porous. Thus, the family has a sense of unity and structure in which the members can identify themselves as belonging individuals; however, this structure should be somewhat open and interactive to allow its members access outside of the family. For instance, the family is not threatened by its members' involvements in social activities outside the family. Thus, its members enjoy a feeling of cohesiveness that comes from well-defined family structures but also are free to venture beyond the boundaries of the family as circumstances or developmental needs arise. It may be helpful for psychotherapists to keep these general principles in mind regarding the family of the ADHD patient.

Negative Identity   One of the major differences between children and adult ADHD patients is that therapy with children assumes that identity (the self) is still in the developing mode. Intervention during the childhood or even the adolescent years may have an advantage in that the patient's identity is still forming and psychotherapeutic influences can be applied to change its course. The path to negative–antisocial identity in adulthood includes numerous intertwining antecedents, often identified as risk factors. These include early childhood experiences of corporal punishment (Straus, 1994; Straus & Yodanis, 1996) and peer relations in early aggressive behaviors (Fischer, Barkley, Fletcher, & Smallish, 1993), as well as the influence of a negative social climate (Owens & Straus, 1975). The motivation for these studies and the identification of risk factors seem to be associated with the need to apply interventions early in life (Loeber, 1991).

The adult patient has most likely crystallized his or her identity by the time psychotherapy begins. The therapist, therefore, is faced with the task of challenging the patient to re-examine and eventually reform the self-identity. This is not an easy task, because even negative identities provide comfort and familiarity to patients that are not easily jettisoned. A special therapeutic balance is highly recommended between disregarding old perceptions and filling the void with new and more adaptive perspectives of the self is highly recommended.

Resistance to change should be considered the rule rather than the exception. A young lady, for instance, had a most difficult time accepting the possibility of interpersonal intimacy in her life. As a teenager she had been most impulsive and rebellious. She saw mainstream life as being "too boring," and she adopted a promiscuous lifestyle that caused her to have a reputation in high school that extended into her adult years. She saw herself as being different from other women, and her identity as a negative person was unfortunately reinforced by her promiscuous activities and the "moral" climate of her community.

Rather than asking the patient to give up a lifestyle she had known for years, focus was placed on some underlying traits that had been quite consistent in her life. For instance, as a rebel she seemed to be very accepting of people who have been rejected by others. She naturally tended to be nonjudgmental and seemed to enjoy rescuing friends in need. Other traits, such as generosity and a capacity to present herself in a nonthreatening manner, were the building blocks to reshaping an identity that apparently did not include a view of the self as capable of a long-lasting and intimate relationship. Some paradoxical approaches were implemented in psychotherapy. For instance, many of the "morally correct" high school peers were discussed, and she realized that they tended to be unforgiving as well as judgmental. As these discussions progressed, this young lady also recognized that she had a better capacity to manage some of the troubles that are normally expected in a relationship. Her more forgiving nature and nonjudgmental style were seen as assets to maintaining long-lasting relationships. Ironically, she began to see herself as being better ready for long-term intimacies than most of her mainstream girlfriends.

A second paradoxical component was introduced into therapy for this young lady. Although much of her impulsivity had subsided, she did not see herself as a mainstream personality because she believed that leading such a life would be too boring for her. She would often state that she needed special challenges in her life, and she did not see herself as giving up her present lifestyle. In fact, she once stated that the bigger the challenge, the better because "it's what makes (her) move." In response, she was asked why she was then avoiding the biggest challenge of her life: living in the mainstream without succumbing to boredom.

Another very common problem with ADHD patients in reforming identity is the limits they place on themselves with respect to achievement and goals. Perhaps the most common example is that of underachievement in school. It is not enough to help individuals develop better study habits. It is important to understand that many patients came from a background in which they were repeatedly told that they could barely graduate high school, let alone find success in college. Even when they intellectually realize that they are capable of much more, the self-image they have developed may not allow them to see themselves as college students. The psychotherapist must be very sensitive to possible inner self-messages that they do not belong or, perhaps more damaging, that they do not deserve. The outward signs of apprehensions may provide some clues, especially if these apprehensions are associated with positive gains.

Some apprehensions may be normal, but it is always prudent to use the time in psychotherapy to explore their origins. An advertising agent (not a patient) once reported that the signing of some major contracts opened the door to financial security, but he hated dealing with all those "stuffed shirts" with whom he must do business. Although he never admitted this, there were strong suspicions that his climb up the socioeconomic ladder placed him in a world that did not fit his self-image, and perhaps he felt that he simply did not belong.

The risks involved in not attending to the need to reform identity is that patients may sabotage themselves. The psychotherapist should be most sensitive to such tendencies, and the therapeutic processes needed to help patients at risk may be the same as those applied to issues of self-esteem. Just as the inner self is separated from all the misdeeds and unsuccessful experiences, it should also be separated from all of the great achievements in life. With issues of self-esteem, it is important for patients not to be self-damning when they come short of goals set for themselves and, in continuation of this same perspective, patients can also learn to accept who they are independent of their achievements.

Social Immaturity   Although there is no set rule, problems related to social development may be best addressed later in therapy, when interpersonal issues are at rest. The development of social skills is usually a childhood task that begins rather early in life (Piaget, 1962). Play activities of toddlers are important in setting the stage for the development of social skills (Feitelson & Ross, 1973; Schwartzman, 1978). There are even outlines of different stages of play, each stage building on the previous one in developing skills of interpersonal cooperation and communication (Roper & Hinde, 1978). Piaget (1962) suggested that the young child moves from independent sensorimotor play, through parallel play, on to cooperative play, with mutual understanding of rules. This development is quite subtle in nature, so much so that the early theorists in child development did not consider much value in play activity with respect to social development. By preschool age, children can be quite sophisticated in sharing toys and developing mutually equitable systems. Their shared rules may be narcissistic, but preschoolers are certainly able to adapt to group activities and their social requirements. By the middle childhood years, rather sophisticated social skills are developed (Gottman, 1977). These children are able to form friendship ties and social skills that are essential for the development of popularity. By this age, observers have clear signs to distinguish the accepted children from the not-accepted children in school settings (Harrist, Zaia, Bates, Dodge, & Pettit, 1997; Younger & Daniels, 1992). Social skills become essential to participate in group activities and to avoid rejection (Rubin, LeMare, & Lollis, 1990).

Children with ADHD unfortunately are handicapped when it comes to the development of the proper social tools to get along with peers (Barkley, 1990). They are unable to clearly interpret the subtle social communications and are more apt to talk out of turn, annoy others during peer group activities, and miss subtle cues vital to the intricate feedback learning that takes place during the growing years. Just as good auditory functioning is necessary to develop speech, attention to the peer group is necessary to develop proper social skills. As the years pass, the problems compound for some ADHD children. They recognize that they are not accepted and may try to compensate. It is not unusual, for instance, for children to give away possessions to win friendships. It is their way to make up for what they lack in social skills. Others may choose to withdraw to avoid embarrassments. This may be particularly so for children who are not predominantly hyperactive. Still others may react to their frustrations with aggression. Regardless of the defensive style, it is well accepted that ADHD children suffer in their capacity to relate to their peers (Barkley, 1990; Ross & Ross, 1976; G. Weiss & Hechtman, 1993). Feelings that they are not in rhythm with their peer group are certainly hurtful psychologically and contribute to a negative self-image.

By the time the ADHD patient is an adult, it is quite possible that numerous embarrassments and struggles have taken place. Thus, the first order of business in psychotherapy is to manage the emotional difficulties associated with a lack of proper social development. Once the emotional issues have been addressed, the patient may be ready to attend to all the missed learning. This task in psychotherapy sessions can often be quite mechanical. The important notation is that psychotherapists may often forget how limited their patient may be, and it is not likely that the patient will feel comfortable enough to ask for specific help. Patients are often naive when it comes to understanding subtle communication, and what may seem obvious to others may be totally missed by the patient.

Some patients may present a special challenge by thinking in very concrete terms. For these patients, communication with the use of metaphors is not recommended. The focus in psychotherapy is to teach the patient in very concrete and literal terms the underlying social rules that most people learned long ago during their childhood years.

Hallowell and Ratey (1994) introduced the idea that the therapist can be a coach for the patient, and this is a very good area in which coaching can be helpful. The description of a coach is someone who can work through the mechanics of day-to-day living. The coach is available to concretely address problem situations and work out a plan to solve them.

Hallowell and Ratey (1994) also pointed out that coaching need not be done by a psychotherapist, and this is an efficient suggestion to consider. Sometimes it may be best to explain the needs and circumstances to a significant other in the patient's life and, if possible, that person can take over the chore of explaining and helping the patient practice ways in which social learning can take place. This task is not difficult, but it can be quite laborious. It is important, therefore, to be sensitive to the possible strains that may take place between the patient and the significant other. Patients with severe social skill problems may have difficulty generalizing. Patients with limited capacity to assimilate will have difficulty transferring what was learned in one situation to the next. Thus, special patience is necessary to point out to patients similarities in circumstances. If interpersonal struggles already exist between the patient and the significant other, it is important to understand that this kind of responsibility may present an added burden to the already-strained relationship. For example, a patient had a habit of saying things innocently, without thinking that such comments might hurt others' feelings. In part, this was due to impulsive tendencies. Among those hurt was his wife, and it was decided that she would not do very well as a coach unless she gained better insights into her husband's social difficulties. Unfortunately, her tendency to take statements personally became an interfering issue.

A coaching relationship with a significant other can have some very good advantages. First, it is certainly more economical, as the patient does not have to pay for the psychotherapist's time for this service. Second, the patient has greater accessibility to the significant other, who sees that patient daily. Thus, day-to-day situations can be addressed promptly with immediate feedback and adjustments.

Separate Treatment of Other Comorbid Conditions

There are a number of conditions associated with ADHD that may require separate treatment attention. That is, apart from efforts to address ADHD, some patients may need independent and separate treatments specifically designed to address comorbid conditions. In fact, for some patients, such as those who have been dependent on street drugs for several years, it may be best to focus treatment efforts on their addiction first; although this condition may be secondary to ADHD, it is often the case that ADHD symptoms are the least of these patient's problems. The purpose of this section is not to provide a comprehensive discussion of treatment for each of the described conditions; rather, the focus is to alert the psychotherapist and suggest some ways in which these special patients can be managed.

Learning Disabilities   The association between ADHD and learning disability (LD) has been noted for at least two decades (e.g., Safer & Allen, 1976). Subsequent studies have identified a high percentage of ADHD children who have also been diagnosed as having LD (Barkley, Fischer, Edelbrock, & Smallish, 1990; R. T. Brown & Borden, 1986; G. Weiss & Hechtman, 1993). Barkley (1990) described the criteria necessary for assessing LD as including a standardized measure of intelligence as well as a standardized measure of academic achievement in subjects such as reading, writing, mathematics, spelling, and so on. Learning difficulties in a given academic subject are identified if achievement scores are below average with respect to normative data and the individual's cognitive ability as measured by standardized tests of intelligence and if the lower scores in achievement are not due to sensory dysfunctions or environmental conditions. For instance, low scores in reading may be due to poor eyesight, or a general lack of achievement is measured because the student was not exposed to the associated education because of illness, poor schooling, or some other reason. The assumption is that LD is due to neurological dispositions. Orton (1937) was one of the pioneers in support of the neurologically based theory of LD. Since then, a number of neuropsychological studies have found that there are numerous cerebral complexities that reflect a wide variety of learning disabilities (Fuster, 1989; Mattis, French, & Rapin, 1975; McKeever & Van Deventer, 1975; Witelson & Rabinovitch, 1972).

The measurement of LD in patients would naturally include much more testing than prescribed for the diagnosis of ADHD. The usual LD testing includes both intellectual and achievement measures and, as indicated above, a significant difference between cognitive functioning and areas of academic achievement should be noted to document learning problems (Barkley, 1990). However, this is not as straightforward as it might seem. Barkley (1990) stated that 1.5 *SD* are necessary to constitute a significant difference but recognized that this is somewhat arbitrary and that the criterion may vary with respect to different school systems and different states.

The criterion that a discrepancy between cognitive and achievement scores must exist at all to identify learning problems can easily be challenged. For instance, it is quite conceivable to have a student who has a real LD in mathematics score quite well in achievement measures of math skills. There have been numerous students who have compensated by putting in the extra time to simply memorize procedures rather than understand the concepts. Thus, they may do well on a math test because of their extra diligence and effort. There have been numerous LD programs in schools that have focused on special skills training to help LD students learn and score well in their areas of weakness. The student's hard work and success do not mean that the LD no longer exists. This is somewhat like the ADHD patient who has applied numerous coping and compensating strategies. Consequently, caution must be exercised in making judgments with respect to differences in scores. Almost a century ago, Alford Binet and his associate Theodore Simon cautioned against diagnostic judgments based solely on numerical profiles. It is interesting to note that their original measures of intelligence consisted of at least 20 subtests—far more than used today—with special emphasis on cognitive patterns and learning preferences. In their work, focus was placed on cerebral organizations and tendencies in each individual; achievement levels on specific subject matter was considered a secondary condition (Hothersall, 1984).

Thus, ADHD adults with specific LDs present a special challenge. The therapist is cautioned to consider additional testing. Regarding treatment issues, special consideration must be given to the patient's circumstances. For younger patients who are still in school, learning problems need special attention. This is also true for older patients who still have interest in pursuing further education. Besides issues related to ADHD, these patients also may need to look at available resources in their community that can help them overcome learning problems. For instance, local community colleges may provide special tutorial assistance through their counseling or resource programs. This separate focus needs to be properly communicated to the patients. Patients need to comprehend that treatment of ADHD symptoms does not result in better understanding of math concepts or any other specific subject matter.

Adults with a dual diagnosis of ADHD and LD should be given special consideration with respect to the practicality of pursuing interventions to take care of the LD. For instance, a patient in his late 40s reported during an interview that he could never quite understand algebra, and there were some suspicions that this was due to a possible LD. However, he seemed to manage quite well with his work-related duties, and the arithmetic necessary for everyday life, such as balancing a checkbook and following a monthly budget, certainly did not require algebra. It was, therefore, decided by both clinician and patient not to pursue additional testing because the patient had no interest in or special need to pursue interventions in this area. By contrast, a nursing student recognized that she had particular problems with the mathematical formulas necessary for dosage adjustments in her course on medications. Clearly, her career responsibilities dictated that a proper assessment and subsequent intervention would be necessary. It is suggested that interventions dealing with LDs are considered separately from interventions addressing ADHD symptoms. Judgments should be made with respect to the needs and circumstances of the patients.

Alcoholism and Other Drug Dependencies   Studies have found significant correlations between substance abuse and ADHD. Wood, Wendor, and Reimherr (1983) found that a sizable percentage of adults who actively abused drugs may suffer with ADHD and are typically undiagnosed as having ADHD. Carroll and Rounsaville (1993) and DeMilio (1989) have also reported an association between ADHD and substance abuse. This association is strengthened by intergenerational correlations. Parents of ADHD children, compared to controls, were more likely to have substance abuse problems (Cantwell, 1972; Jones, Smith, Ulleland, & Streissguth, 1973). For instance, alcohol consumption during pregnancy has been suggested as a risk factor for ADHD in the baby (Shaywitz, Cohen, & Shaywitz, 1980; Streissguth et al., 1984). At present it is unclear whether ADHD and substance abuse share a common underlying disposition or if the correlations found are due to one condition influencing the other.

Wood et al. (1983) suggested that a number of substance abusers may have been undiagnosed with ADHD, and it is possible that they turned to drugs to self-medicate. This was a retrospective analysis, and caution must be taken in interpreting the findings because of the lack of rigorous controls. Barkley et al. (1990), in a more recent prospective study, found that ADHD children with a history of conduct problems were most likely to develop substance abuse problems. The more important predictive factor seemed to be the conduct disorder rather than ADHD.

The hypothesis presented by Wood et. al. (1983) that many substance abusers do so to self-medicate ADHD symptoms has at least been supported by clinical observations. Prescribing stimulant medications to ADHD adults with a history of drug abuse can be helpful for this subset of patients, who clearly present a pattern of drug abuse as a means to self-medicate ADHD symptoms. This subset of ADHD patients turns to drugs to help control tendencies to be overwhelmed by stimuli and impulsive dispositions. A history of drug abuse dictates the need to monitor these patients closely, but this particular subset should receive the opportunity to at least try stimulant medication. By contrast, there may be a risk of using stimulant medication on patients who use drugs for recreation rather than to medicate themselves.

Research is certainly necessary in this area of study to provide more definitive directions for treatment. However, a distinction between substance *abuse* and substance *dependence* is crucial to the course of treatment. ADHD patients with a dependency on drugs need special intense treatments, and this should be the primary focus of intervention. ADHD, in many of these cases, is the least of their problems. Even if the ADHD disposition has led to substance abuse and subsequent dependency, the addictive component of the dependency dictates that special interventions addressing the drug dependencies be executed first. Thus, it is not a matter of sequence in etiology but that of the most debilitating dysfunction. Drug dependencies, by definition, take on a life of their own. Even if the primary problem is solved, the addictions have a way of remaining and seem to stabilize maladaptive behavioral patterns. For many patients, intensive psychotherapeutic interventions, including group therapy, AA meetings, and perhaps residential forms of treatment, are necessary.

Personality Disorders   ADHD children have been described as being at risk of developing antisocial features for several decades now (Barkley, 1981). However, it was not until recently that qualifications with respect to subcategories of ADHD were reported that weakened the theme of a direct link between ADHD and development of antisocial personality. For instance, the psychological stability of parents (Frick et al., 1992; Patterson, DeBaryshe, & Ramsey, 1989) and experience of peer rejection (Parker & Asher, 1987) have been cited as possible intervening variables. Hinshaw (1992) reported on the combination of attention difficulties and other related factors, such as aggression and academic failures; he suggested that the development of antisocial features is a result of a number of interacting factors. Conduct problems in childhood, rather than ADHD, seem to have a tighter causal connection to antisocial traits later in life (Barkley, Guevremont, Anastopoulos, DuPaul, & Shelton, 1993). However, Barkley et al. (1993) were able to show that children with ADHD are more likely to develop conduct problems than non-ADHD children and they estimated that, by adolescence, up to 50% of the ADHD population present some problems in conduct. It seems ADHD is not directly responsible for antisocial features, but it can set the stage for the development of other problems, which, in turn, increase the risk of antisocial personality later in life.

It is important to understand that these studies are very behaviorally oriented and that descriptions of antisocial features refer to the behavioral styles observed, such as aggression, defiance of authority, and so on. The studies presented fit into present-day diagnostic criteria of antisocial personality disorder, which are also very behavioral (American Psychiatric Association, 1994), and one could argue that ADHD adults with similar behavioral features may have problems related to the negative identity discussed earlier in this book. In fact, treatment of many of the subjects may very well be the same as that suggested for individuals with a negative identity, low self-esteem, or both.

Thus, a distinction should be made between behavioral components of antisocial personality and an enduring antisocial personality disorder. Millon (1981) provided much insight into this very important distinction. Three distinguishing features are presented. First, he stated that, unlike the Axis I diagnoses, all the personality disorders are placed on Axis II to emphasize stability of symptoms and underlying psychological dispositions that may not be easily notable through behavioral observations. Second, Millon emphasized "the traits that comprise personality patterns have an inner momentum and autonomy; they are expressed with or without inducement or external participation" (p. 10). This is an important feature, because maladaptive behaviors are described as not being mere reactions to environmental influences and are not stimulus specific. By contrast, it is quite reasonable to understand that many ADHD patients with a history of maladaptive–antisocial behaviors have had a long history of uncontrolled reactions to changing environmental conditions. Third, Millon described the enduring personality patterns as being ego-syntonic, as opposed to ego-dystonic. This is also an extremely important feature when considering ADHD patients. People with personality disorders who are ego syntonic tend to communicate a sense of comfort with their own personality features, however irrational or maladaptive they seem to others. Even when confronted, they tend to express feelings of suitability regarding their own behaviors and feel quite justified in continuing on with their maladaptive patterns. Motivation for behavioral adjustments are usually associated with specific environmental conditions. For instance, an individual diagnosed with antisocial personality disorder may be able to present model behaviors while incarcerated so that he or she can influence a parole board into granting him or her early release. However, the old tendencies quickly re-emerge once the specific goal is accomplished.

From clinical experiences, none of these characteristics described by Millon (1981) are prominent in ADHD adults. For instance, the ADHD symptoms are often described as being ego dystonic; patients have never found comfort in experiencing these symptoms, and they often communicate much frustration over the impotent efforts to extinguish them. Even among ADHD patients who have accepted a negative identity of themselves, ego-dystonic characteristics can be noted. They often share feelings that they wish their lives were easier or, in some way, different. ADHD adult patients may have accepted the negative interpretations of others, but there is often an inner longing for a more acceptable social self.

Although much of the literature has focused on the risk of antisocial personality disorder, it is easy to recognize similar behavioral patterns that could associate ADHD patients with borderline and histrionic personality disorders. People with borderline personalities also may present a long history of disruptive and self-defeating behaviors. Like the ADHD patient, there may be a tendency to react impulsively to different environmental conditions. People with histrionic personalities can be similar to ADHD patients as they also tend to overreact and perhaps appear impulsive. However, unlike the ADHD patient, both people with borderline personalities and those with histrionic personalities seem to thrive on the conflicts and the disruptions in their lives. Although they may claim otherwise, they seem to perpetuate problems and may not be happy unless some form of conflict or problem exists. Although the ADHD patient may find much relief in resolving problems, people with borderline and histrionic personalities may become bored when all is calm. Although one could argue that ADHD patients tend also to experience boredom, it is important to understand that this feeling is usually activity specific. For instance, they may grow bored with long-term projects and cannot follow through adequately. It is rare that ADHD patients would report boredom when things are going smoothly for them. For people with borderline and histrionic personalities, feelings of boredom are associated with a lack of disruptiveness in their lives. Tragically, these people have feelings of boredom that are associated with a real emptiness in their own personal lives and, in fact, it can be hypothesized that the ego-syntonic characteristic of perpetual conflicts and problems is an unconscious defensive strategy to escape the sense of inner emptiness and superficiality of life.

For the person with antisocial personality disorder, it is important to keep in mind that open defiance toward authority figures, impulsive aggressiveness, and open verbal hostility—features often associated with ADHD patients with a history of conduct disorder—need not exist at all. The underlying sociopathic features may very well include nonaggressive behaviors or, in some cases, quite charming behavioral features. Unlike the ADHD patients, the antisocial personalities tend not to become anxious or overly distressed over maladaptive tendencies; again, the distinction is made between ego-dystonic (ADHD) and ego-syntonic (antisocial personality) characteristics. Behaviorally, ADHD patients can be seen as having a long history of disruptive behaviors that are quite self-defeating. The ADHD patient may even present some insights into this self-defeating pattern along with the frustrations of not being able to find appropriate relief. By contrast, antisocial personalities may very well be quite deliberate with their self-serving behaviors. Their frustrations are usually associated with unsuccessful attempts to take advantage of and use others for their own personal benefits.

Of course, it is quite possible that some patients have attention problems along with a personality disorder. If so, long-term psychotherapeutic interventions are advised. Exclusive focus on problems with attention will most likely not be very effective, and whatever positive changes that are measured might be superficial and short lived. Thus, psychotherapeutic efforts for these patients must take into account the underlying maladaptive personality as the primary focus of intervention.

Temperament Problems   Because a number of ADHD adults tend to have impulse-control problems, recent popular writings have associated ADHD with temperament issues (Hallowell & Ratey, 1994; Wender, 1995). In fact, Hallowell and Ratey (1994) included "hot-tempered" (p. 201) in their 20-item list of symptoms for their suggested criteria in diagnosing adults with ADHD. This is unfortunate, because it has misled many patients and relatives of patients into believing that temperamental problems are due to ADHD. In this section, a brief overview of the temperament literature is presented, and some very important distinctions are made between ADHD and problems related to temperamental issues. As in the previous topics of this section, the psychotherapist is directed toward differential psychotherapeutic treatment approaches.

Traditionally, the study of temperament was delegated to developmentalists interested in sensory thresholds and adaptations in neonates. Margaret Fries, a pioneer pediatrician and later a psychiatrist, systematically observed children to document individual constitutional differences (Fries, 1944; Fries & Woolf, 1953). She was perhaps the first to propose a standard method of observation and began to recognize distinctive behavioral differences in infants. For instance, some babies were extremely active and highly sensitive to auditory stimuli, whereas others tended to be quiet and somewhat sluggish to respond to environmental stimuli. Documentation and support were gathered for the hypothesis that individuals do come into the world with their own set of sensory thresholds, which makes a difference in the way they interact with their environment.

Later studies began to develop temperamental factors based on observations of infants (Thomas & Chess, 1977; Thomas, Chess, & Birch, 1968; Thomas, Chess, Birch, Hertzig, & Korn, 1963). Babies were categorized as being either easy or difficult to manage on the basis of behavioral observations. Easy babies seem to be very adaptive to changing environmental circumstances. They were able to tolerate minor discomforts and eventually could develop a pattern in which both caregiver and child fell into a rhythm of stimulus exchange. These babies responded quickly to efforts by the caregivers, and the caregivers, in turn, were better able to predict the different needs of the child (e.g., diaper change, food, etc.).

The difficult babies were least predictable. They seemed to have significant problems finding comfort in their environment. Often, they were described as being hypersensitive, and caregivers felt somewhat frustrated meeting the babies' needs. Regardless of attention given, these babies still cried and fussed.

Other temperamental factors were noted. For instance, some babies had difficulty warming up to caregivers. They tended to reject caregivers' attempts to cuddle, and they did not seem to need much touching for reassurance and warmth. These babies were few in frequency, but their temperaments seemed quite striking, because the normal human touch, warmth, and cuddling most other babies enjoyed actually seemed to be an annoyance and discomfort to these few infants.

By the late 1960s and early 1970s it was believed that, whatever constitutional conditions exist during early infant life, they can be shaped by environmental stimuli (Mussen, Conger, & Kagan, 1969; Stern, 1977). Kagan (1971) began to write about caregiver influences on infant development. He hypothesized that the difficult child is no more at risk of psychological problems later in life than the easy child, given the correct environmental conditions. The theme of matching child with caregiver became important. For instance, a difficult child with a very soothing and warm caregiver can learn to temper overreactions and find a stimulus balance between environmental challenge and comfort. At the same time, a baby who tends to be somewhat sluggish and disengaged from environmental stimuli may be best matched by a very stimulating and active caregiver. This interactional component with the environment suggested a tendency to regress toward a universal mean, and whatever difference existed in early infancy was shaped by the environmental influences enough to reject the notion that early temperamental dispositions can predict behaviors later in life. Even the babies who were described as being difficult to warm up were given hope.

This new theme countered any notions that some children are doomed to a negative life because of constitutional dispositions, but it may have arrested prematurely further research attending to temperament in the later years of life. At present, for instance, there are to my knowledge no studies that have investigated potential temperamental issues dealing with later childhood and adolescence, let alone looking at the adult population.

There may very well be adults who can be characterized as being hot-tempered and perhaps difficult to manage. However, it is important to distinguish this set of traits from ADHD symptomotology. The symptoms related to ADHD must cut across different environments and circumstances. Thus, as discussed quite extensively earlier in this book, problems should exist in normative day-to-day activities, even those activities that the individual considers enjoyable and relaxing. By contrast, volatile and perhaps explosive personalities present problematic behaviors only during times of frustration. In essence, when these people are doing tasks they enjoy or prefer to do, they display no problems in attending to that task or with being distracted. Therefore, these individuals present problems only when they are not getting their way or when events are not happening as planned. This is an important point to consider to differentiate ADHD from temperamental problems.

Psychotherapeutic interventions for these individuals may include a combination of cognitive and psychopharmacological treatments. Kellner (1982) suggested that cognitive strategies may be helpful in the development of an awareness in the patient with maladaptive temperamental tendencies. The goal is to help the patient learn to temper his or her emotions by engaging in self-reflective strategies and self-monitoring exercises. These same strategies may be helpful for ADHD patients, but it must be clear that the problems of individuals with impulse control due to temperamental issues necessitate different treatment priorities, such as control of anger. For many individuals with temperamental problems, interventions must take into account possible narcissistic features. Again, hot-tempered individuals will present no problems for long periods of time—weeks or months at a time—as long as their wishes are met and others successfully serve them. Only when impediments arise or when others are given priority over them, do they display their temper.

REFERENCES

American Psychiatric Association. (1994). *Diagnostic and statistical manual of mental disorders* (4th ed.). Washington, DC: Author.

Barkley, R. A. (1981). *Hyperactive children: A handbook for diagnosis and treatment.* New York: Guilford Press.

Barkley, R. A. (1990). *Attention deficit hyperactivity disorder: Handbook for diagnosis and treatment.* New York: Guilford Press.

Barkley, R. A., Fischer, M., Edelbrock, C. S., & Smallish, L. (1990). The adolescent outcome of hyperactive children diagnosed by research criteria: An eight year prospective follow-up study. *Journal of the American Academy of Child and Adolescent Psychiatry, 29,* 546–557.

Barkley, R. A., Guevremont, D. C., Anastopoulos, A. D., DuPaul, G. J., & Shelton, T. L. (1993). Thriving-related risks and outcomes of attention deficit hyperactivity disorder in adolescence and young adults: A three to five year follow-up survey. *Pediatrics, 92,* 212–218.

Barkley, R. A., Guevremont, D. C., Anastopoulos, A. D., & Fletcher, E. E. (1992). A comparison of three family therapy programs for treating family conflicts in adolescents with attention-deficit hyperactivity disorder. *Journal of Consulting and Clinical Psychology, 60,* 450–462.

Beck, A. T. (1993). Cognitive therapy: Past, present, and future. *Journal of Consulting and Clinical Psychology, 61,* 194–198.

Bellack, A. S., & Hersen, M. (Eds.). (1979). *Research and practice in social skills training.* New York: Plenum.

Bielski, R. J., & Friedel, R. O. (1976). A prediction of tricyclic antidepressant response: A critical review. *Archives of General Psychiatry, 33,* 1479–1489.

Brewin, C. R. (1989). Cognitive change processes in psychotherapy. *Psychological Review, 96,* 379–394.

Brown, C. S., & Cooke, S. C. (1995, March). Attention deficit hyperactivity disorder: Clinical features and treatment options. *Current Therapeutics,* pp. 57–64 .

Brown, R. T., & Borden, K. A. (1986). Hyperactivity at adolescence: Some misconceptions and new directions. *Journal of Clinical Child Psychology, 15,* 194–209.

Burrows, G. E. (1977). *Handbook of studies on depression.* New York: Elsevier.

Cantwell, D. P. (1972). Psychiatric illness in the families of hyperactive children. *Archives of General Psychiatry, 27,* 414–417.

Carroll, K. M., & Rounsaville, B. J. (1993). History and significance of childhood attention deficit disorder and treatment seeking cocaine abusers. *Comprehensive Psychiatry, 34,* 75–82.

Castonguay, L. G., Goldfried, M. R., Wiser, S., Raue, P. J., & Hayes, A. M. (1996). Predicting the effects of cognitive therapy for depression: A study of unique and common factors. *Journal of Consulting and Clinical Psychology, 64,* 497–504.

Chambless, D. L., & Hollon, S. D. (1998). Defining impaircally supported therapies. *Journal of Consulting and Clinical Psychology, 66,* 7–18.

Cole, J. O., & Schatzbergaf Frazier, S. H. (1976). *Depression: Biology, psychodynamics and treatment.* New York: Plenum.

DeMilio, L. (1989). Psychiatric syndromes in adolescent substance abusers. *American Journal of Psychiatry, 146,* 1212–1214.

DeRubeis, R. J., & Crits-Christoph, P. (1998). Empirically supported individual and group psychological treatments for adult mental disorders. *Journal of Consulting and Clinical Psychology, 66,* 37–52.

Dobson, K. S. (1989). A meta-analysis of the efficiency of cognitive therapy for depression. *Journal of Consulting and Clinical Psychology, 57,* 414–419.

Ellis, A. (1962). *Reason and emotion in psychotherapy.* New York: Lyle Stuart.

Erikson, E. H. (1950). *Childhood in society.* New York: W. W. Norton.

Feitelson, D., & Ross, G. (1973). The neglected factor: Play. *Human Development, 16,* 202–223.

Fischer, N., Barkley, R. A., Fletcher, K. E., & Smallish, L. (1993). The adolescent outcome of hyperactive children: Predictors of psychiatric, academic, social and emotional adjustment. *Journal of the American Academy of Child and Adolescent Psychiatry, 32,* 324–332.

Framo, J. L. (1981). The integration of marital therapy with sessions with family of origin. In A. S. Gurman & D. P. Kniskern (Eds.), *Handbook of family therapy* (pp. 133–158). New York: Brunner/Mazel.

Framo, J. L. (1992). *Family-of-origin therapy: An intergenerational approach.* New York: Brunner/Mazel.

Frick, P. J., Lahey, B. B., Loeber, R., Stouthamer-Loeber, M., Christ, M. G., & Hanson, K. (1992). Familial risk factors to oppositional defiant disorder and conduct disorder: Parental psychopathology and maternal parenting. *Journal of Consulting and Clinical Psychology, 60*(1), 49–55.

Fries, M. E. (1944). Psychosomatic relationships between mother and infant. *Psychosomatic Medicine, 6,* 159–162.

Fries, M. E., & Woolf, P. J. (1953). Some hypotheses on the role of the congenital activity type in personality development. *Psychoanalytic Study of the Child, 8,* 48-62.

Fuster, J. N. (1989). *The prefrontal cortex: Anatomy, physiology and neuropsychology of the frontal lobe* (2nd ed.). New York: Raven Press.

Gotlib, I. H. (1981). Self reinforcement in recall: Differential deficits in depressed and nondepressed psychiatric patients. *Journal of Abnormal Psychology, 90,* 521–530.

Gottman, J. M. (1977). Toward a definition of social isolation in children. *Child Development, 59,* 976–988.

Gurman, A. S., & Kniskern, D. P. (1981). *Handbook of family therapy.* New York: Brunner/Mazel.

Gurman, A. S., & Kniskern, D. P. (1991). *Handbook of family therapy* (2nd ed.). New York: Brunner/Mazel.

Haley, J. (1963). *Strategies of psychotherapy.* New York: Grune & Stratton.

Haley, J. (1976). *Problem-solving therapy.* San Francisco: Jossey-Bass.

Hallowell, E. M., & Ratey, J. J. (1994). *Driven to distractions.* New York: Random House.

Harrist, A. W., Zaia, A., Bates, J. E., Dodge, K. A., & Pettit, G. S. (1997). Subtypes of social withdrawal in early childhood: Sociometric status and social–cognitive differences across four years. *Child Development, 68,* 278–294.

Hartmann, H. (1958). *Ego psychology and the problem of adaptation.* New York: International Universities Press.

Hinshaw, S. P. (1992). Academic underachievement, attention deficits and aggression: Comorbidity and implications for intervention. *Journal of Consulting and Clinical Psychology, 60,* 893–903.

Hollon, S. D., DeRubeis, R. J., & Evans, M. D. (1987). Causal mediation of change in treatment for depression: Discriminating between nonspecificity and noncausality. *Psychological Bulletin, 102,* 139–149.

Hollon, S. D., Shelton, R. C., & Davis, D. D. (1993). Cognitive therapy for depression: Conceptual issues in clinical efficiency. *Journal of Consulting and Clinical Psychology, 61,* 270–275.

Hothersall, D. (1984). *History of psychology.* New York: Random House.

Johnson, F. N., & Johnson, S. (1978). *Lithium in medical practice.* Baltimore: University Park Press.

Jones, K. L., Smith, D. W., Ulleland, C. N., & Streissguth, A. P. (1973). Pattern of malformation in offspring of chronic alcoholic mothers. *Lance, 1,* 1267–1271.

Joyce, P. R., & Paykel, E. S. (1989). Predictors of drug response and depression. *Archives of General Psychiatry, 46,* 89–99.

Kagan, J. (1971). *Change in continuity in infancy.* New York: Wiley.

Kellner, R. (1982). Disorders of impulse control (not elsewhere classified). In J. H. Greist, J. W. Jefferson, & R. L. Spitzer (Eds.), *Treatment of mental disorders* (pp. 398–418). New York: Oxford University Press.

Lane, M. (1970). *Introduction to structuralism.* New York: Basic Books.

Loeber, R. (1991). Development and risk factors of juvenile antisocial behaviors and deliquency. *Clinical Psychology Review, 10,* 1–42.

Maddi, S. R. (1980). *Personality theories: A comparative analysis* (4th ed.). Homewood, IL: Dorsey Press.

Maslow, A. (1968). *Toward a psychology of being.* New York: Van Nostrand.

Mattis, S., French, J. H., & Rapin, I. (1975). Dyslexia in children and young adults: Three independent neuropsychological syndromes. *Developmental Medicine in Child Neurology, 17,* 150–163 .

McKeever, W. F., & Van Deventer, A. D. (1975). Dyslexic adolescence: Evidence of impaired vision in auditory language processing. *Cortex, 11,* 361–378.

Menninger, K. (1964). *The vital balance.* New York: Viking Press.

Millon, T. (1981). *Disorders of personality DSM–III: Axis II.* New York: Wiley-Interscience.

Minuchin, S. (1974). *Families and family therapy.* Cambridge, MA: Harvard University Press.

Murphy, K. R., & LeVert, S. (1995). *Out of the fog: Treatment options and coping strategies for adult attention deficit disorder.* New York: Skylight Press.

Mussen, P. H., Conger, J. J., & Kagan, J. (1969). *Child development and personality* (3rd ed.). New York: Harper & Row.

Nadeau, K. G. (1995). *Comprehensive guide to attention deficit disorder in adults: Research, diagnosis, and treatment.* New York: Brunner/Mazel.

Orton, S. T. (1937). *Reading, writing, and speech problems in children.* New York: Norton.

Overmier, J. B. L., & Seligman, M. E. P. (1967). Effect of inescapable shock upon subsequent escape in avoidance learning. *Journal of Comprehensive Physiological Psychology, 63,* 28–33.

Owens, D. M., & Straus, M. A. (1975). The social structure of violence in childhood and approval of violence as an adult. *Aggressive Behavior, 1,* 193–211.

Parker, J. G., & Asher, S. R. (1987). Peer relations and later personal adjustment: Are low-accepted children at risk? *Psychological Bulletin, 102,* 357–389.

Patterson, G. R., DeBaryshe, B. D., & Ramsey, E. (1989). A developmental perspective on antisocial behavior. *American Psychologist, 44,* 329–335.

Piaget, J. (1962). *Play dream and imitations in childhood.* New York: Norton.

Quinn, P. O. (1994). *ADD and the college student.* New York: Magination Press.

Rapaport, D. (1951). *Organization and pathology of thought.* New York: Columbia University Press.

Raps, C. S., Peterson, C., Reinhard, K. E., & Seligman, M. E. P. (1982). Attributional style among depressed patients. *Journal of Abnormal Psychology, 91,* 102–108.

Ratey, J. J., Greenberg, M. S., Bemporad, J. R., & Lindem, K. J. (1992). Unrecognized attention deficit hyperactivity disorder in adults presenting for outpatient psychotherapy. *Journal of Child and Adolescent Psychopharmacology, 2,* 267–275.

Rehm, L. P., Fuchs, C. Z., Roth, D. M., Kornblith, S. J., & Romano, J. M. (1979). A comparison of self control and assertion skills treatment of depression. *Journal of Behavior Therapy, 10,* 429–442.

Rogers, C. R. (1951). *Client-centered therapy.* Cambridge, MA: Riverside Press.

Rogers, C. R. (1961). *On becoming a person.* Boston: Houghton Mifflin.

Roper, R., & Hinde, R. A. (1978). Social behavior in a play group: Consistency and complexity. *Child Development, 49,* 570–579.

Ross, D. M., & Ross, S. A. (1976). *Hyperactivity: Research, theory, and action.* New York: Wiley.

Rubin, K. H., LeMare, L., & Lollis, S. (1990). Social withdrawal in childhood: Developmental pathways to peer rejection. In S. R. Asher & J. D. Coie (Eds.), *Peer rejection in childhood* (pp. 217–252). New York: Cambridge University Press.

Safer, D. J., & Allen, R. P. (1976). *Hyperactive children.* Baltimore: University Park Press.

Sahakian, W. (1974). *Psychology of personality: Readings in theory.* Chicago: Rand McNally.

Satir, V. (1972). *People making.* Palo Alto, CA: Science and Behavior Books.

Schatzberg, A. F., & Cole, J. O. (1991). *Manual of clinical psychopharmacology* (2nd ed.). Washington, DC: American Psychiatric Press.

Schou, M. (1979). Artistic productivity and lithium prophylaxis in manic-depressive illness. *British Journal of Psychiatry, 135,* 97–103.

Schwartzman, H. B. (1978). *Transformations: The anthropology of children's play.* New York: Plenum.

Seligman, M. E. P. (1975). *Helplessness: On depression, development and death.* San Francisco: Freeman.

Seligman, M. E. P., & Maier, S. F. (1967). Failure to escape traumatic shock. *Journal of Experimental Psychology, 74,* 1–9.

Shaywitz, S. E., Cohen, D. J., & Shaywitz, B. E. (1980). Behavior and learning difficulties in children of normal intelligence born to alcoholic mothers. *Journal of Pediatrics, 96,* 978–982.

Solden, S. (1995). *Women with attention deficit disorder.* Grass Valley, CA: Underwood Books.

Stern, D. (1977). *The first relationship.* Cambridge, MA: Harvard University Press.

Straus, M. A. (1994). *Beating the devil out of them: Corporal punishment in American families and its effects on children.* San Francisco: Jossey-Bass/Lexington.

Straus, M. A., & Yodanis, C. L. (1996). Corporal punishment in adolescence and physical assaults on spouses in later life: What accounts for the link. *Journal of Marriage and the Family, 58,* 825–841.

Streissguth, A. P., Martin, D. C., Barr, H. M., Sandman, B. M., Kirchner, G. L., & Darby, B. L. (1984). Intrauterine alcohol and nicotine exposure: Attention and reaction time in four-year-old children. *Developmental Psychology, 20,* 533–541.

Sullivan, H. S. (1947). *Conceptions of modern psychiatry.* New York: Norton.

Teasdale, J. D., & Fennell, J. V. (1982). Immediate effects on depression of cognitive therapy interventions. *Cognitive Therapy and Research, 6,* 343–352.

Thomas, A., & Chess, S. (1977). *Temperament and development.* New York: Brunner/Mazel.

Thomas, A., Chess, S., & Birch, H. G. (1968). *Temperament and behavior disorders in children.* New York: New York University Press.

Thomas, A., Chess, S., Birch, H. G., Hertzig, M. E., & Korn, S. (1963). *Behavioral individuality in early childhood.* New York: New York University Press.

Tzelepis, A., Schubiner, H., & Warbasse, L. H. (1995). Differential diagnosis and psychiatric comorbidity patterns in adult attention deficit disorder. In K. G. A. Nadeau (Ed.), *Comprehension guide to attention deficit disorder in adults: Research, diagnosis, and treatment* (pp. 35–57). New York: Brunner/Mazel.

Weiss, G., & Hechtman, L. T. (1993). *Hyperactive children grow up* (2nd ed.). New York: Guilford Press.

Weiss, L. (1992). *Attention deficit disorder in adults.* Dallas, TX: Taylor.

Wender, P. H. (1995). Attention-deficit hyperactivity disorder in adults. New York: Oxford University Press.

Williams, J. M. G. (1984). *The psychological treatment of depression.* New York: Free Press.

Winokur, G., Clayton, P., & Weich, T. (1969). *Manic depressive illness.* St. Louis, MO: C. V. Mosby.

Witelson, S. F., & Rabinovitch, N. S. (1972). Hemispheric speech lateralization in children with auditory–linguistic deficits. *Cortex, 8,* 412–426.

Wood, D., Wendor, P., & Reimherr, F. W. (1983). The prevalence of attention deficit disorder, residual type, or minimal brain dysfunction in a population of male alcoholic patients. *American Journal of Psychiatry, 140,* 95–98.

Younger, A., & Daniels, T. M. (1992). Children's reasons for nominating peers as withdrawn: Passive withdrawal versus active isolation. *Developmental Psychology, 28,* 955–960.

Chapter 7

Pharmacotherapy

INTRODUCTION

The use of medication to treat ADHD patients is the most popular, the most common, and the oldest form of intervention. The systematic observation of behavior-problem children on medication perhaps dates back to Bradley's (1937) account of the effects of benzedrine.

With the advent of looking at ADHD as a life span problem, the tradition of medication has remained intact for the adult ADHD population (Ratey, Greenberg, Bemporad, & Lindem, 1992; Wender, 1987, 1995; Wilens, Biederman, Mick, & Spencer, 1995). The psychopharmacological literature for the adult ADHD population has followed the same patterns as those found for the child ADHD population. Wilens and his colleagues (Wilens, Spencer, & Biederman, 1995; Wilens, Biederman, Spencer, & Prince, 1995) have provided a pharmacotherapy review of the literature on adults with ADHD and, just as was found in the child literature (Dulcan, 1990), the most rigorous and empirically designed studies have been conducted on stimulant medication (Wilens & Biederman, 1992; Wilens, Biederman, Spencer, & Prince, 1995).

The literature on adults, however, does seem to include a greater interest in looking at nonstimulant medications, at least more so than the literature on children with ADHD. Also, there seems to be a divergent trend when comparing child and adult populations, with respect to nonstimulant medications. For children with ADHD, antipsychotic agents, especially thioridazine (Mellaril), have been considered in the literature (Aman, Marks, Turbott, Wilsher, & Merry, 1991; Klein, 1990), mainly to help manage acting-out tendencies in children who have a dual diagnosis of ADHD and intellectual impairments (Alexandris & Lundell, 1968; Aman et al., 1991). For similar reasons of control of acting-out behaviors, Clonidine, an antihypertensive agent, has been considered and suggested effective (Hunt, 1987; Hunt, Kapper, & O'Connell, 1990; Hunt, Lau, & Ryu, 1991; Hunt, Minderaa, & Cohen, 1985). By contrast, nonstimulant medication treatment for adults tends to focus on comorbid mood conditions, and the nonstimulant drug of choice seems to be the antidepressant (Magee, Maier, & Reesal, 1992; Wilens, Biederman, Mick, & Spencer, 1995; Wilens, Biederman, Spencer, & Prince, 1995).

Studies that measure effects of nonstimulant medication tend to be less empirically sound; Wilens, Biederman, Spencer, and Prince's (1995) review noted that the majority of double-blind investigations examined psychostimulants and that the investigations of nonstimulant agents, mostly antidepressants, often were assessed under open conditions. Nevertheless, there seems to be a greater interest in looking at nonstimulant medications when treating ADHD adults, as opposed to the child and adolescent populations. Regardless, the overall findings strongly suggest that stimulant medications are the most effective agents for treating both children and adults. The second-order agents along this hierarchy are antidepressants, followed by rather minor considerations in the literature of other agents, such as neuroleptics and adrenergics.

The structure of this chapter will follow this hierarchy. In addition, some time will be spent discussing agents that have not been found to be effective in relieving ADHD symptoms. Also, this chapter will include some discussion on the merits of combining medications. These discussions are based on clinical speculations and observations. Thus, although they may be useful in forming logical and reasonable hypotheses, they are certainly limited by the lack of empirical support. Finally, some practical recommendations will be presented regarding medication management and treatment of ADHD patients.

STIMULANT MEDICATIONS

In a recent review of the literature it was noted that there have been well over 100 controlled studies of stimulant treatment effects in children and adolescents but only 6 controlled investigations on adults with ADHD (Wilens, Biederman, Spencer, & Prince, 1995). One of three psychostimulants typically have been prescribed to children with ADHD; these are methylphenidate (Ritalin), dextroamphetamine (Dexedrine), and pemoline (Cylert). In more recent years, four amphetamines in a single tablet form have been marketed under the brand name of Adderall (Richwood Pharmaceutical Company, Inc., Florence, Kentucky 41042). The four amphetamines include dextroamphetamine saccharate, amphetamine aspartate, dextroamphetamine sulfate USP, and amphetamine sulfate USP, each in equal amounts. To date, Adderall has been marketed for children with ADHD only. Of the stimulants prescribed to children, only methylphenidate and pemoline have been studied in adults under controlled conditions. Because pemoline has a longer sustained effect than methylphenidate, it has traditionally been used on older children and adolescents with ADHD to circumvent the problem with consistent compliance, especially if second dosages are necessary throughout the day during school hours (Conners & Taylor, 1980). Consequently, ADHD children who were prescribed methylphenidate originally may have been switched to pemoline during their older years, if they began to resist afternoon dosages because of peer pressure and fear of ridicule. This section reviews methylphenidate and pemoline studies on adults with ADHD. It also discusses Conners et al.'s (1996) study on the use of nicotine, a drug that is considered for adults exclusively.

Methylphenidate

Although an age-related preference shift away from methylphenidate and toward pemoline may have been carried out to the adult population, more recent views suggest that methylphenidate is the preferred stimulant medication, or at least it is the most studied (Wilens, Spencer, & Biederman, 1995). Researchers from the University of Utah pioneered investigations of methylphenidate use with the hypothesis that adults with ADHD will experience similar positive effects as were found previously with ADHD children (Wood, Reimherr, Wender, & Johnson, 1976). A subsequent investigation of methylphenidate response in adults did not support initial findings (Mattes, Boswell, & Oliver, 1984). However, this report was followed by a second controlled study of methylphenidate on adults by the University of Utah researchers (Wender, Reimherr, Wood, & Ward, 1985), and again positive effects were reported, with significant improvement in attention capacity, reduction in impulsivity, and general decreases in motor overactivity. Although the effects of methylphenidate on adult ADHD were questioned in the early years (Gauthier, 1984; Mattes et al., 1984), the more recent findings support the use of this stimulant for adults with ADHD. Spencer et al. (1995) provided more recent support for the use of methylphenidate. They conducted a randomized 7-week crossover trial to measure the effects of methylphenidate on ADHD symptoms, along with additional secondary dispositions, such as depression and anxiety. Using standardized instruments for dependent measures, they demonstrated methylphenidate's effectiveness in reducing ADHD symptoms.

Clinicians may be reluctant to treat ADHD with methylphenidate if a comorbid substance abuse condition exists. However, Khantzian and his associates (Khantzian, Gawin, Kleber, & Riordan, 1984) noted that three adult subjects who were diagnosed with attention deficit disorder (ADD), residual type, and had a history of cocaine dependence, improved with methylphenidate treatment. They suggested that cocaine dependence may have been secondary to attention-related problems and that cocaine was used to self-medicate. Methylphenidate, in effect, replaced cocaine as a more appropriate treatment. It was interesting to note that the three subjects experienced a reduction in craving behaviors as well as a reduction in tension-related symptoms. It is important to note that methylphenidate treatment for cocaine abuse in itself is not successful. Gawin and associates (Gawin, Riordan, & Kleber, 1985) prescribed methylphenidate to five cocaine abusers without any reported attention-related problems. Unlike their previous patients with ADD, none of the five cocaine abusers decreased their use of cocaine and, in fact, methylphenidate treatment may have caused an increase in the use of cocaine over a 5-week period.

The results of these open studies suggest that methylphenidate may be effective for ADHD adults who are also cocaine dependent, but the positive effects may be limited to patients who have turned to inappropriate drug use as a way to find relief from ADHD symptoms. Further studies under more controlled conditions will be needed in order to draw more definitive conclusions. For now, it may be best to monitor these patients closely if methylphenidate is prescribed. It was interesting to learn that the positive effects of methylphenidate included a reduction of symptoms related to cocaine abuse as well as symptoms associated with attention problems.

There have been other case results testifying to the benefits of methylphenidate beyond ADHD symptomotology; for instance, Hooberman and Stern (1984) reported that methylphenidate treatment helped a 21-year-old woman with a dual diagnosis of ADD and borderline personality disorder. The medication helped reduce the symptoms related to borderline personality disorder as well as those related to ADD. These kinds of findings should be tested under controlled conditions, with particular emphasis on differentiating between ADHD symptoms and personality disorder symptoms.

The overall impression to date is that methylphenidate can be quite effective in managing ADHD symptoms experienced by adults. Earlier inconsistencies may have been due to a number of problems. First, the diagnostic criteria have changed over the years, rendering comparison of the effects of several studies difficult. Second, the authors of the more recent support for methylphenidate treatment (Spencer et al., 1995) suggested that previous studies have been rather conservative in dosage levels; they advocated for more robust doses of methylphenidate to reach effective treatment levels. Third, the study conducted by Mattes et al. (1984) used a number of neuropsychological tests as the dependent measures. These tests have not been proven to provide the sensitivity necessary for proper assessment of ADHD functioning (Barkley, Grodzinsky, & DuPaul, 1992; Wilens, Biederman, Spencer, & Prince, 1995).

Review of both open and controlled studies of methylphenidate indicates that side effects are minimal. Like those found in the child population, the most frequent side effects include insomnia and diminished appetite. Weight loss, headaches, and feelings of dysphoria have also been reported, along with nausea and other gastrointestinal problems. These latter side effects are extremely infrequent.

Pemoline

To date, only one controlled study has measured the effects of pemoline on adults with ADHD (Wender, Reimherr, & Wood, 1981) and, when they compared it with methylphenidate, Wilens et al. (1996) found no major difference between the two. It was concluded that the effects on adults with ADHD are similar. Similar positive effects were also noted on patients with chronic cocaine abuse and attention-related problems. Just as found with methylphenidate, case reports indicate that pemoline can signficantly reduce the use of cocaine as well as reduce ADHD symptoms (R. D. Weiss, Pope, & Mirin, 1985). Again, the theoretical perspective given is that of patients who have turned to cocaine as a way of self-medicating, and pemoline can also be used as a more appropriate treatment for ADHD symptom relief. Although Wender (1995) reported that pemoline is effective on fewer ADHD patients, when compared to methylphenidate, he did point out some of pemoline's advantages. First, many patients respond well to just one dose per day, and this eliminates the inconvenience and possibly reduces the risk of noncompliance. Second, pemoline is classified as a Schedule IV drug; he went on to suggest that there is minimal risk of its use for recreational purposes. This second advantage may be useful in treating ADHD adults with a history of drug abuse. R. D. Weiss et al. (1985) measured the effects of pemoline on two ADHD adults with a chronic history of cocaine abuse. Pemoline was prescribed after both patients failed conventional drug abuse treatment, and this drug treatment was described as being successful in reducing cocaine use as well as attention-related symptoms.

Nicotine

Conners et al. (1996) hypothesized that nicotine treatment may be effective in reducing ADHD symptoms. They reported that ADHD adults smoke more frequently than non-ADHD adults or patients with other psychiatric conditions. The reason given was that ADHD adults use smoking as a form of self-medication, and this led Conners et al. to test the therapeutic effects of nicotine. A transdermal patch at a dosage of 7 mg/day for nonsmokers and 21 mg/day for smokers was administered in a double-blind crossover design. Compared with placebo, significant improvements were noted, and the authors concluded that nicotine treatment is worthy of further study.

At present, Conners et al.'s (1996) study stands alone. Unlike the other stimulants, nicotine treatment has not been considered appropriate for children. Conners et al. recognized the need for the study of long-term effects. There may be some concern in regard to negative side effects from long-term use. Also, the researchers recognized a need to compare the effects of nicotine with those of other stimulants.

ANTIDEPRESSANT MEDICATIONS

The use of antidepressants in the treatment of ADHD adults has become increasingly popular (Biederman et al., 1993; Rapport, Carlson, Kelly, & Pataki, 1993). Unfortunately, the empirical literature has not kept pace with the growing popularity. It was rather disappointing to learn that most of the support for the use of antidepressants with ADHD adults comes from case studies and open trials. It is quite difficult to validate conclusions drawn from an inadequate number of subjects in the sample, because the small sample size severely limits the generalizability of results. Nevertheless, the number of antidepressants available seems to increase each year, and there may be a strong temptation for practitioners who have traditionally worked with adults to prefer antidepressant medications over stimulant medication.

Tricyclic Antidepressants

The only controlled study that measured the effects of antidepressant medication on adults with ADHD examined desipramine (Wilens et al., 1996). The researchers chose desipramine because it was cited as an effective medication for treating ADHD children. The adult ADHD patients chosen for the study fulfilled the *DSM–III–R* (American Psychiatric Association, 1987) criteria for ADHD; patients in the treatment group received a daily dose of 200 mg, and they were followed biweekly for a 6-week period. Dependent variables included symptoms of depression and anxiety as well as ADHD. By the end of the sixth week, significant reductions in 12 out of the 14 symptoms of ADHD were noted; this included symptoms in all of the three main ADHD categories: inattentiveness, hyperactivity, and impulsivity. No significant changes over time were noted in the patients who received placebo treatment. Overall, approximately 68% of the patients in the treatment group were described as positive responders, whereas none of the patients in the placebo group were described as such after the 6-week period was completed. The researchers concluded that similar positive effects can be expected in the adult ADHD population as have been found in children and adolescents with ADHD.

All other reports on desipramine and, for that matter, other tricyclic medications, have not included controlled methodological properties. For example, Magee et al. (1992) reported that desipramine was helpful in treating a 37-year-old woman diagnosed as having ADHD. It was important to note that improvements were found in four areas of functioning (irritability, mood, anxiety, and impulsivity) and only one, impulsivity, was central to ADHD symptomatology. Nevertheless, the authors argued that antidepressants may have an advantage over stimulant medication, and positive effects were maintained over a 3-month period. Similar impressions were drawn by Satel, Southwick, and Denton (1988) supporting the use of imipramine, another tricyclic antidepressant. This was also a case study, and the authors argued that the antidepressant helped with comorbid conditions. In this case, the patient had a dual diagnosis of ADHD and borderline personality disorder.

By contrast, Wender (1995) raised significant questions regarding the utility of tricyclic antidepressants on ADHD patients. He reported that ADHD patients have a greater sensitivity to the tricyclic side effects, at least compared to patients who are diagnosed with depression and not ADHD. These side effects can include constipation, weight gain, dry mouth, decreased libido, and impaired sexual functioning. In addition, he expressed caution about the use of tricyclic antidepressants on ADHD patients who have a particular history of hyperactivity. He cited Gittelman-Klein's reports on imipramine treatment in which she observed new difficulties emerging, such as temper outbursts and aggressiveness (Klein, Gittelman, Quitkin, & Rifkin, 1980). Wender concluded that tricyclic antidepressants do not have any major positive effects on ADHD patients and that there may be a higher risk of more intense than usual side effects as well as the emergence of new unwanted symptoms. It is important to keep in mind the lack of controlled conditions in these reports. Also, it is not known if temper outbursts and other agressive reactions are side effect risks mainly for the hyperactive–impulsive type, rather than the inattemptive type.

Selective Serotonin Reuptake Inhibitors (SSRIs)

This class of antidepressants was first introduced in the United States in the 1980s after a series of comparative studies concluded that SSRIs were just as effective as tricyclics but had fewer side effects (Schatzberg & Cole, 1991). Fluoxetine (Prozac) is perhaps the best-known SSRI; it was first released in 1988 for patients with major depressive disorder, but uncontrolled clinical trials have been reported to support its use for a variety of other mental disorders, such as panic attacks, generalized anxiety, obsessive–compulsive disorder, and even personality disorder (Schatzberg & Cole, 1991). Recently, fluoxetine, along with paroxetine (Paxil) and setraline (Zoloft), have been discussed with respect to their usefulness for ADHD patients (Pliszka, 1995).

The attraction for SSRIs stems from two advantages. First, these drugs are relatively neurotransmitter specific. Although not absolute, this class of drugs primarily affects the chemistry involved in the reuptake of the neurotransmitter serotonin. By contrast, tricyclics are described as being "messy" (Pliszka, 1995) because they involve the functioning of several neurotransmitters, such as norepinephrine, acetylcholine, and histamine, along with serotonin and numerous others. Second, it has been theorized that serotonin is an important neurotransmitter associated with positive mood stabilization. The SSRIs are particularly effective in chemically blocking the reuptake of serotonin, with an efficiency factor approximated to be 15–60 times greater than other drugs (Schatzberg & Cole, 1991). Finally, SSRIs are better tolerated than tricyclics because they do not cause the drowsiness, constipation, dry mouth, and libido dysfunctions reported by patients on tricyclics. (In clinical practice, SSRIs have been discontinued, however, because of complaints of side effects that affect sexual functioning.) More important, although proper long-term effects have not been measured, they do not present the potential for cardiovascular risks of tricyclic medication (Schatzberg & Cole, 1991).

Unfortunately, information on the use of these medications for ADHD patients is based on case studies only. Wender's (1995) experience treating ADHD adults with fluoxetine led him to conclude that it is ineffective, but he went on to suggest that the high frequency of depression in ADHD adults warrants further exploration of the use of these medications. On the other hand, Sabalesky (1990) presented two cases in which hypersomnolence was noted after treatment with fluoxetine. These subjects were 25- and 39-year-old men who had been diagnosed previously as having residual ADD with hyperactivity.

Perhaps the best support for the use of fluoxetine with ADHD patients was provided by Barrickman, Noyes, Kuperman, Schumacher, and Verda (1991). This was an open-trial study, and the subjects were both children and adolescents. Consequently, its findings are certainly limited, especially in regard to adults with ADHD. Nevertheless, it seems to be the most extensive follow-up study on the treatment of ADHD with fluoxetine. Subjects were medicated for a 6-week period, and pre- and posttreatment comparisons were made with objective instruments such as a continuous-performance task, standardized behavioral questionnaires, and tests of cognitive functioning. The results were relatively positive, with 88% of the children showing at least a moderate improvement after 6 weeks of drug treatment. However, the greatest improvements were noted on the least objective measures, such as the physician's and parent's rating scales, and the least significant improvements were noted on the more objective instruments, such as the continuous-performance task and the cognitive tests. Considering the open conditions of this study, the findings, though highly significant stastically, may be due to experimental bias.

On the other hand, it was interesting to note that all except two of the subjects had at one time been on other medications. Over 50% were on stimulants, and most of the rest were on tricyclic antidepressants or antipsychotic medications. Barrickman et al. (1991) reported that "most of the subjects were treatment resistant or only partially responsive" (p. 764) to these prior medications, and they were encouraged to learn that fluoxetine had a relatively positive effect on subjects who had not responded well to the more typical medications.

Monoamine Oxidase Inhibitors (MAOIs)

This class of antidepressants was reviewed as having moderate positive effects on adult ADHD patients, but studies again have been limited to open trials and case reviews (Wilens, Spencer, & Biederman, 1995). Wender (1995) reported successful treatment of adult patients who were prescribed phenelzine (Nardil) and tranylcypromine (Parnate). He suggested that a major advantage over stimulant medication may be the capacity for these medications to produce 24-hr control of symptoms. Apparently, this is needed for some patients who act dangerously, if they are at any time without the influence of medication. This special condition presents a liability for fast-acting stimulant medications. For instance, one of Wender's patients set fire to his own property in the middle of the night, a time when stimulant medication is typically out of the system.

However, Wender (1995) also pointed out that MAOIs are quite intolerable because of their very unpleasant side effects, such as hypotension, weight gain, insomnia, decreased libido, and a need for dietary restrictions. Wilens, Biederman, Spencer, and Prince (1995) noted that these antidepressants are impractical because "robust doses" (p. 274) may be necessary to significantly reduce ADHD symptoms. Even when relatively positive results are obtained, researchers have pointed out that patients' compliance is poor (Wilens, Biederman, Spencer, & Prince, 1995). For instance, Wood, Reimherr, and Wender (1983) reported favorable symptom reductions on selegiline (Eldepryl), but when the subjects were given a trial of stimulant medication almost all of them preferred the stimulant to selegiline.

In conclusion, this class of antidepressant medication should be considered secondary to stimulant medication and prescribed only if other choices are inappropriate. For instance, Jankovic (1993) found selegiline to be an appropriate alternative treatment to stimulant medication for 20 patients with Tourette's syndrome and ADHD. ADHD patients with Tourette's syndrome may experience an increase in the frequency and intensity of symptoms of this nervous disorder while on stimulant medication. The patients in the study tolerated up to 15 mg/day of selegiline, and improvements were noted in approximately 80% of the patients. Many of these improvements were maintained after 1 year. Of course, this was also an open study, and the measures taken were quite subjective.

Other Antidepressants

Bupropion   Bupropion (Wellbutrin) is a unicyclic antidepressant that has been prescribed as an alternative to other antidepressants, usually because of its favorable side effect profile (Schatzberg & Cole, 1991). Wender and Reimherr (1990) found positive effects of this medication in 4 out of 19 adult ADHD patients. All of the patients were previously treated by either stimulant medication or MAOIs. Of the 14 patients who experienced positive effects from bupropion, 10 chose to continue with this medication treatment rather than return to their original medication.

Barrickman et al. (1995) conducted a controlled study in which they compared the effects of bupropion with the effects of methylphenidate. The dependent variables included standardized measures of behaviors and performance on neuropsychological instruments. They concluded that both medications were equally effective in managing ADHD symptoms. Unfortunately, this study was conducted with children and adolescents only. Thus, it would be risky to generalize these findings to the adult ADHD population.

Wender (1995) reported that bupropion is similar to the MAOI medications in that it provides 24-hr-a-day effect without the dietary restriction necessary for MAOI antidepressants. He suggested that this medication may be quite helpful for ADHD adults who have comorbid symptoms of depression. He did warn that bupropion is more effective in managing affective symptoms than classical ADHD symptoms; although patients have reported some improvements in concentration and other attention-related functions, bupropion was not considered superior to stimulant medication in the provision of relief from ADHD symptoms.

Venlafaxine   Findling, Schwartz, Fannery, and Manos (1996) introduced venlafaxine as a newly released, structurally novel medication that has been described as being superior to tricyclic antidepressants because of fewer side effects. Findling et al. (1996) ran an 8-week open trial of this agent on 10 ADHD patients. All but 1 patient completed the entire 8-week study period and, out of the 9 remaining patients who did complete it, 7 were considered positive responders. Significant effects were measured in the reduction of hyperactivity–impulsivity, inattention, and anxiety. It was noted that there was no major difference in depressive symptoms because there was an absence of these symptoms in this population. Findling et al. presented their finding as "preliminary evidence that venlafaxine may be a safe and effective treatment for adults who suffer from ADHD" (p. 187); they also recommended further studies under more controlled conditions to validate their preliminary findings.

CONSIDERATION OF ALTERNATIVE MEDICATIONS

At present, the use of alternative medication seems to be motivated by comorbid conditions or by neurotransmitter theories of ADHD. Wender (1995) reported on the use of amino acids as possible treatment for ADHD. Trials first included L-dopa and later phenylalanine. It was hypothesized that the introduction of amino acids would increase the action of neurotransmitters and, on the basis of the theory that ADHD patients are characterized as having lower levels of neurotransmitter functioning, amino acids can act as precursors to increasing neurotransmitter levels. Significant and, more important, sustained levels of functioning were not found. In a relatively controlled design, the Wender group (Wood, Reimherr, & Wender, 1985) attempted to assess the effects of phenylalanine. Within a week, positive drug effects approached statical significance, but a 3-month follow-up indicated that these effects were not sustained. The power of the research design was limited because of the small sample size. Subsequent open trials, however, supported the initial impression that effects of amino acids are short term, at best. Similar findings were noted with the use of L-tyrosine by Reimherr et al. (1987). Not all patients showed positive effects, and those who did seemed to develop a tolerance that negated initial therapeutic effects.

On the basis of the same neurotransmitter theory of ADHD with specific activation of dopamine, bromocriptine was considered as a possible effective treatment because of its dopamine receptor agonist properties (Cavanagh, Clifford, & Gregory, 1989; Cocores, Davies, Mueller, & Gold, 1987). Cavanagh et al. (1989) studied the effects of bromocriptine on two inpatient men with a dual diagnosis of ADD and a chemical dependency. These young adults, ages 18 and 24, showed some improvement in concentration and inhibition of restlessness, but the overall attention-related symptoms were not reduced significantly with this drug. On the other hand, Cocores et al. (1987) reported that bromocriptine was useful in treating patients with a dual diagnosis of ADHD and cocaine addiction. They hypothesized that the patients turned to cocaine abuse as a way of self-medicating themselves to find relief from ADHD symptoms. They suggested that bromocriptine can be used as a substitute for cocaine, by reducing ADHD symptoms, at least during the course of their rehabilitation. The limitations of their study, however, made it difficult to measure symptom reduction appropriately and, again, treatment effects were limited to short-term follow-up.

Shekim, Masterson, Cantwell, Hanna, and McCracken (1989) conducted an open trial of nomifensine maleate on 18 ADHD adults. Nomifensine maleate is a direct dopamine agonist, and Shekim et al. also were basing their hypothesis of positive medication effects on the dopamine theory of ADHD. Effects were measured at the end of the first and fourth weeks of treatment. No standardized measures were used. All data were collected on the basis of a structured interview designed to address ADHD symptoms. Of the 18 adults medicated, decreases in symptoms were reported by 15 patients. However, reports of side effects were quite prominent; they included dry mouth, nausea, headaches, and drowsiness. Again, the usual limitations regarding open trial studies need to be considered, and the reported side effects may compromise the use of this drug for a condition that is lifelong.

In a later study, Shekim, Antun, Hanna, McCracken, and Hess (1990) reported slightly more promising results on eight males given S-adenosyl-L-methionine (SAM). Eight males diagnosed as having ADHD, residual type, were clinically assessed, and six of them improved clinically with this medication. The authors also reported that side effects were both minimal and transient. Also, it was noteworthy that two of the patients who had improved on SAM had not shown any significant improvements while previously on methylphenidate. It would certainly be interesting to follow up on this finding by specifically looking at ADHD patients who have not responded to stimulant medication.

Balon (1990) studied the use of buspirone (BuSpar) on a 45-year-old man with a dual diagnosis of ADHD and generalized anxiety disorder. Again, the motivation was to provide a medication that has crossover effects that cover both sets of symptoms. Buspirone is an anti-anxiety agent with possible dopamine antagonist effects. The combination of anxiety-reducing effects and possible increases of dopamine at the synapses, as theorized to be lacking among ADHD patients, could suggest that buspirone can be an effective medication for ADHD patients who also experience much anxiety. The single case study presented by Balon (1990) may support this hypothesis, but further study is certainly needed.

Wender (1995) assessed the use of several other medications, such as clonidine, nadolol, lithium, and even thioridazine (Mellaril), a common neuroleptic usually given to children who are behaviorally uncontrollable and often aggressive. With the exception of lithium, all of these medications are prescribed to patients in addition to stimulant medication. Combined pharmacotherapy is discussed in the next section. For now, it is important to note that these medications have not been found to be effective on ADHD adults by themselves. Lithium was described as being ineffective in managing ADHD symptoms in adults. Wender reported that he has seen a number of ADHD patients who were first prescribed lithium because of a misdiagnosis, apparently bipolar disorder, and these patients did not report any relief from ADHD symptoms.

COMBINED PHARMACOTHERAPY

Combined pharmacotherapy seems to always include a stimulant medication. No more than two medications have been discussed in the literature, and dual prescriptions are given for one of two main reasons. First, clinicians believe that they may enhance control of symptoms. Second, a second medication may be prescribed to counter the side effects of stimulant medication.

Wilens and colleagues (Wilens, Biederman, Mick, & Spencer, 1995; Wilens, Spencer, & Biederman, 1995) discussed the use of stimulants and antidepressants in combination. A trend was reported in which patients reported enhanced functioning. These were all case study reports, and the ADHD patients seemed to have comorbid conditions of mood disturbances.

Ratey, Greenberg, and Lindem (1991) reported on three cases in which the prescription of nadolol, a beta antagonist, was used to enhance the effects of methylphenidate. Problems with impulsivity were reportedly reduced, temper outbursts were controlled, there was a decrease in distractibility, and there was greater improvement in attention. All of these descriptions were subjective reports, apparently from the patients themselves. In addition, the authors reported that the added prescription of nadolol tended to decrease inner tensions and anxiety. Although it was not clear, these symptoms may sometimes be seen as side effects of methylphenidate. In essence, the secondary prescription was perhaps viewed as being helpful in relieving unwanted effects from stimulant medication.

Increased therapeutic efficiency was also reported by Wender (1986, 1995). He found that small doses of either thioridazine or clonidine have been useful in patients who report insomnia while on stimulant medication. Clonidine may also be useful for patients with mild hypertension.

There are no systematic controlled studies available. All of the reports in this area stem from case observations with very subjective analyses. All of these reports reflect acute functioning; long-term effects are unavailable at this time.

CONCLUSIONS AND PRACTICAL RECOMMENDATIONS
Stimulants as Primary Pharmacotherapy

Although the systematic study of stimulant medication on adults is not as advanced as that found in the child population, preliminary findings strongly support the thesis that stimulant medication effects on ADHD adults are quite comparable to the effects reported on ADHD children (Wilens, Biederman, Spencer, & Prince, 1995). To date, psychostimulants are virtually the only medications that have been studied under controlled conditions. With a few exceptions in the literature examining the effects of antidepressants, the most objective data on medication effects are on psychostimulants. Therefore, with the exception of nervous disorders, which are discussed later in this section, psychostimulants should be considered first. This recommendation is mostly directed toward clinicians who are more accustomed to treating adults for depression and anxiety. If a comorbid condition of depression exists, there may be a temptation to begin pharmacotherapy with an antidepressant. According to present objective data, this may be a mistake. Many of the mood- and anxiety-related problems are secondary to a long history of ADHD symptom tolerance. Once the ADHD symptoms subside with the help of stimulant medication, it is possible that secondary symptoms also will subside. For instance, someone who is anxious about his or her job performance because of inattentiveness and forgetfulness may find some relief from anxiety once job performance improves because of the alleviation of ADHD symptoms.

This scenario is not a guarantee, however, because it is also likely that symptoms that were originally secondary may take on a life of their own, independent of the primary conditions (see discussions of comorbid conditions in Chapter 6). Furthremore, the use of stimulant medication can exacerbate anxiety- and mood-related problems. Stimulant medication should still be considered the primary pharmchotherapy, but careful monitoring is highly recommended. Alternative agents should be considered as secondary and only when clinical observation suggests poor response to stimulant medication. It is important to keep in mind that, even when combined pharmacotherapy is considered, the stimulant drugs are considered the primary agents.

The only exception to the use of stimulant medication as the primary pharmacotherapy is when patients present with nervous disorders. Patients suffering from tics, Tourette's syndrome, seizure disorder, tremor, and so on may be at risk of exacerbating their nervous condition if stimulants are prescribed. In these cases only, it may be prudent to consider alternative medications as the primary pharmacotherapy treatment.

Limitations of Pharmacotherapy

Even under the best of conditions, pharmacotherapy alone is not enough to provide appropriate intervention. The strength in using pharmacotherapy is in its ability to provide quick relief from symptoms. Especially in consideration of the fast-acting stimulant medications, patients very acutely can discover that their attention improves, they have become less distractible, they can concentrate on tasks for greater periods of time, and they are able to organize their lives. However, the findings measured stem from short-term studies. ADHD is a lifelong condition, and the literature does not provide adequate insights into the long-term effects of medication treatment.

G. Weiss and Hechtman's (1993) 20-year follow-up reports of ADHD patients strongly suggest that pharmacotherapy alone is insufficient. As discussed earlier, many patients have confirmed the importance of professional support and human resources to help them throughout the long years. In consideration of the fact that G. Weiss and Hechtman's subjects most likely have been treated better than most other ADHD adults because of their extensive follow-up attention, these reports should be considered conservative. It is quite likely that ADHD adults, many of whom have not received much professional contact other than perhaps medication review, may have greater needs than those described in G. Weiss and Hechtman's reports.

Much emphasis has already been given to the special comorbid conditions of adult ADHD patients. The theme presented was that of patients who do not present uncomplicated cases. There is often a temptation to manage multiple problems by means of polypharmacotherapy. Wender (1995), as discussed earlier in this chapter, provided reports of some success. However, these findings are based on open trials. Future research, under more controlled conditions, may provide more definitive recommendations for polypharmacotherapy. Ultimately, however, the clinician must understand that intervention should include much more than drug management. Even if the only intervention received by the patient is pharmacotherapy, the special long-term aspect of ADHD dictates that special attention be given to issues such as long-term compliance, effects of medication treatment during life-changing events, and the long-term physical well-being of patients.

Research Limitations

As noted earlier, there are very few controlled studies that can provide the clinician proper guidance and direction. Unfortunately, it is much easier to conduct open trials, and there seems to be an unhealthy ratio between the number of controlled and the number of open-trial studies. For many clinicians in the field, the conclusions drawn from open trials are often considered definitive rather than as hypothesis formulation for further study. With only a few exceptions, most researchers in this field do not follow up their preliminary findings based on case studies.

Even in double-blind studies, there have been some questions raised that suggest that it is difficult to maintain blind conditions. Margraf et al. (1991) reported that subjects and researchers in control studies are able to use subtle cues to guess correctly experimental conditions (treatment or control group). Medications with significant side effects are the most difficult to disguise.

Also, present standards that require proper informed consent of subjects compromise the placebo condition. The experience of a true placebo includes the belief that it is an effective medication, although it is not. In a true placebo condition, the subjects should believe that their treatment is real and will take care of their ailments effectively. Thus, by definition, the placebo experience is a deception. This condition no longer exists, because subjects must be informed ahead of time that they have a given probability of being placed in a placebo group. In essence, the stage is set for arousal of the subjects' curiosity and subsequent detective work that could confound results.

Avoid Trial-and-Error Medication Management

One of the most frustrating experiences as a clinician is to hear patients report that they have been prescribed six or seven different medications in about as many months. Clearly, the contribution of science in this field is limited; the number of objective investigations is too small to understand the utility of pharmacotherapy comprehensively. With so many different medications available, there is a strong temptation to switch gears quickly in search of the best effects. However, it is quite possible that many medications have not been fully explored before they are given up.

Although the lack of research almost predisposes clinicians to the trial-and-error method, two principles may be helpful in curbing this tendency. First, before a medication is prescribed, all possible alternatives should be explored to the fullest. If there is a reason for choosing a particular medication, then there must also be a reason (or reasons) for rejecting all the others. A careful review of the literature can be helpful in eliminating much of the randomness. Later, if alternatives need to be reconsidered, at least the changes are made in a more systematic manner. Second, especially with stimulant medications, it may be best to consider dosage adjustments before turning to alternative drugs. Again, many clinicians who feel more comfortable prescribing antidepressants than stimulant medication may be somewhat conservative when it comes to the dosage levels of stimulants. There have been a number of patients who were originally given low dosages of methylphenidate (10 mg bid) and later switched to an antidepressant. Especially if some relief from symptoms is reported, an increase in dosage may be more appropriate than a change to a new drug. Also, there have been numerous examples in which the methylphenidate prescription had been effective but was not believed to be effective because of poor assessments. On closer examination of the patient's daily functioning, most of the problems reported were in the morning hours, when he or she was getting ready for work, and in the later afternoon hours, when the medication had worn off completely. A close examination of the symptoms, especially the intensity and circumstances and settings in which they occur, is essential to clinical judgments.

Take the Time to Listen

It is extremely important to realize that ADHD does not lend itself well to the medical model, which is very mechanical and quite functional for ailments such as broken bones, tumors, and other physical anomalies. The problem is clearly identified because it is foreign to the normal condition, and a precise treatment is prescribed to take care of it. However, as discussed earlier, ADHD patients do not present symptoms that are foreign to the normal condition, and science has just begun to provide information with respect to the treatment of ADHD patients. Consequently, many of the procedures of managing patients in a busy physician's office may very well be counterproductive for the ADHD patient. Perhaps the most common complaint received from patients is that professionals have not taken the time to listen and fully understand their problems. It is imperative not to forget that many ADHD adults have already experienced numerous negative professional contacts that usually date back to their early school years, such as experiences with teachers who either did not understand the problems or were simply too insensitive to take the time to try to understand.

These same feelings can easily be triggered by clinicians if the patients perceive or believe that proper time and energy are not being expended to understand their problems. The usual procedure of having multiple patients with the same appointment time and spending just a few minutes per patient as the physician moves from one examining room to the next is not conducive to the needs of ADHD patients. There have been numerous complaints from ADHD patients who have had to wait hours in the waiting room, followed by another long waiting period in an examining room, and then have only a few short minutes to interact with their physician. These complaints are quite legitimate, because it takes extra time to listen and appreciate fully the many issues that these patients present. The choice of medication may depend on a variety of details regarding daily functioning and changing life events. A simple detail such as that explained earlier in a patient who continued to present symptoms only during the times that the medication was perhaps out of the system could easily prevent the frustration of a long series of ineffective trial-and-error experiences. A little extra time to ask more defining questions could make all the difference. Unlike other dysfunctions, treatment is not definitive, and the variety of options available requires time-consuming consideration.

REFERENCES

Alexandris, A., & Lundell, F. W. (1968). Effects of thioridazine, amphetamine and placebo on the hyperkinetic syndrome and cognitive area in mentally deficient children. *Canadian Medical Association Journal, 98,* 92–96.

Aman, M. G., Marks, R. E., Turbott, S. H., Wilsher, C. P., & Merry, S. N. (1991). Clinical effects of methylphenidate and thioridazine in intellectually subaverage children. *Journal of the American Academy of Child and Adolescent Psychiatry, 30,* 246–256.

American Psychiatric Association. (1987). *Diagnostic and statistical manual of mental disorders* (3rd ed., rev.). Washington, DC: Author.

Balon, R. (1990). Buspirone for attention deficit hyperactivity disorder? *Journal of Clinical Psychopharmocology, 10,* 77.

Barkley, R. A., Grodzinsky, G., & DuPaul, G. J. (1992). Frontal lobe functions in attention deficit disorder with and without hyperactivity: A review and research report. *Journal of Abnormal Child Psychology, 20,* 163–188.

Barrickman, L. L., Noyes, R., Kuperman, S., Schumacher, E., & Verda, M. (1991). Treatment of ADHD with fluoxetine: A preliminary trial. *Journal of the American Academy of Child and Adolescent Psychiatry, 30,* 762–767.

Barrickman, L. L., Perry, P. J., Allen, A. J., Kuperman, S., Arndt, S. V., Herrmann, K. J., & Schumacher, E. (1995). Bupropion versus methylphenidate in the treatment of attention deficit hyperactivity disorder. *Journal of the American Academy of Child and Adolescent Psychiatry, 34,* 649–657.

Biederman, J., Faraone, S. V., Spencer, T., Wilens, T. E., Norman, D., Lapey, K. A., Mick, E., Lehman, B., & Doyle, A. (1993). Patterns of psychiatric comorbidity, cognition and psychosocial functioning in adults with attention deficit hyperactivity disorder. *American Journal of Psychiatry, 150,* 1792–1798.

Bradley, C. (1937). The behavior of children receiving benzedrine. *American Journal of Psychiatry, 94,* 577–585.

Cavanagh, R., Clifford, J. S., & Gregory, W. L. (1989). The use of bromocriptine for the treatment of attention deficit disorder in two chemically dependent patients. *Journal of Psychoactive Drugs, 21,* 217–220.

Cocores, J. A., Davies, R. K., Mueller, P. S., & Gold, M. S. (1987). Cocaine abuse in adult attention deficit disorder. *Journal of Clinical Psychiatry, 48,* 376–377.

Conners, C. K., Levin, E. D., Sparrow, E., Hinton, S. C., Erhardt, D., Mack, W. H., Rose, J. E., & March, J. (1996). Nicotine and attention in adult attention deficit hyperactivity disorder (ADHD). *Psychopharmocology Bulletin, 32,* 67–73.

Conners, C. K., & Taylor, E. (1980). Pemoline, methylphenidate, and placebo in children with minimal brain dysfunction. *Archives of General Psychiatry, 37,* 922–930.

Dulcan, N. K. (1990). Using psychostimulants to treat behavioral disorders of children in adolescence. *Journal of Child and Adolescent Psychopharmacology, 1,* 7–20.

Findling, R. L., Schwartz, N. A., Fannery, D. J., & Manos, M. J. (1996). Venlafaxine in adults with attention-deficit/hyperactivity disorder: An open clinical trial. *Journal of Clinical Psychiatry, 57,* 184–189.

Gauthier, M. (1984). Stimulant medications in adults with attention deficit disorder. *Canadian Journal of Psychology, 29,* 435–440.

Gawin, F. H., Riordan, C., & Kleber, H. D. (1985). Methylphenidate treatment of cocaine abusers without attention deficit disorder: A negative report. *American Journal of Drug and Alcohol Abuse, 11,* 193–197.

Hooberman, D., & Stern, T. A. (1984). Treatment of attention deficit and borderline personality disorders with psychostimulants: Case report. *Journal of Clinical Psychiatry, 45,* 441–442.

Hunt, R. D. (1987). Treatment effect of oral and transdermal clonidine in relation to methylphenidate: An open pilot study in ADD-H. *Psychopharmacological Bulletin, 23,* 111–114.

Hunt, R. D., Kapper, L., & O'Connell, P. (1990). Clonidine in child and adolescent psychiatry. *Journal of Child and Adolescent Psychopharmacology, 1,* 87–102.

Hunt, R. D., Lau, S., & Ryu, J. (1991). Alternative therapies For ADHD. In L. L. Greenhill & B. B. Osman (Eds.), *Ritalin: Theory and patient management* (pp. 75–95). New York: Merry Ann Liebert.

Hunt, R. D., Minderaa, R. B., & Cohen, D. J. (1985). Clonidine benefits: Children with attention deficit disorder in hyperactivity: Report of double-blind placebo-crossover therapeutic trial. *Journal of the American Academy of Child Psychiatry, 24,* 617–629.

Jankovic, J. (1993). Deprenyl in attention deficit associated with Tourette's syndrome. *Archives of Neurology, 50,* 286–288.

Khantzian, E. J., Gawin, F., Kleber, H. D., & Riordan, C. E. (1984). Methylphenidate (Ritalin) treatment of cocaine dependence: Preliminary report. *Journal of Substance Abuse Treatment, 1,* 107–112.

Klein, R. G. (1990). Thioridizine effects on the cognitive performance of children with attention-deficit hyperactivity disorder. *Journal of Child and Adolescent Psychopharmacology, 1,* 263–270.

Klein, R., Gittelman, F., Quitkin, F., & Rifkin, A. (Eds.). *Diagnosis and drug treatment of adults and children.* (2nd ed.). New York: Willliams and Wilkins.

Magee, R., Maier, D., & Reesal, R. T. (1992). ADHD and desipramine. *Canadian Journal of Psychiatry, 37,* 149–150.

Margraf, J., Ehler, A., Roth, W. T., Clark, D. B., Sheikh, J., Agras, W. S., & Taylor, C. B. (1991). How "blind" are double-blind studies? *Journal of Consulting and Clinical Psychology, 59,* 184–187.

Mattes, J. A., Boswell, L., & Oliver, H. (1984). Methylphenidate effects on symptoms of attention deficit disorder in adults. *Archives of General Psychiatry, 41,* 1059–1063.

Pliszka, S. R. (1995). The serotonin re-uptake blockers: Do they have a role in the treatment of ADHD? *The ADHD Report, 3*(5), 3–5.

Rapport, M. D., Carlson, G. A., Kelly, K. L., & Pataki, C. (1993). Methylphenidate and desipramine in hospitalized children: I. Separate and combined effects on cognitive function. *Journal of the American Academy of Child and Adolescent Psychiatry, 32,* 333–342.

Ratey, J. J., Greenberg, M. S., Bemporad, J. R., & Lindem, K. J. (1992). Unrecognized attention-deficit hyperactivity disorder in adults presenting for outpatient psychotherapy. *Journal of Child and Adolescent Psychopharmocology, 2,* 267–275.

Ratey, J. J., Greenberg, M. S., & Lindem, K. J. (1991). Combination of treatments for attention deficit hyperactivity disorder in adults. *Journal of Nervous and Mental Disease, 179,* 699–701.

Reimherr, F. W., Wender, P. H., Wood, D. R., & Ward, M. (1987). An open trial of L-tyrosine in the treatment of attention deficit disorder, residual type. *American Journal of Psychiatry, 144,* 1071–1073.

Sabalesky, D. A. (1990). Fluoxetine in adults with residual attention deficit disorder and hypersomno-lence. *Journal of Neuropsychology and Clinical Neurosciences, 2,* 463–464.

Satel, S., Southwick, S., & Denton, C. (1988). Use of imipramine for attention deficit disorder in a borderline patient. *Journal of Nervous and Mental Disease, 176,* 305–307.

Schatzberg, A. F., & Cole, J. O. (1991). *Manual of clinical psychopharmocology* (2nd ed.). Washington, DC: American Psychiatric Press.

Shekim, W. O., Antun, F., Hanna, G. L., McCracken, J. T., & Hess, E. B. (1990). S-adenosyl-L-methionine (SAM) in adults with ADHD, RS: Preliminary results from an open trial. *Psychopharmacology Bulletin, 26,* 249–253.

Shekim, W. O., Masterson, A., Cantwell, D. P., Hanna, G. L., & McCracken, J. T. (1989). Nomifensine maleate in adult attention deficit disorder. *Journal of Nervous and Mental Disease, 177,* 296–299.

Spencer, T., Wilens, T., Biederman, J., Faraone, S. V., Ablon, J. S., & Lapey, K. (1995). A double-blind, crossover comparison of methylphenidate and placebo in adults with childhood onset of attention-deficit hyperactivity disorder. *Archives of General Psychiatry, 52,* 434–443.

Weiss, G., & Hechtman, L. T. (1993). *Hyperactive children grow up* (2nd ed.). New York: Guilford Press.

Weiss, R. D., Pope, H. G., & Mirin, S. M. (1985). Treatment of chronic cocaine abuse and attention deficit disorder, residual type, with magnesium pemoline. *Drug and Alcohol Dependence, 15,* 69–72.

Wender, P. H. (1986). Concurrent therapy with d-amphetamine and adrenergic drugs. *American Journal of Psychiatry, 143,* 259–260.

Wender, P. H. (1987). *The hyperactive child, adolescent and adult: Attention deficit disorder through the life span.* New York: Oxford University Press.

Wender, P. H. (1995). *Attention-deficit hyperactivity disorder in adults.* New York: Oxford University Press.

Wender, P. H., & Reimherr, F. W. (1990). Bupropion treatment of attention-deficit hyperactivity disorder in adults. *American Journal of Psychiatry, 147,* 1018–1020.

Wender, P. H., Reimherr, F. W., & Wood, D. R. (1981). Attention deficit disorder ("minimal brain dysfunction") in adults. *Archives of General Psychiatry, 38,* 449–456.

Wender, P. H., Reimherr, F. W., Wood, D., & Ward, M. (1985). A control study of methylphenidate in the treatment of attention deficit disorder, residual type in adults. *American Journal of Psychiatry, 142,* 547–552.

Wilens, T. E., & Biederman, J. (1992). The stimulants. In D. Shafer (Ed.), *The psychiatric clinics of North America* (pp. 191–222). Philadephia: W. B. Saunders.

Wilens, T. E., Biederman, J., Mick, E., & Spencer, T. (1995). A systematic assessment of tricyclic antidepressants in the treatment of adult attention-deficit hyperactivity disorder. *Journal of Nervous and Mental Disorders, 183,* 48–50.

Wilens, T. E., Biederman, J., Prince, J., Spencer, T. J., Faraone, S. V., Warburton, R., Schliefer, D., Harding, N., Linehan, C., & Geller, D. (1996). Six-week, double-blind, placebo-controlled study of desipramine for adult attention deficit hyperactivity disorder. *American Journal of Psychiatry, 153,* 1147–1153.

Wilens, T. E., Biederman, J., Spencer, T. J., & Prince, J. (1995). Pharmocotherapy of adult attention deficit/hyperactivity disorder: A review. *Journal of Clinical Psychopharmocology, 15,* 270–279.

Wilens, T. E., Spencer, T. J., & Biederman, J. (1995). Pharmocotherapy of adult ADHD. In K. G. Nadeau (Ed.), *A comprehensive guide to attention deficit disorder in adults: Research, diagnosis, and treatment* (pp. 168–188). New York: Brunner/Mazel.

Wood, D. R., Reimherr, F. W., & Wender, P. H. (1983). The use of L-deprenyl in the treatment of attention deficit disorder, residual type. *Psychopharmocology Bulletin, 19,* 627–629.

Wood, D. R., Reimherr, F. W., & Wender, P. H. (1985). Treatment of attention deficit disorder with DL-phenylalanine. *Psychiatry Research, 16,* 21–26.

Wood, D. R., Reimherr, F. W., Wender, P. H., & Johnson, G. E. (1976). Diagnosis and treatment of minimal brain dysfunction in adults. *Archives of General Psychiatry, 33,* 1453–1460.

Chapter 8

Future Advancements

One of the most fundamental characteristics of science is objectivity. The historical presentation of ADHD in Chapter 1 introduced the theme that progress has not been linear. Much of this may be due to the influence of subjective trends at different times in history. These influences could be subtle, such as the cultivation of research generated by the assumptions of the time (e.g., cognitive revolution, emphasis on environmental factors, etc.). They could also be quite overt, as research funding dictates which proposals are accepted and which are not. Constant self-reflective vigilance is perhaps the only guard against being swept away with the subjective winds of the time. It may also be advantageous to turn against the trend of the time. For instance, Tom Hartmann's normative perspective (see Chapter 2) of ADHD, although highly questionable, provides fertile ground for some interesting hypotheses that have yet to be tested. At present, it may be easier to receive research funds from a pharmaceutical company to run a study that measures the short-term effects of a particular drug rather than it is to receive funds to conduct a more global cross-cultural study. The macroperspective of ADHD may have been neglected, and it would be interesting to see if future endeavors will take on this challenge.

Fundamental to the study of the adult ADHD population is the understanding of the developmental course ADHD takes throughout the growing years and into adulthood. It is not known how and why symptoms change over time. Again, these are complex research questions that need to take into account the multifactor matrix of time, biology, and environment. A fundamental model to systematically observe and record data was offered in Chapter 2. However, this is only a starting point to a very challenging set of research issues. It would be interesting to see which symptoms or aspects of ADHD remain relatively stable over time and, in turn, how these findings shape future theoretical perspectives. Future research, for instance, may identify several divergent and convergent properties of ADHD that help fundamentally redefine ADHD.

Future research in the diagnosis of ADHD must be more sensitive to the adult population. For instance, field studies designed to refine diagnostic criteria should include adults as well as children. In Chapter 4 I hypothesized that measures of inconsistency and long-term persistence toward goals may be fundamental to the adult ADHD population, more so than hyperactivity–impulsivity and inattention. These last two components were developed on the basis of child studies. It would be interesting to see how the conceptual landscape of ADHD changes, if at all, as more adult studies are included.

The diagnostic process introduced in Chapter 4 is designed to increase diagnostic reliability. The intention is to help practitioners unravel numerous intertwining factors, typical of ADHD adults, that have accumulated over the years. However, this process needs to pass the empirical test. Specifically, can it provide a significant increase in reliability? If so, can future empirical studies provide greater insight into the diagnostic weight of each component of the process? Which component, or combination of components, best explains the between-group (ADHD vs. non-ADHD) variance?

Perhaps there is no greater challenge than the future study of treatment effects. The theme presented in this text is that the complexity of ADHD requires a combination of treatments, which are best administered by a multidisciplinary team of professionals. At present, there are no definitive studies that can explain which treatment, under what conditions, is most effective. Once these issues approach resolution, it may be prudent to look at the possible increase in effectiveness due to different treatment combinations.

As presented in Chapter 6, psychotherapeutic interventions involve a great variety of circumstances and life conditions. The range of needs and personalities within the adult ADHD population may very well be equivalent to the range found in the general population. Consequently, future research in this area may need to be sensitive to within-group variabilities, and its challenge is to properly account for the multifactor interactions generated by this variance.

On a more fundamental level, it is hoped that future research in pharmacotherapy will include fewer case studies and more controlled designs. Also, it is hoped that future research can address the long-term—as opposed to short-term—outcomes of pharmacotherapy. Further study on the combination of different drugs, especially within the adult ADHD population, is needed. The sensitivity to multiple interaction effects can be most helpful to practitioners who must deal with multiple comorbid conditions.

As stated in Chapter 1, this book was written to help practitioners who work with ADHD adults. It is obvious that this field of study is quite young, and there are still numerous unanswered questions. Unfortunately, ADHD adults cannot be put on hold until all of the questions are answered. Consequently, the practitioner is charged with the care of these patients with whatever information is available. Much of the focus in this book has been on building a bridge between research findings and the practical problems faced by clinicians in private practice. Admittedly, much of this bridge lacks extensive empirical support. However, there is much hope that future research will provide the needed empirical support and that the distance across the bridge to good clinical practice will be shortened. To make this a reality, research efforts must be sensitive to the practical needs of the practitioner. More extensive studies are needed to aid in the development of better diagnostic procedures and more effective interventions. In turn, clinicians need to be good consumers of research, and this includes close critical review of studies. They also need to be more sensitive to the utility of research findings so they can move toward clinical services that assure greater objectivity and reliability. If, after these difficult tasks are accomplished, none of the clinical practices proposed in this text are significantly challenged, it would be a great disappointment.

Index